Because My Soul Longs for You

Because My Soul Longs for You
Integrating Theology into Our Lives

Edited by
RABBI EDWIN C. GOLDBERG
RABBI ELAINE S. ZECHER

Historical Introduction by
RABBI JOSEPH A. SKLOOT, PhD

CCAR PRESS · NEW YORK

LIBRARY OF CONGRESS CATALOGING-IN-PUBLICATION DATA
Names: Goldberg, Edwin C., editor. | Zecher, Elaine, 1961- editor.
Title: Because my soul longs for you : integrating theology into our lives / edited by Rabbi Edwin C. Goldberg, Rabbi Elaine S. Zecher.
Description: New York : Central Conference of American Rabbis, 2021. | Summary: "Contributors to this volume share how they welcome God's presence into their lives, as well as the theological language they use to think and speak about this presence. Chapters explore how we experience God through prayer, text study, poetry, food, music, service, movement, meditation, interpersonal connection, and more'—Provided by publisher.
Identifiers: LCCN 2020049424 (print) | LCCN 2020049425 (ebook) | ISBN 9780881233728 (trade paperback) | ISBN 9780881233735 (ebook)
Subjects: LCSH: God (Judaism) | Reform Judaism.
Classification: LCC BM610 .B365 2021 (print) | LCC BM610 (ebook) | DDC 296.3/11--dc23
LC record available at https://lccn.loc.gov/2020049424
LC ebook record available at https://lccn.loc.gov/2020049425

Book interior design and composition
by Scott-Martin Kosofsky at The Philidor Company, Rhinebeck, NY.

10 9 8 7 6 5 4 3 2 1 0

Reform Judaism Publishing, a division of CCAR Press
355 Lexington Avenue, New York, NY 10017
(212) 972-3636 · ccarpress@ccarnet.org
www.ccarpress.org

Contents

Acknowledgments

WE ARE GRATEFUL this book has come to fruition. Its genesis was in the work of Rabbi Elyse Frishman and Rabbi Judith Abrams, z"l, in preparation for *Mishkan T'filah* and its adoption of integrated theology, a term coined by Rabbi Elaine Zecher, partner in this current book. Rabbi Zecher, joined by Rabbi Edwin Goldberg, Rabbi Janet Marder, Rabbi Sheldon Marder, Rabbi Leon Morris, and Cantor Evan Kent along with Rabbi Peter Berg, were instrumental in the creation of *Mishkan HaNefesh* and the continued incorporation of integrated theology into CCAR books. At the center of everything was and remains the insights and steady leadership of Rabbi Hara Person. She believed that the idea of integrated theology deserves more focused attention. This book was created at her urging. We are also grateful to the essential editorial leadership of Rabbi Dr. Sonja Pilz, Editor at CCAR Press, and the helpful assistance of Rafael Chaiken, Director of CCAR Press. We also wish to thank Rabbi Dr. Lawrence Hoffman for important guidance in the development of the theological perspectives; his wisdom and insight have shaped our thinking about integrated theology. Rabbi Zecher also wishes to thank Rabbi Lawrence Kushner, who opened her eyes to welcome the sacred by experiencing the Divine without having to attach a specific theology to it.

I, Rabbi Goldberg, wish to thank my wife, Melanie Cole Goldberg, for her support in this project and for contributing a chapter to the book, as well as to express my gratitude to all the writers. Finally, thank you to the membership of Congregation Beth Shalom of The Woodlands.

I, Rabbi Zecher, wish to thank my husband, David M. Eisenberg, for his enthusiastic support and encouragement and for his groundbreaking work in integrative medicine that informed how to understand an integrated theology. I am also grateful for my three thoughtful adult children, whose ideas and vast knowledge inform and challenge my thinking. My gratitude extends to clergy colleagues—past and present—at Temple Israel of Boston, as well as to the leadership and members of the congregation. They have trusted my crazy ideas, helped make them happen, and encouraged my work with the Central Conference of American Rabbis.

INTRODUCTION

Experiencing the Divine in Our Lives

RABBI EDWIN C. GOLDBERG and RABBI ELAINE S. ZECHER

"CAN YOU SPEAK TO MY CHILD ABOUT GOD?" The concern showed on her face. She had no idea how to explain who, what, why, and how God is.

She is not alone. God is the other three-letter word that makes some parents cringe when they are asked about it. Actually, it sometimes feels like explaining sex is easier and more rehearsed in our minds than getting involved in a conversation about God. The truth is, many people feel uncomfortable having this conversation.

Why is it difficult to talk about God? Is God like a mathematical equation that we would be able to solve if only we could get the right definition? There are many ways to describe God. Judaism is a monotheistic religion founded on the principle that all the disparate gods are really One God. There is no god of the seas, or the sky, or even the underworld. Our biblical ancestors Abraham and Sarah found one God uniting the universe and united by the universe. Jewish tradition teaches that their tent was open on all four sides in order to receive wayfarers from any direction.[1] The image of the tent serves another purpose as well: it signifies that there are countless paths to come closer to this One God. Within our own tradition, many passageways lead us to an experience of the Divine—an experience that so many of us are longing for.

The title of this book, *Because My Soul Longs for You*, comes from an old Sabbath hymn, formally called *Shir HaKavod* ("Song of Glory") and also known by its first two words, *Anim Z'mirot*. It is ascribed to Judah HeChasid of Regensburg (d. 1217). The entire song features a number of original verses and some language from the Bible. Our title is taken from the first stanza, אַנְעִים זְמִירוֹת וְשִׁירִים אֶאֱרֹג, כִּי אֵלֶיךָ נַפְשִׁי תַעֲרֹג (*Anim z'mirot v'shirim e·erog, ki eilecha nafshi ta·arog*, I seek pleasing melodies and thirst for songs because my soul longs for You), itself a reference to Psalm 42:2. The tradition is to open the Torah ark before reciting this prayer, a way of suggesting that God's spirit is summoned when it is sung.

It is human nature to long for God's presence in our lives. However, many of us do not know what to do with this longing. The subtitle of this book is *Integrating Theology into Our Lives*. There are many and diverse Jewish paths to experience and think about God, and we as Reform Jews have the privilege of having more than one path open to us. With a little bit of study and a lot of living, our soul's longing can be addressed. All we need is intention, some humility, and the honesty that open up before us a warm and redolent world.

Shir HaKavod includes these words:

> And so I tell your glory, yet never have seen you;
> Imagine you, find names for you, yet never have known you.
>
> By hand of those who prophesied and throngs who worshipped you,
> You gave imagination to the glory beyond view.[2]

Within these pages, we hope you will discover the One in the different forms described and experienced in the many and diverse paths by talented writers, rabbis, cantors, scholars, and seekers who allow and welcome God into their lives. In their wisdom, we hope you are inspired to allow and welcome God into your own life, too, while also drawing God out—in the path that is yours.

What words do we and the authors of this book use to describe our own paths to, experiences of, and ideas of the Divine? The word "God" is just a placeholder for an idea—the ineffable, the never-ending extension of our breath.[3] No one knows how to pronounce God's name, *YHVH*, let alone offer an exact definition. Those four Hebrew letters *yod, hei, vav, hei*, can all be read as consonants, which makes it difficult to pronounce the word in prayer. The letters sound like the way we breathe, so we say "God" or "*Adonai*" instead.

In chapter 3 of the Book of Exodus, we read about Moses's experience of God in the form of the Burning Bush—a *theophany*, a "manifestation of the Divine." Moses wants to have a name for this sacred encounter. There he is—reinventing himself after a life in Pharaoh's palace, setting up a new home in Midian, marrying, and developing his resume as a shepherd—when he unexpectedly stumbles upon a shrub burning but not burning up. A divine voice calls out to him with a new mission to free the Israelites from Egypt. When Moses asks for a reference, God invokes this unpronounceable name: *Ehyeh-Asher-Ehyeh*, "I will be what I will be" (Exodus 3:14). What kind of name is this?

Moses's experience provides a clue to getting closer to describing and, perhaps then, defining God. Those Hebrew letters in God's self-proclaimed name can also be read as vowels: *eeh-aah-ooh-aah*. Consonants are closed sounds. Vowels are open ones. Watch what your mouth does when you pronounce a vowel. The sound is not confined. For us, this is the first step in describing and then defining God. The medium is the message. God is fluid; God is in a dynamic state. God is becoming known, becoming understood and explored. It is a wonderful component of our tradition that the consonant-based language of Hebrew provides us with a name for God that can be read as all vowels. To us, there must have been a cosmic intention to allow for the open sounds of possibility when describing and defining the Divine.

We can try to imagine what the ancients sensed about God. They must have felt the force in the universe manifesting in their world, primarily through nature. The powerful windstorms, the droughts, and the magnificence of rebirth each spring must have brought to them a sense of wonder, awe, and mystery—mixed with fear of the unknown and unknowable. They must have had their own questions about the ways their world functioned when they pondered life and death. Like Adam, the first human, who had all living things paraded in front of him to name and understand them (*B'reishit Rabbah* on Genesis 2:19), the ancients began to name God, too, in order to understand the nature of God's presence in their lives. But naming and defining often create limitations and boundaries. Our ancestors used metaphors and images based on their human understanding. They equated the likeness of God to the likeness of human beings, which in turn mirrored a likeness of

God. It is no wonder that humans like pharaohs or emperors would then mistake themselves for gods throughout history.

And so, while each act of definition and naming was made in an attempt to understand God, it moved God further away from a possible personal, intimate, spiritual, and evolving experience of God. We lost that direct sense of mystery, wonder, and fear.

Let's retrace our steps, not to oversimplify God's complexity, but to regain the capacity to sense God's presence in our lives. Might it not be possible that in earlier times, our ancestors felt God's presence but lacked the skills to study God? Is it possible that more recently, we have become skilled at studying God but may have lost the ability to sense and experience God's presence in our lives?

Maybe the challenge all along has been that we work too hard to speak *about* God instead of *experiencing* God.

Philosophers and theologians have diligently created constructs through which to understand the Divine. These constructs are carefully distinguished from one another. Process Theology, Religious Humanism, Deism, Limited Theism, Predicate Theology, and God as Encounter are among the many philosophical and theological constructs that make up the names and definitions of who, what, and how God is.

These are important ideas, but we have missed an essential step.

Abraham Joshua Heschel distinguishes between theology and an idea he called "Depth Theology": "Theology is the content of believing and depth theology calls upon our experience out of which arises belief, some of which defy definition." He recognizes that "theology declares, depth theology evokes. Theology demands believing and obedience; depth theology hopes for responding and appreciation."[4] The Psalmists, long ago, did not espouse a particular theology to reach God. They simply addressed God and allowed the longings of their hearts to emerge. Heschel called this "the birthpangs of theology"—our own experiences revealing God to us at all times.

Before we can name or define God, we need to encounter and experience God in our lives.

Many teachers have engaged in an exercise in which they ask their students, "Who here believes in God?" No one raises a hand. And then, the next question is posed: "How many of you have experienced God?" Everyone raises a hand. How can that be possible?

We can talk a lot about food, but only when we taste it do we understand its texture, flavor, and the enjoyment it gives us. The same is true about God. Only when we experience God in our own lives—when we experience that same kind of mystery, beauty, and challenge the ancients experienced as well—do we begin to think and talk about God and our own theology. We begin to integrate theological ideas and conversations into our lives.

We created this book as a demonstration of "Integrated Theology," to show how our personal and embodied experiences can lead to the integration of many different kinds of theologies and theological metaphors into one unified whole. Exploring the chapters, readers will discover a story revealed, a story of the human experience of God: by gazing at the stars (part 1); by diving into our Jewish and human traditions (part 2); by being in relationship with others (part 3); by experiencing the Divine with and within our own bodies (part 4); and finally, by deeply listening to an experience of God within (part 5). Our readers will be able to ask themselves how each author came to experience and understand the sacred and its meaning for their lives and beliefs. How can sharing poetry, justice work, the experience of sickness and health, and the myriad of other ways to experience God presented in this book become bridges across the breach of our souls' longing?

Integrating theology into our lives means being open to the possibility that our own experiences of God might develop, deepen, and change over the course of our lives. We do not need to marry ourselves to a single theology. As a result of our ever-changing experiences of God, we integrate different theologies into our own; we are creating what we call our own Integrated Theology. Our Integrated Theologies gather some of the theological ideas garnered, developed, and postulated over the centuries. All of them are available to us all the time—in all their beauty and tastes.

Our lives take many turns down a circuitous route. We are multifaceted. If we are made in God's image, then God must be diverse and multifaceted, too. The created is only a reflection of the Creator, and we, human to the core, are filled with varied experiences that evolve over a lifetime.

In the Reform Movement, the development of the prayer book *Mishkan T'filah* reflects a Depth Theology experience of prayer. Rabbi Elyse Frishman, its editor, understood that we do not need to choose one particular way of naming or defining God; neither do we need to build a service around that one idea. As a result, her design of the prayer book allowed for a two-page paradigm, with multiple prayers, readings, and poems on the left page accompanying the traditional prayers on the right page. This resulted in a polyphonic theology and expression of the Divine, inviting readers and prayer leaders to reflect on their own Integrated Theologies. An Integrated Theology juxtaposes and places different theological ideas in relationship. Each theology can stand alone, but together—"integrated" into each other—they offer a stronger, deeper, and more complex understanding of God.[5]

We hope this book serves its purpose, not by defining God or offering another series of theological insights, but by inspiring all of us to integrate experiences of the sacred into our lives and thoughts. The possibilities are open like the sounds of the vowels that make up God's name offered to Moses in Midian by the bush on fire that did not burn up. What beckons each of us is the moment in which we live to feel and to experience God integrated in our lives.

No one has all the answers. But every one of us is asked the questions. So, let our very lives be one possible answer. For here is the best thing of all: Our souls long for God. And God may long for us as well.

Notes
1. Rabbeinu Yonah on Pirkei Avot 1:5.
2. Translation by Joel Rosenberg, in *Kol Haneshamah: Shabbat Vehagim* (Wyncote, PA: Reconstructionist Press, 1994), 452.
3. Marcia Falk, *The Book of Blessings: New Jewish Prayers for Daily Life, the Sabbath, and the New Moon Festival* (New York: CCAR Press, 2018).
4. Abraham Joshua Heschel, *The Insecurity of Freedom: Essays on Human Existence* (New York: Schocken Books, 1959), 117–18.
5. "Preparing for the New Machzor and the High Holidays," special issue, *CCAR Journal*, Summer 2013.

Reanimating Jewish Theology:
A Historical Introduction

RABBI JOSEPH A. SKLOOT, PhD

"AT THE AGE OF 75 my father became a golem," writes the historian Nathanial Deutsch. "He was suffering from kidney failure, only the latest in a series of medical complications related to diabetes. When I asked him what he meant, my father groaned, 'I have become a golem. An out-of-control body.'" Deutsch identifies the proximate cause of his father's decline as a lifetime of physical neglect. That neglect, he says, was a consequence of a certain mental disposition instilled over years of Jewish education: "In the yeshivas that my father attended, students were encouraged to cultivate their minds and souls but not their bodies. Indeed, they were taught that their bodies were things to be ignored, subdued or enlisted to perform *mitzvot* ["commandments"] but not indulged or exercised."[1] Jews, according to this way of thinking, are corporeal beings to the extent that they perform obligatory acts but are otherwise abstract entities, purely intellectual. The body is Other, alien; it is a demon, a phantom, a golem.

Deutsch's memoir recounts the human consequences of dichotomizing mind and body: illness and suffering. But in the world of Jewish ideas, this same dichotomy has enfeebled the field of modern Jewish theology. In other words, Jewish thinkers have spent the last centuries disembodying Jewish theology by seeking truth in the abstract propositions of human reason—rationalism—rather than in lived Jewish life. They believed that universal truth could not be derived from indigenously Jewish sources—namely, Scripture, tradition, and embodied practice—and Jewish theology thus became disconnected from the lives of praying, studying, mourning, rejoicing, embodied Jews. Jewish theology became a golem, alien to the Judaism that supposedly brought it into existence.

But the story does not end there. Over the course of the twentieth century, there was a counter-reaction: beginning with Martin Buber, some Jewish theologians rejected the rationalist approach and began to revivify Jewish theology by reconnecting it to lived experience. This book, composed at the start of a new century, may be seen as a culmination of that project, undertaken not by academics but by teachers of Torah and Jewish living, reflecting on the theological assumptions behind the practice that shapes their daily lives.

Theology Defined

It is worth reflecting briefly at the start of this essay on the term "theology" and its application in a Jewish context.[2] Theology, as a distinct field of scholarly activity, emerged within medieval Christianity as the project of systematically articulating the basic principles of that faith. Only in the nineteenth century, as Jews began to enter European universities, did Jewish scholars adopt the term and use it to describe the task of articulating the fundamentals of Judaism. In principle, today, theology—for both Jews and Christians—has come to define a much broader project: investigation into the nature of God and God's relationship to the universe and humankind. This is how the term will be used in this essay. As such, moreover, it is closely related to two other disciplines: philosophy and Jewish thought.

While theology's Christian origins limited its appeal until the era of Emancipation, some Jews adopted the term "philosophy" in the Middle Ages under the influence of Muslim scholars, themselves immersed in reviving the classics of Ancient Greece.[3] In this tradition, philosophy came to signify the pursuit of wisdom through the use of abstract reasoning—the origin of which was the Active Intellect, or God's omniscient mind—often in accordance with the methods of Plato and Aristotle. In the words of the fictional philosopher in Judah HaLevi's (1075–1141) dialogue The Kuzari, "The philosopher . . . is equipped with the highest capacity, [and] receives through it the advantages of disposition, intelligence and active power, so that he wants nothing to make him perfect. . . . In the perfect person a light of divine nature, called Active Intellect, is with him, and its Passive Intellect is so closely connected therewith that both are but one."[4] The mind of the philosopher, therefore, is of such superior quality that it receives its conceptions directly from God, the source of all truth.

The restriction of philosophical study to abstract ideas, however, has meant that philosophers have generally demoted alternative sources of authority—scripture, prophecy, religious experience, for example—to secondary status, if not irrelevance. As Moses Maimonides (1138–1204) declared in the introduction to his *Guide for the Perplexed*, "Natural science borders on divine science, and its study precedes that of divine science." And further, "The internal meaning of the *words of the Torah* is a pearl whereas the external meaning of all parables *is* worth *nothing*."[5] In other words, Maimonides argued that "natural science"—which proceeds according to the dictates of logic and reason—precedes in importance "divine science"—namely, exegesis and theology. "Divine science" teaches the same truths as "natural science" but does so cryptically, in "riddles and parables." The literal meaning of these parables "is worth nothing," but the symbolic meaning is in accordance with reason. Thus, scripture should be read as a post facto justification for reason but not as a source of truth in and of itself.

If the disciplines of "philosophy" and "theology" are rooted in antiquity and the Middle Ages, "Jewish thought" is a twentieth-century coinage, meant to encompass a range of fields, from philosophy and theology, to mysticism, literature, and political theory. As the religion scholar Paul Mendes-Flohr has noted, scholars of Jewish thought have indicated "a pronounced preference for the methods of intellectual history," seeking to situate Jewish texts and their authors contextually and in relation to each other.[6] As such, as much as this essay focuses on theology in the sense described above, it is in practice a work of intellectual history, and thus Jewish thought: an attempt to describe the sway of rationalism over Jewish theology for several centuries and more recent attempts to overcome it.

Finally, the precise scope of this essay should be noted: it is not a broad survey of Jewish theology or philosophy over five centuries. Significant topics and figures will not be discussed or will receive only cursory mention. For instance, the Eastern European religious movement Chasidism will not be explored here in any detail. This is the case despite its transformative significance in Jewish life from the eighteenth century onward and, most especially, despite its articulation of the concept of "the worship of God through corporeality" (*avodah bagashmiyut*). The reason for this conspicuous absence is twofold: first, the complexity of Chasidism as a religious movement would require an essay of its own, and second, while Chasidic texts engage numerous theological and philosophical themes, their idiom—often that of homily, exegesis, and narrative—differs significantly from the systematic treatises that are the foci of this essay.[7]

Reason and Ethics
Maimonides, Spinoza, and Mendelssohn

Maimonides was taken to task by his contemporaries for elevating reason over revelation, science over religion, but he laid the groundwork for Benedict de Spinoza (1632–77) several centuries later. This Dutch child of Portuguese Conversos argued that reason was the sole criterion of truth. Even in matters of theology, "God's eternal word and covenant and true religion are divinely inscribed upon the hearts of men, that is *upon the human mind*."[8] He developed a philosophical system that equated God with nature, and religion with ethical behavior in service of the state. He read the Bible as if it were any text—"The method of interpreting Scripture does not differ from the [correct] method of interpreting nature, but is wholly consonant with it"—and sought to discern the political message of its authors.[9] He stated categorically that the Bible was not a source of objective truth: "The Bible does not teach philosophical matters but only piety."[10] If it possessed any value, it was as an ethical curriculum meant to inspire good deeds ("piety," in Spinoza's terms): "If we want to attest the divine character of Scripture objectively, we must establish from the Bible alone that it offers true moral doctrines."[11] That was the limit of its influence.

As a consequence of this iconoclasm, Spinoza was excommunicated by the Sephardic community of Amsterdam and became *persona non grata* in the early modern Republic of Letters. However, more recently, over the last century, scholars and admirers have transformed him into a symbol of the first stirrings of modernity.[12] He has become synonymous with the principles that would define modern European philosophy beginning in the eighteenth century, not to mention Jewish theology: the sovereignty of human reason, the separation of the state from religion, and the rejection of the Bible as a source of philosophical truth.[13] Jewish theologians thereafter ceded responsibility for asking ultimate questions about God and the universe to scientists. They determined they could write coherently only about what God demanded of human beings—ethics—but not about God's nature. Further, they accepted the principle that truth, whether in mathematics or in ethics, was universal: demonstrable in any context—past, present, or future; accessible to all reasonable, reasoning people; distillable into axiomatic principles.

Moses Mendelssohn (1729–86), anxious not to be perceived as one of the heretic Spinoza's disciples, nonetheless followed in Spinoza's footsteps toward the end of the eighteenth century.[14] Mendelssohn, in a lifetime spent in dialogue with Christian theologians often hostile to Judaism, tried to prove the reasonableness of Judaism and make the case that Jews should be granted rights as citizens of the emerging European nation-states. If Spinoza made religion subservient to the state, Mendelssohn got religion out of the theology business entirely. In his treatise *Jerusalem*, the Socrates of Berlin, as he was known, argued that God and the universe could be understood only through reason and that Judaism made no theological claims; it possessed "no doctrinal opinions, no saving truths."[15] Reason was all that was necessary for human beings to attain individual salvation and for society to achieve the common good. This is what Mendelssohn called "the universal religion of mankind" or natural law and ethics.[16] Judaism, perhaps counterintuitively for his non-Jewish readers, was not a religion but "a divine legislation—laws, commandments, ordinances, rules of life."[17] Through this divine legislation, Jews could discern the truths of natural law and ethics without having to engage in complex philosophical reasoning themselves. They thereby possessed a shortcut to salvation, but salvation was nonetheless achievable for all people through the exercise of their reason. According to the religion scholar Leora Batnitzky,

Mendelssohn's embrace of natural law and ethics and articulation of Judaism as "divine legislation" reduced its sphere of influence in the lives of its adherents to the areas of religious ritual and practice—and denied it authority in the theological realm, which was simply a subsidiary of philosophy.[18]

Geiger, Kant, and Cohen

Ethics found another champion in Abraham Geiger (1810–74). The chief ideologue of nineteenth-century Reform Judaism in Germany, and the first Jew to employ the term "theology" to describe his scholarly project, Geiger wrote evocatively of human beings' ethical obligations: "The full devotion, the intensity of feeling, wherewith moral man attaches himself to the Highest Moral Purity, to God's holiness, the expression of such a relation to the Most High, determines also the relation of men to each other."[19] Human beings serve God through their "self-ennoblement" and "loving devotion" to ethical commitments. This truth distinguished Judaism from other religions, ancient and modern, and meant that its message could one day be embraced by all people: "This Religion has also in its very nature the impulse to offer its blessings as the religion of humanity."[20] If Spinoza made religion about ethical service to the state, Geiger made Judaism ethical service to a transcendent God, what in subsequent years became known as "ethical monotheism."

Lurking behind Geiger's ethical monotheism was the specter of Immanuel Kant (1724–1804). Kant's influence in Jewish theology was and remains pervasive. A younger contemporary of Mendelssohn, Kant sought to deduce an ethical system from the concepts of pure reason—like the axioms of mathematics—without reference to any particular context or external authority (such as Scripture or the state). His ethics was rooted in what he termed the "categorical imperative," which he phrased in one iteration: "Act only in accordance with that maxim through which you can at the same time will that it become a universal law."[21] Religion for Kant was the "repeated arousing of this feeling of the sublimity of one's moral vocation," meaning regular public rituals that reminded individuals of right and wrong.[22] In this way, Kant, like

Spinoza, instrumentalized religion, fashioning it solely as a means to ethical action rather than an end in and of itself, and in so doing ignored the many aspects of religious life that serve purposes other than ethical education.

Kant, like many European intellectuals of his day, was hostile to Judaism. While Protestant Christianity was, for Kant, an allegorization or spiritualization of ethics, Judaism was nothing but a national cult. Hermann Cohen (1842–1918), on the other hand, Kant's foremost interpreter at the turn of the twentieth century, applied the Königsberg philosopher's insights to Judaism. For Cohen, the professor of philosophy at Marburg, in opposition to Christianity, Judaism was the best instantiation of the kind of religion Kant had advocated a century earlier. It was a "religion of reason," the best means of "arousing" in a person "one's moral vocation" or "duty." But Cohen went a step further too, equating ethics with theology: God was not a being, as God was for Geiger, but rather an idea—one synonymous with humanity's most perfect ethical aspiration: "God's essence is morality, and morality only," he wrote.[23] Built on Kant's categorical imperative and his instrumentalized understanding of religion, Cohen reconceptualized Judaism as the most-perfected form of ethical monotheism and transformed God into an abstraction.

Romanticism and Its Critics

As the eighteenth century turned toward the nineteenth, rationalism weathered an increasingly fierce critique. The poets, novelists, philosophers, and ideologues of the movement known as romanticism began to explore the terrain of human emotion and intuition, which seemed more true than cold, analytical reason. This romantic critique of reason was foreshadowed in the early work of the Genevan philosopher Jean-Jacques Rousseau (1712–78), who wrote with characteristic flamboyance, "Sublime science of simple souls, are there so many difficulties and so much preparation necessary in order to know you? Are your principles not engraved in all hearts, and is it not enough, in order to learn your laws, to commune with oneself and, in the silence of the passions, to listen to the voice of one's conscience?"[24]

Rousseau's call to explore the varied terrain of the human heart rather than the universal logic of the mind sparked a movement that found many adherents in Jewish literary circles, especially in the Russian Empire.[25] Thoroughly indoctrinated in rationalism, however, romanticism found little purchase among Jewish philosophers until the rise of Zionism at the end of the century. In the face of ascendant antisemitism, Zionists sought to reanimate Jewish national consciousness, long atrophied as a result of apathy from within and persecution from without. Zionists put their faith in the Jewish nation and devoted their energies to its service.

Early in his life, Martin Buber (1878–1965), the Austrian interpreter of Chasidism, spoke of a Zionist movement that would "above all restore a unified, unbroken sense of Jewish life to the throne" and "will once more encourage Jews to feel like an organism and to strive for a harmonious unfolding of their strength, to invest as much energy into walking, singing, and working as in the analysis of intellectual problems and to take pride and joy in a healthy and perfect body."[26] For Buber, Jewish nationalism was one facet of a larger twentieth-century springtime of nations, a "rebirth in which every person and every people will participate, each according to his kind and his values."[27] The theology of turn-of-the-century Zionism thus made the Jewish nation the focus of inquiry and adoration.

In the years since the Second World War, romanticism has come under withering critique. To many observers, Nazism was the apotheosis of the romantic veneration of emotion, subjectivity, and the nation. To be a rationalist was to advocate objectivity and universalism, which, in the face of the horror of Auschwitz, endowed the position with both logical and moral superiority. Abraham Joshua Heschel (1907–72), a poignant witness to the power of religious emotion, wrote derisively of romanticism: "The sublime is not enough."[28] Even more pointedly, Joseph Soloveitchik (1903–93), the leading theologian of American Orthodoxy, equated romanticism with nihilism. Jewish religious life was grounded in rational calculation, lived with fidelity to "Jewish law" (halachah), and "is not at all concerned with a transcendent world."[29] Soloveitchik applied rational analysis—the mathematical enumeration of universal principles—to halachah, which he described as a totalizing system governing every aspect of existence for the religious Jew.

Relation, Revelation, and Experience
Buber and Rosenzweig

Buber had given up romanticism long before the Nazi terror, however, in the wake of the Great War. Confronted by the human cost of nationalism run amok, he began to articulate what has become known as his philosophy of dialogue.[30] Buber's work is a sustained challenge to rationalism and an attempt to draw theological conclusions from everyday experience, an approach that cleared a path for others to follow.

Buber's philosophy of dialogue is most famously elucidated in his *I and Thou*. In it, he argues that the proper state of human affairs is one of reciprocity or relation. Human beings come to know God, come to recognize their place in the universe, and come to understand their moral vocation through what Buber calls "I-Thou" relations. He compares these relations to the experience of a fetus within its mother's womb, an experience of connectedness that can occur among people, between a person and nature, and between a person and ideas or works of art. Contained in these experiences, which are often fleeting, is the stuff of genuine encounter that Buber identified with divinity.

Rationalism, by contrast, with its cool objectivity, led to what Buber termed "I-It" relations. These relations were the antithesis of the "I-Thou," for in them human beings instrumentalize and objectify each other and the world. In rationalism's abstractness and universalism, there is no encounter, no reciprocity, only exploitation. Buber lambasted capitalism and secularism for reducing human life to the condition of the "I-It." By treating human beings and the natural world as abstract quanta, by denying the metaphysical dimension of human relationships, European society had raised a generation that could not know the possibility of the "I-Thou," a psychological precondition for the horror of modern warfare.

Buber's philosophy of dialogue, further, draws theological conclusions from human life as it is lived and experienced in community. Buber writes poetically of the power of the "I-Thou"—what he calls the "basic word"—to imbue our consciousness with divinity, even when it comes to our relationships with morally repugnant indivuals: "Relation is reciprocity. My You acts on me as I act on it. Our students teach this, our works form us. The 'wicked' become a revelation when they are touched by the sacred basic word. How are we educated by children, by animals! Inscrutably involved, we live in the currents of universal reciprocity."[31] What is crucial here is that Buber defines this reciprocity, when activated and experienced by human beings, in theological terms: it is "revelation," God made manifest in the world.

While Buber's philosophy of dialogue represented a reengagement with everyday experience of personhood and human interaction, Mendes-Flohr has shown that it was also an indictment of romanticism. While romantics emphasized human subjectivity as the source of truth, Buber recognized that it was only through relation—individual subjectivities in dialogue—that truth was achieved and God encountered.[32] In other words, the presence of a "Thou" in relation to an "I" kept the subjective "I" honest—prevented a descent into solipsism. God was not revealed outside the world, in ecstatic emotion or lonely flights of the soul, as romantics contended, but within the world in the presence of an Other.

Buber's philosophy of dialogue has been critiqued by Jewish readers as not sufficiently rooted in Jewish sources, and far too individualistic (indeed antinomian), to be understood as Jewish theology. If revelation can occur in any I-Thou relation, then what need for Sinai, Scripture, or Jewish practice? For this reason, it is necessary to read *I and Thou* alongside Buber's work on Chasidism, which can be seen as a working out of the philosophy of dialogue through Jewish sources. In a late essay, Buber remarked that through his study of Chasidism, "It was necessary . . . to take into my own experience as much as I actually could of what had been truly exemplified for me there [i.e., Chasidism], that is to say, of the realization of that dialogue with being whose possibility my thought had shown me."[33]

Nevertheless, if the theological implications of Buber's philosophy of dialogue are deemed insufficiently Jewish, it is worth considering Buber's German collaborator and thought partner, Franz Rosenzweig (1886–1929). Rosenzweig's philosophy, as detailed in his *The Star of Redemption*, may be deemed an attempt to validate the traditional Jewish concept of revelation in the terms of early twentieth-century speculative philosophy. And while the meaning and implications of *The Star of Redemption* are much debated, it is worth noting that in his letters to Buber and in his more popular writings, Rosenzweig emphasized the theological implications of Jewish religious practice. When Jews see themselves as bound by the force of "religious duty" (mitzvah) and bound to other Jews in community, they become aware of the One who unifies the universe—God. God is revealed, made manifest in the lived, embodied life of the Jew through ritual observance and practice and thereby in the world.[34]

Thus, in the first half of the twentieth century, Rosenzweig and Buber, each in his own way, charted a new course in Jewish theology that led away from rationalism toward interpersonal relations and religious ritual. On this foundation, a new nonrational Jewish theology began to emerge, and Jewish theology entered a new era: postmodernity.

Borowitz, Plaskow, and Benjamin

A generation later, Eugene Borowitz (1924–2016) also recognized the dubiousness of the rationalist project. Shaken by the Nazi genocide of European Jewry carried out in the name of progress, Borowitz considered the attempt to describe God in purely rational terms—to make our theology consistent with the latest science—a fool's errand, given human beings' penchant for justifying the most patently false or repugnant ideas. God *was* not an idea, but lest human society descend into nihilism, God *was* a necessary "ground" for ideas of value, of goodness, and of truth. "If we," Borowitz wrote, "have even a dim, troubled, barely verbalizable acknowledgement of an unshakable demand for value at the heart of the universe, one that we must, to remain human, answer and exemplify, then we have found our personal way to what our tradition in various ways called 'God.'"[35] Moreover, Borowitz argued that the Jewish people were bound in reciprocal relationship to God through the duties imposed on them by Jewish tradition. Borowitz encapsulated this relationship in biblical terminology: "covenant."

Writing at the end of the twentieth century, Borowitz was not sanguine about the benefits of Jewish acculturation and assimilation. He asserted that Jewish peoplehood was more than an ethnic construct—it was an existential reality; he "affirmed the intrinsic truth of Jewish particularity and knew it had to do with our people's response to God's 'commanding.'"[36] Borowitz argued that covenant entailed both human freedom and divine imperative: "The God whom we encounter is real, and great enough to ground our values, and yet respects us enough to give us personal freedom in our relationship with God, the Covenant."[37] Jews, possessing God-given free will, willingly choose to "carry out the Torah's injunctions continually. A Jewishly adequate idea of God would move Jews to do this by indicating the cosmic authority behind the Torah life and thus the ultimate significance of its required acts."[38] In this way, Borowitz squared the circle between Buber's philosophy of dialogue and Rosenzweig's philosophical justification of revelation: Jews become aware of their relation to God, the "Divine legislator" as it were, in the context of a communal engagement in the life of religious practice.

Borowitz, in the shadow of the Holocaust, rejected rationalism because it could harbor within it duplicity and falsehood. His feminist contemporary, Judith Plaskow (b. 1947), offers a similar argument against rationalism but on different grounds. She zeroes in on the person of the theologian: "Named by a male community that perceives itself as normative, women are part of the Jewish tradition without its sources and structures reflecting our experience. Women are Jews, but we do not define Jewishness. . . . The central categories of Torah, Israel, and God all are constructed from male perspectives."[39] Jewish theology, in other words, fashioned from its earliest days by men, claims the status of universal truth but was, in reality, born out of men's assumptions, men's experiences, and men's social position. Jewish theology thus is one facet of longstanding patriarchal oppression of women. With postmodernity and feminism, Jewish theologians, Plaskow asserts, have to accept the reality of the human body and human subjectivity, that all theology emerges from the person of particular author and within a particular social context. Plaskow made her project a refashioning of the essential patriarchal concepts of Judaism as reflective of Jewish women's experiences and realities.

Born of this awareness of subjectivity, Plaskow rejects as idolatry theological approaches that seek to discern God's nature in absolute terms. Instead, Plaskow argues "a broad and changing variety of metaphors brings home on the nonrational level on which images function that God has many guises, no one of which is final."[40] With this pragmatic proviso, Plaskow writes of a God (or Goddess) that is "always moving in and through the shifting web of life, enabling and necessitating continual growth and change" and who is "found in the elements that surround us: earth, ocean, stars, air, sky, moon, flowers, trees."[41] Most importantly, in contrast to patriarchal descriptions of God in the Bible and Rabbinic tradition that glorify domination, Plaskow writes of "the presence of God in empowered, egalitarian community." Drawing on Buber's philosophy of dialogue and her experience in feminist consciousness-raising groups and dynamic Jewish communities, Plaskow asserts that "community is the location and vehicle for the experience of God": "It is when we join with others, in a way that only human beings can, in shared engagement to a common vision, that we find ourselves in the presence of another presence that is the final source of our hopes and intentions, and that undergirds and sustains them."[42]

Most recently, Mara H. Benjamin (b. 1972) has taken up Plaskow and other feminists' challenge to shift the terms for God in Jewish theology to ones that speak to women's experiences. Plaskow argued for the rejection of the theology of domination and argued for egalitarian and communitarian imagery that spoke to her experience of feminist communities. Without limiting or equating women's experience to maternity, Benjamin asserts that the maternal feelings of attraction, obligation, resistance, freedom, consent, and submission are emblematic of the relationship of the Jewish people and God. Again drawing on Buber and Rosenzweig, Benjamin explains that love "can be commanded, and this commanded love is performative. A daily praxis of service constitutes the proper response to divine love."[43] She therefore analogizes the embodied "daily praxis of service" to one's child to the embodied "daily praxis of service" to God enumerated in Jewish law and tradition. Benjamin's exploration of maternal metaphors leads her to reengage with Rabbinic texts. While Judaism and Western culture have generally identified bearing and raising children as a hallmark of women's subjugation, Benjamin reclaims that tradition and at the same time turns it on its head: she sees in motherhood the exact "dialectical movement between freedom, or agency, and the boundedness of the conditions of existence" emblematic of the Jewish people's covenant with God.[44]

Benjamin's work is not simply a call to refashion Judaism in a feminist lens and reinterpret Jewish texts in light of women's experiences; it is also a sustained critique of the legacy of rationalism in Jewish theology. She asserts that even Buber and Rosenzweig described the divine aspect of reciprocal human relations in "decidedly abstract terms. The 'other' they envision has no specific social location or set of needs."[45] Benjamin, by writing in detail about the dynamics of mothering, does just that, emphasizing its embodied, everyday nature and the power of such encounters to help us "understand the nature of the divine, or at least the tools with which to investigate the human relationship to the divine."[46] Moreover, Benjamin embraces the subjectivity of her own reflections: "Subjectivity . . . acts simultaneously as a landscape to be explored and as a resource to be excavated. . . . I investigate that which occurs or appears in the everyday experience of consciousness in the subjective, social realm, and I include, and at times begin from, my own subjective experience in the aim of unearthing knowledge that reaches beyond myself."[47] Benjamin argues that knowledge of God can only be unearthed where one is—in her case, from her position as a mother. By exploring the content of this experience and identity, she develops a theology that both reengages with traditional Jewish sources and speaks to the realities of early twenty-first-century American Jewish life.

Maimonides, Revisited

If Maimonides and his successors transformed Jewish theology into a golem, the efforts of Jewish theologians over the last century, and most especially in recent decades, have led to its reanimation. Beginning with Martin Buber, Jewish theologians sought to reconnect theology to lived experience—relation, revelation, community, and practice. In so doing, moreover, they sought to reinterpret traditional Jewish sources that the rationalists had dismissed or to which they paid only cursory attention. It is fitting then, at the beginning of a new century, that historians of Jewish ideas have begun also to reassess the place of Maimonides in Jewish philosophy and theology. In his recent work on medieval German Jewish pietism, David Shyovitz has emphasized that Maimondes's rationalism was "well beyond the mainstream" among medieval Jewish thinkers, and it is incorrect to assume that his novel ideas had the purchase they would later acquire in the early modern period and beyond.[48]

By contrast, Shyovitz has written extensively about how German Jews "located theological profundity specifically in the routine, mundane components of the natural order," how nature and its inner workings—from the animal kingdom to the human body—encapsulated theology. In Shyovitz's words, "Given that the Pietists also saw the natural order as imbued with spiritual profundity, it should come as no surprise that the body which reflected and encapsulated that order was seen as reflection of God's goodness, as theologically meaningful—indeed, as the very linchpin of creation."[49] This medieval understanding of the "routine and prosaic" possessing theological worth goes hand in hand with Benjamin's postmodern call for theology to be rooted in a "specific social location or set of needs."

Embodied Theology

As I stated at the outset, what I have tried to do in this essay is identify a tendency, indeed a pronounced tendency, in the systematic treatises of a number of Jewish theologians: the attraction of rationalism and the desire to overcome it. The scope of this essay necessarily prevents me from considering the works of several other significant Jewish theologians, past and present, as well as theologically rich works in other genres, such as exegesis and narrative. It is worth noting, however, in closing that the embrace of subjectivity and embodiment that so marks twentieth- and twenty-first-century Jewish theology is mirrored in a number of popular trends in Jewish culture, including renewed interest among liberal Jews in embodied ritual practice—from dietary regulations to Sabbath observance—and the adoption and transformation of embodied practices in other traditions, such as yoga and mindfulness meditation.[50] This book, as an anthology of "autoethnographies"—reflections on the lived Jewish experiences of a number of rabbis—is similarly an example of the attempt to locate theological meaning in the everyday embodied experiences.

At the start of a new century, therefore, a new kind of consensus has emerged in the realm of both academic Jewish theology and popular Jewish culture: Jews are more than minds. Jews are bodies rooted in context and culture, time and space. Jewish theology thus requires that God be more than an abstract proposition to be cognized by the mind. God must be understood and experienced in lived human experience and in the embodied practices that make up a Jewish life.

NOTES

1. Nathaniel Deutsch, "My Father, the Golem," *Guilt & Pleasure* 1, no. 3 (2006): 19.

2. See Rachel Adler's reflection on the significance of the term "theology" for Jews in the introduction to *Engendering Judaism* (Boston: Beacon Press, 1998), xvi–xviii.

3. The adoption of philosophy by Jews in the Middle Ages provoked a strong backlash; see Idit Dobbs-Weinstein, "The Maimonidean Controversy," in *History of Jewish Philosophy*, ed. Daniel H. Frank and Oliver Leaman (London: Routledge, 1997), 275–91.

4. Judah Hallevi, *Book of Kuzari*, trans. Hartwig Hirschfeld (New York: Pardes, 1946), 32–33.

5. Moses Maimonides, *The Guide of the Perplexed*, vol. 1, trans. Shlomo Pines (Chicago: University of Chicago Press, 1963), 7–9. Emphasis original.

6. See Paul Mendes-Flohr, "Jewish Philosophy and Theology," in *The Oxford Handbook of Jewish Studies*, ed. Martin Goodman, Jeremy Cohen, and David Sorkin (Oxford: Oxford University Press, 2002), 765.

7. Similarly, a number of important figures in Jewish theology will not be accounted for here. Some, such as Abraham Joshua Heschel, will be mentioned only briefly, and others, such as Rachel Adler, Leo Baeck, Emil Fackenheim, and Arthur Green, not at all. The reason for these absences generally has to do with the necessity for brevity and the desire to stake out the essay's argument without overwhelming the reader with an abundance of proof texts. Sometimes, as in the case of Heschel, they do not fit neatly into the dialectic that is at the heart of this essay.

8. Benedict de Spinoza, *Theological-Political Treatise*, trans. Michael Silverthone and Jonathan Israel (Cambridge: Cambridge University Press, 2007), 163; emphasis mine.

9. Spinoza, *Theological-Political Treatise*, 98.

10. Spinoza, *Theological-Political Treatise*, 168.

11. Spinoza, *Theological-Political Treatise*, 165.

12. See two recent hagiographic treatments: Rebecca Newberger Goldstein, *Betraying Spinoza: The Renegade Jew Who Gave Us Modernity* (New York: Schocken Books, 2009); and Rachel Kadish, *The Weight of Ink* (Boston: Mariner Books, 2018).

13. On Spinoza's pivotal role in European intellectual history, see Jonathan I. Israel, *Radical Enlightenment: Philosophy and the Making of Modernity 1650–1750* (New York: Oxford University Press, 2002). On the various ways Spinoza has been understood in Jewish thought, see Daniel B. Schwartz, *The First Modern Jew* (Princeton, NJ: Princeton University Press, 2013).

14. On the relationship of Mendelssohn's thought to Spinoza's, see Michah Gottlieb, *Faith and Freedom* (Oxford: Oxford University Press, 2011).

15. Moses Mendelssohn, *Jerusalem: Or on Religious Power and Judaism*, trans. Allan Arkush (Waltham, MA: Brandeis University Press, 1983), 89–90.

16. Mendelssohn, *Jerusalem*, 97.

17. Mendelssohn, *Jerusalem*, 89.

18. Leora Batnitzky, *How Judaism Became a Religion: An Introduction to Modern Jewish Thought* (Princeton, NJ: Princeton University Press, 2011), 23–27.

19. Abraham Geiger, *Judaism and Its History*, trans. Charles Newburgh (New York: Bloch, 1911).

20. Geiger, *Judaism and Its History*, 37.

21. Immanuel Kant, *Groundwork for the Metaphysics of Morals*, trans. Allen W. Wood (New Haven, CT: Yale University Press, 2002), 37.

22. Immanuel Kant, *Religion within the Bounds of Bare Reason*, trans. Werner S. Pluhar (Indianapolis: Hackett, 2009), 57.

23. Hermann Cohen, *Reason and Hope: Selections from the Jewish Writings of Hermann Cohen*, trans. Eva Jospe (Cincinnati: Hebrew Union College Press, 1971), 83. See also Hermann Cohen, *Religion und Sittlichkeit* (Berlin: M. Poppelauer, 1907).

24. Jean-Jacques Rousseau, "Discourse on the Arts and the Sciences," in *The Basic Political Writings*, 2nd ed., trans. Donald A. Cress (Indianapolis: Hackett, 2011), 14, 25.

25. Olga Litvak, *Haskalah: The Romantic Movement in Judaism* (New Brunswick, NJ: Rutgers University Press, 2012).

26. Martin Buber, "Jewish Renaissance," in *The First Buber: Youthful Zionist Writings of Martin Buber*, trans. Gilya G. Schmidt (Syracuse, NY: Syracuse University Press, 1999), 33. Originally published as "Jüdische Renaissance," *Ost und West*, 1, no. 1 (January 1901).

27. Buber, "Jewish Renaissance," 34.

28. Abraham Joshua Heschel, *God in Search of Man: A Philosophy of Judaism* (New York: Schocken Books, 1976).

29. Joseph B. Soloveitchik, *Halakhic Man* (Philadelphia: Jewish Publication Society, 1983), 32.

30. On Buber's transformation, see Paul R. Mendes-Flohr, *From Mysticism to Dialogue: Martin Buber's Transformation of German Social Thought* (Detroit: Wayne State University Press, 1989); and more recently, *Martin Buber* (New Haven, CT: Yale University Press, 2019).

31. Martin Buber, *I and Thou*, trans. Walter Kaufmann (New York: Touchstone, 1996), 67.

32. Mendes-Flohr, *From Mysticism to Dialogue*, 101–19.

33. Martin Buber, "Hasidism and Modern Man," in *Hasidism and Modern Man*, trans. Maurice Friedman (Princeton, NJ: Princeton University Press, 2016), 3.

34. Franz Rosenzweig, "The Builders," in *On Jewish Learning* (Madison: University of Wisconsin Press, 1955), 85–86.

35. Eugene B. Borowitz, *Renewing the Covenant* (Philadelphia: Jewish Publication Society, 1996), 60.

36. Borowitz, *Renewing the Covenant*, 207.

37. Borowitz, *Renewing the Covenant*, 131.

38. Borowitz, *Renewing the Covenant*, 58.

39. Judith Plaskow, *Standing Again at Sinai* (New York: HarperCollins, 1991), 3.

40. Plaskow, *Standing Again at Sinai*, 154.

41. Plaskow, *Standing Again at Sinai*, 144, 155.

42. Plaskow, *Standing Again at Sinai*, 157.

43. Mara H. Benjamin, *The Obligated Self: Maternal Subjectivity and Jewish Thought* (Bloomington: Indiana University Press, 2018), 23.

44. Benjamin, *The Obligated Self*, 15.

45. Benjamin, *The Obligated Self*, 13.

46. Benjamin, *The Obligated Self*, xv.

47. Benjamin, *The Obligated Self*, xviii.

48. David I. Shyovitz, *A Remembrance of His Wonders: Nature and the Supernatural in Medieval Ashkenaz* (Philadelphia: University of Pennsylvania Press, 2017), 50

49. Shyovitz, *A Remembrance of His Wonders*, 75.

50. The former was given official sanction in the 1999 "A Statement of Principles for Reform Judaism"; see Gunther W. Plaut, *The Growth of Reform Judaism: American and European Sources*, 2nd ed. (Philadelphia: Jewish Publication Society, 2015), 296–99. The widespread embrace of the latter is chronicled, most recently, in Emily Sigalow, *American JewBu: Jews, Buddhists, and Religious Change* (Princeton, NJ: Princeton University Press, 2019). Related to both of these trends is the increasing prominence of neo-Chasidic theologies; see Ariel Evan Mayse and Arthur Green, *A New Hasidism*, 2 vols. (Philadelphia: Jewish Publication Society, 2019).

PART 1

Creation

Every blade of grass has its angel that bends over it
and whispers, "Grow, grow."
—*B'reishit Rabbah* 10:6

CHAPTER I

Experiencing God While Watching the Universe

Rabbi John L. Rosove

I REMEMBER lying on my back in my childhood home's backyard, looking up into the blue sky with my older brother. One day, he said, "You know that there is no ceiling." That was the first time I got a sense of the infinite nature of the universe. I felt overcome with awe and wonder, as it is written in Job (37:14–17):

> Hearken to this, O Job, stand,
>   and take in the wonders of God.
> Do you know when God directs them,
>   and His thunderhead's lightning shines?
> Do you know of the spread of cloud,
>   the wonders of the Perfect in knowledge,
> when your garments feel warm
>   as the earth is becalmed from the south?[1]

That childhood experience of awe and wonder was the beginning of my lifelong religious and spiritual quest.

In many religions, and in some Jewish communities, "Do you believe in God?" is a threshold question. Answer yes, and you are one of the fold. Answer no, and you have a problem. So it is with reticence or a mildly defiant tone that many Jews tell me, "Rabbi, I don't believe in God!" I sometimes think that on some level, they expect someone (i.e., me!?) to hear that statement and "cast them out." The conversation gets interesting if we talk about the nature of the God they find so incredible. Often it turns out to be the white-haired figure touching fingers with Adam on the Sistine Chapel ceiling—a commanding, rewarding, and punishing God. Most liberal Jews do not accept the notion of such a God, especially given the evidence all around us that innocent people do suffer and that therefore the all-knowing, all-powerful, and all-good God of tradition either has turned the Divine back on us, ignores us, or does not exist.

When people tell me that they do not believe in God either because they have seen no empirical proof for God's existence or they cannot accept the God of the Bible and medieval rabbis, I understand completely—because I don't believe in that God either. I say this as one who has spent decades thinking about God, faith, and the insights and truths Jewish tradition offers us. I have studied Torah seriously for more than forty years and have enjoyed the spiritual gifts of some of our greatest thinkers, mystics, and poets. And so I can see clearly that we live in a vastly different world from that of our ancestors, whose God ideas evolved from the social models surrounding them, the world of feudal kings and vassals.

Enlightenment thinkers and reformers tended to reject the teachings of the great Jewish mystics because their writings and teachings carried people into nonrational, nonlinear, intuitive thinking. But we today are hungry for the spiritual answers that our linear, rational minds cannot deliver—and the embracing sense of community that their openness can help create. We are new and different kinds of Jews, some of whom neither our mystical nor our rational ancestors would recognize as particularly Jewish or rational at all. One says, "I'm a religious person in that I feel a connection to something eternal and infinite that's in my soul and in yours. But I don't believe in a personal God, and all this talk about God as King and me as servant is meaningless to me." Another says, "I'm grateful for the gifts of health, meaningful work, and love. Sometimes I feel overwhelmed by gratitude and a sense of inadequacy to express how much I feel blessed, and that's about as close as I come to prayer. But that prayer is addressed to life itself and to no one in particular, and surely not to 'God.'" Many Jews have spiritual yearnings, but too often they do not bother to look for a spiritual home within the Jewish community. They do not assume that Jewish tradition and community can offer them spiritual depth. They do not expect to be touched in their souls.

We all share in their yearning, but we can actually satisfy those yearnings by pulling inspiration from both contemporary Jewish thinkers and writers and from the mystical and philosophical traditions of Judaism, which speak about God not in terms of thunderbolts but rather as an inner spark. The question that is most pertinent to us now is not "Do I believe in God?"; it is *"How do I and how can I experience myself as a spiritual being?"*

A search that starts with that question does not ask us to marshal empirical evidence for a God-force existing somewhere outside of us, but instead shifts our focus to our own experiences. When we embark on an interior search, we can live as fully spiritual beings without having to concern ourselves with, affirm, or deny belief in God at all. Instead, we open ourselves to awe, wonder, and gratitude; and in the vastness of all of that, we connect with our souls and with the ancient mysteries threaded through our lives.

Here's a small example of what I am talking about: On September 5, 1977, NASA launched a small 1,590-pound spacecraft called *Voyager 1*. The mission's purpose was to study the outer solar system and beyond. The small craft carried both observational equipment and messages intended for any future "finders": a golden record of greetings in fifty languages, including one whale language; a twelve-minute sound essay that included the music of a kiss, a baby's cry, and the meditations of a young woman in love; 116 encoded pictures meant to show our science and civilization; and ninety minutes of the Earth's greatest hits, eastern and western, classical and folk, including a Navajo night chant, a Pygmy girl's initiation song, a Peruvian wedding song, Bach, Beethoven, Mozart, Stravinsky, Louis Armstrong, and Chuck Berry's "Johnny Be Good." If, by some infinitesimally slight chance, sentient beings were to intercept the craft at some point on its travels, these artifacts of our civilization were meant to give them an idea of who we were, we occupants of planet Earth in the Milky Way galaxy in this era.

I got my best sense of this mission, and the scale of its aspirations, in an eight-minute video written and narrated by the astronomer and astrophysicist Carl Sagan for his 1980 television series *Cosmos: A Personal Voyage*. Describing the *Voyager 1* and its twin, *Voyager 2*, which had been launched a month earlier, Sagan said:

> The *Voyagers* ... barreling along at almost a million miles a day ... will take hundreds of centuries until they escape the gravitational shackles of our solar system and make for the open sea of interstellar space. ... The spacecraft will wander for ages in the calm cold interstellar blackness where there is almost nothing to erode them. Once out of the solar system they will remain intact for a billion years or more as they circumnavigate the center of the Milky Way galaxy, essentially forever. ... In five billion years none of our artifacts will have survived on earth ... humans will have become extinct or evolved into other forms, and the evolution of the sun will have burned the earth into a crisp or reduced it to a whirl of atoms. And far from home, untouched by these remote events, the *Voyagers*, bearing the memories of a world that is no more, will fly on.[2]

Imagine a human-made object filled with recorded memories traveling through interstellar space ... forever. How are we supposed to wrap our minds around such expansions in time, space, and emotional depth—all part of the mysterious and wondrous creation all of us are a part of—except to be struck dumb in awe and amazement?

The awe and amazement I feel does not require any sort of belief in a God-figure pulling the *Voyagers* through space. The part of us that is so moved by the wonder and poetry of life—I would call this part the soul—does not seem to require grandeur of a *Voyager* scale to be awakened, I have realized. These days, I seem to experience it frequently—when walking in my neighborhood, reading something beautifully written, hearing magnificent music, spending time with my family, communing sweetly with my little dog, and sitting quietly on our deck above the tree-tops drinking red wine in late afternoon, feeling the breeze on my face, and hearing the rustling of leaves.

Over the years, I have found that my capacity to experience awe and wonder, first experienced when I was five years old and that I later discovered in Job, has grown in direct proportion to how grateful I feel for the gifts in my life.

It is the mystics' God, the God of "inwardness," that expands us in this way and allows us to tap into the hidden spiritual waters inside us. The truth of the mystics is that the individual is not separate from God. God is the mystery within us, inside our very soul. Reb Nachman of

Bratzlav taught that the Divine Presence flows constantly as the light of awareness into the world, but that an inner vessel needs to be created within every human being to receive that light. The vessel of our soul—once we are in touch with it—receives the light in moments of awe and wonder over the miracles of the universe, as well in moments of deep love and connection with others. Reb Nachman taught that a vessel is made whenever the heart opens to give in love to others. This is one meaning of the verse וְעָשׂוּ לִי מִקְדָּשׁ וְשָׁכַנְתִּי בְּתוֹכָם—"And let them make Me a sanctuary that I may dwell among them" (Exodus 25:8).

This mystical experience of godliness is not only revitalizing, it breaks down unnecessary barriers and enables a far more inclusive and expansive vision of Jewish life and humankind as a whole. Reaching across time, space, and human distinctions, it inspires the understanding that divinity shines everywhere.

Here is what I think is important to know: Every peak emotional moment of joy, awe, and gratitude is similar to the classic religious and prophetic moments recorded in the great books of Jewish literature—it is a revelation of some deeper spiritual truth. Recognizing that, as we contemplate the depths of space or each other's eyes, we are reminded that we are part of something far greater than ourselves.

Rabbi Abraham Joshua Heschel, among our people's greatest poets of the soul, describes what the spiritual experience is all about:

> Our radical amazement responds to the mystery, but does not produce it. You and I have not invented the grandeur of the sky nor endowed the human being with the mystery of birth and death. We do not create the ineffable, we encounter it. . . . The awareness of the ineffable is that with which our search must begin. . . . The search of reason ends at the shore of the known; on the immense expanse beyond it only the sense of the ineffable can glide . . . reason cannot go beyond the shore, and the sense of the ineffable is out of place where we measure, where we weigh.[3]

Heschel said as well:

> Left-brain thinking will never bring us into God's presence nor give us a glimpse of God's reality. It is only through the non-rational, intuitive,

symphonic, aesthetic, creative, and imaginative faculties that we can suspend time, reason and logic enough to glimpse a moment of God's eternity.

Jewish tradition does many things, and two of the most important are that it feeds the mind and inspires the soul. I do not think we need to put aside our left-brain training as we open ourselves to what the mystics can teach us. Rather, we can ask the question that will take us closer to our souls: *"How do I and how can I experience myself as a spiritual being?"* How can we connect to what is eternal and infinite in ourselves and the world? How can we connect with the sense of awe and wonder over the miracles of our universe on the one hand, and gratitude for very simple facts of our very existence on the other? Our search for answers, whether we use the word "God" or not, pulls us into the deep and vital current of Judaism. It does not demand that the atheists and agnostics among us suspend their doubts and disbeliefs. It does not ask us to slink away if we do not believe in God. Instead, it asks all of us to become more aware of the musings of the right hemisphere of our brains and to think about the spiritual significance of the hours and days, months and years of our lives: our ability to fall in love; our ability to celebrate and rejoice at weddings, births, *b'nei mitzvah* celebrations, conversions, anniversaries, and yes, also our family gatherings; our ability to treasure and enjoy our alone time; our ability to create and enjoy the creations of human hands, hearts, minds, and souls in art, film, music, literature, poetry, dance, and architecture; our ability to engage in good works in the community; and our ability to respond with gratitude to the miracles we enjoy every day.

We do not need to believe in a removed, plague- and miracle-wielding God to be Jews and spiritual beings. Our task instead is to be more than secular actors in our human drama as it unfolds, to understand that we are not separate willful beings making our way in a chaotic, meaningless existence, but a unique glow of light in our souls—the beautiful, inexplicable, and awe-inspiring spark of life. It is by seeing the light in one another and then drawing our separate lights together into a larger glow that we reveal to ourselves and to each other, discover and understand the deeper truth about the world. It may be true, as one Chasidic sage once noted, that "the human being is the language of God,"[4] because God is present in each of our souls, each longing to know the Source from which we come and to which we return.

Whether we speak of that Source as God or Nature or Life or Love, we and the mystics and the scientists are all talking about the same thing, and Judaism is embracing enough to welcome us all.

There is a traditional Jewish blessing for every experience. Upon seeing the large-scale wonders of nature, such as lightning, shooting stars, vast deserts, high mountains, hills, seas, long rivers, earthquakes, the sunrise and sunset, and the sky in its purity, we say:

בָּרוּךְ אַתָּה, יי אֱלֹהֵינוּ, מֶלֶךְ הָעוֹלָם, עוֹשֶׂה מַעֲשֵׂה בְרֵאשִׁית.

Baruch atah, Adonai Eloheinu, Melech haolam, oseh maaseih v'reishit.

Praised are You, Adonai our God, Ruler of the universe, Maker of the work of creation.

Upon seeing the small-scale wonders of nature, such as beautiful trees and flowers, animals, and human beings, we say:

בָּרוּךְ אַתָּה, יי אֱלֹהֵינוּ, מֶלֶךְ הָעוֹלָם, שֶׁכָּכָה לוֹ בְּעוֹלָמוֹ.

Baruch atah, Adonai Eloheinu, Melech haolam, shekachah lo b'olamo.

Praised are You, Adonai our God, Ruler of the universe, that such as these are in God's world.

May the sense of awe and wonder never leave us as we encounter the small and large miracles of the world we inhabit—from the sky above us to moments of love.

Notes

1. Robert Alter, trans., *A Hebrew Bible—A Translation with Commentary, The Writings Volume 3* (New York: W. W. Norton & Company, 2019), p. 562.
2. Carl Sagan, *Pale Blue Dot: A Vision of the Human Future in Space* (New York: Random House, 1994), 152–53.
3. Abraham Joshua Heschel, *Between God and Man: An Interpretation of Judaism* (London: Collier Macmillan, 1959), 47.
4. Rabbi Menachem Mendel of Vitebsk (1730–88) was an early third-generational leader of Chasidic Judaism and the primary disciple of the Maggid of Mezeritch. He lived in Minsk and served his Chasidim in Belarus.

This chapter is based on Rabbi John L. Rosove, *Why Judaism Matters: Letters of a Liberal Rabbi to His Children and the Millennial Generation* (Nashville: Jewish Lights, 2017), 3–9.

PART 2
Traditions

So you want intimacy with the One who
spoke the world into being?
Then study your stories.
—*Sifrei D'varim* 49

Experiencing God While Praying:
X-rays to God

Ilana Kurshan

For as long as I can remember, I have brought books to read in synagogue. Concentrating on prayer has never come easily. I struggle to find meaning in the recitation of the same words day after day, and so inevitably at some point in the prayer service I reach down sheepishly into my bag, pull out a novel, and nestle it inside my siddur as discreetly as possible. Sometimes I turn around to check who is sitting in the row behind—I would not want to set a bad example for young children sitting attentively in shul with their parents—but what troubles me most is not the people who might be observing me, but the words embroidered in gold on the ark covering that hangs before me: "Know Before Whom You Stand."

We come to synagogue to stand before God. Prayer is an opportunity to engage with the Divine—to speak, or whisper, our hopes and fears, acknowledge our mistakes, express our regrets, reflect on what makes us feel grateful, and thank God for our blessings. It is also an opportunity to reach within ourselves and ask the deep and difficult questions that often get lost in the rush of the urgent, the immediate, the mundane. To focus on our prayers is to try and formulate answers to some of life's fundamental questions: What do I regret about my behavior this morning, yesterday, this past year, this past decade? What are my dreams for this next stage of life? What are my unique talents, and how can I use them to contribute to others around me? How would I like to see the world transformed?

Granted, there are many people who make time on a weekly or even daily basis to think about these questions. They write in a journal every morning, or meditate alone in their bedrooms, or attend a yoga class, or go off on silent retreats. But as a lover of language and as someone who has always felt deeply at home in Jewish tradition, I have set myself the challenge of trying, at least for a few hours each week, to put aside my novel, open my siddur, and draw out the connections between my own inner world—my hopes, fears, dreams, regrets—and the words of the liturgy. The siddur is the language of the human heart. The Kotzker Rebbe famously teaches that we are commanded in the *Sh'ma* prayer that "these words shall be on your heart" because if we place them on our hearts, then in those moments when our hearts open, the words will fall in. My heart is not always open to prayer, but when it is, these are some of the words that have fallen in.

Modeh Ani

> I thank You, living and eternal King, for giving me back my soul in mercy.
> Great is Your faithfulness.

The moment I emerge from sleep is generally one of anxiety. I feel the stresses of the day that lies ahead—the decisions that must be made, the tasks that must be completed, the people who are awaiting a response. I reach for my phone to see who wants my attention or needs something of me, but in that moment before the artificial light of the backlit screen casts its glow in our still-dark bedroom, I restrain myself. There is enough to take in already—the early-morning light, the warm blanket pulled up to my neck, the beep of the neighbor's van backing out just a few feet from my bedroom window. Before inviting more, I want to turn back to those pre-sensory moments when my eyes have not yet opened and the weight of the day has not yet descended on me. My soul shrinks from all that it has just remembered, from what poet Richard Wilbur describes as "the punctual rape of every blessed day."[1] I want to return to those untarnished moments when I can see the light only because I feel it dancing on my still-shut eyelids.

Wilbur imagines that the soul wakes up before the body and descends reluctantly to accept its physical form, like the air filling the blouses and bedsheets fluttering on a laundry line on a windy day. As Wilbur would have it, every day begins with the soul's bitter disappointment at having to assume physical form once again. But the earliest Jewish prayers recited in the morning regard the restoration of the soul to the body as an occasion for gratitude and hope. And so I try to remember to utter these words before opening my eyes and before the anxiety sets in. This prayer serves to ward off the dread—there may be much that concerns and distresses me about the day that is dawning, but I thank God for having faith in me and deeming me deserving of yet another day.

In our home, mornings are never easy. There seems no point in setting an alarm because one of the children will inevitably jump into our bed at the crack of dawn. My daughter Liav is generally the first to wake up; she comes into our room as soon as she sees the first rays of sunlight peeking under the bottom of her shade and snuggles under the covers with us. She knows that in our family, individual attention is hard to come by—especially since she is a twin and shares her bedroom (and her bedtime routine) with her sister. So she has learned to steal the pre-dawn hours for herself.

Soon it is time to wake the other kids. I tread softly into their rooms and open the shades, flooding their room with light. I try not to speak a single "secular" word before singing to them the *Modeh Ani* prayer: "I thank You, living and eternal King…" I want my children to wake up in gratitude. Afterward I can tell them to get dressed and make their beds and not to forget to brush their teeth. All that can wait. Better that their first image should be one of the soul descending into the body to allow another day of potential and possibility. Better that they, unlike me, should wake each day in hope and not in anxiety.

Elohai N'shamah

My God, the soul You have placed within me is pure.
You formed it within me,
You breathed it in me,
 and You guard it while it is within me.
One day You will take it from me and restore it within me
 in the time to come.
As long as the soul is within me, I thank You,
O Lord my God and God of my ancestors,
Master of all worlds,
Lord of all souls.
Blessed are You, O Lord,
Who restores souls to lifeless bodies.

Modeh Ani is a relatively late addition to the Jewish liturgy; it is first found in prayer books from the sixteenth century. But it echoes many of the themes of *Elohai N'shamah*, a prayer mentioned in the Babylonian Talmud (*B'rachot* 60b) and included at the very beginning of the siddur.

David Abudarham, a fourteenth-century Sephardic commentator on the siddur, points out that each line in this prayer echoes a biblical verse. The opening lines, about God fashioning our souls, recall the sixth day of Creation, when God created Adam and breathed the spirit of life in him. Every morning hearkens back to the creation of the world. We wake up and our souls are placed back inside us in much the same way that God first breathed life into Adam's nostrils. "My God, the soul You have placed within me is pure"—as if every night God launders each soul and returns it clean and fresh. Abudarham connects the notion of "You formed it in me" to a verse from Zechariah (12:1): "The Eternal, who stretches out the heavens, who lays the foundation of the earth, and who forms the human spirit within a person." The Hebrew term used for "spirit" is *ruach*, which also means "wind." The spirit fills the body much like the wind filling the clothing on Wilbur's laundry line, and once animated again, the body can move and dance like the laundry in the breeze.

"One day You will take it from me," we acknowledge in *Elohai N'shamah*. Abudarham links this line to a verse from Ecclesiastes (12:7): "Then shall the dust return to the earth as it was, and the spirit shall return to God who gave it." We remind ourselves of our mortality immediately upon awakening because if our lives were not bounded—if we had all the time in the world—then we might be tempted to crawl back under the covers and do nothing at all. Like many parents, I am constrained by my children's school hours, yet without that time pressure, I might never get anything done. It is the knowledge of how short the day is that propels me forward. We speak the words of *Elohai N'shamah* to remind ourselves that we cannot know how many mornings we have left; we do not know how many more times God will faithfully restore our souls to our bodies. But we have been granted this morning on this day in this life, and so let us arise and embrace it.

Baruch Atah, Adonai . . .

Blessed are You, Lord our God, King of the Universe
Who has not made me a heathen.
Blessed are You, Lord our God, King of the Universe,
Who has not made me a slave.
Blessed are You, Lord our God, King of the Universe,
Who has not made me a woman.
  (Women say: Who has made me according to His plan.)

In the traditional liturgy, the morning benedictions begin with three blessings of personal status in which we thank God for not making us who we are not—a heathen, a slave, and a woman. More progressive prayer books word these blessings in the positive form—thanking God for making us a Jew, a free person, and someone created in God's image. But the shadow of their precursors enables us to appreciate the fates we have been spared.

One morning when I was in a synagogue that follows the traditional liturgy, I heard the male prayer leader recite the words "Who has not made me a woman." At the time I was five months pregnant; I had just begun feeling the baby kick, and though I did not yet know that she would be a girl, I could swear that the fetus thrashed violently in response to hearing the words of that blessing. And I recoiled as well, not in disgust but in surprise. I realized for the first time that the prayer I ought to be saying every morning was not thanking God for making me according to God's plan—which suggests a sort of second best—or even thanking God for making me in God's image, a prayer that both men and women can recite together. Rather, I wanted to thank God for making me a woman.

So many of my most profound spiritual experiences would not have been possible if I had been born male. In carrying human life inside me and bringing children into the world, I have felt closest to God as creator. I prayed with the most intention and fervor throughout my pregnancies, conscious of how much was beyond my control even as it was taking place just millimeters beneath the surface of my skin. Especially in those early months, I could not know with any certainty from hour to hour if the baby inside me was healthy or even still alive.

In moments of doubt or concern, there was nothing to do but place my hand on my belly and plead with God. And then, on those most joyous days of my life, amid the terror and elation of birthing my children, I felt so blessed to have this role as God's partner in creation. The liturgy of *Avodah* service recited on Yom Kippur evokes the terror and elation with which the high priest entered and exited the Holy of Holies, with the whole nation waiting outside in fear and trepidation. It is not an experience any woman will ever have, let alone a woman living in the modern era—but in giving birth, I feel I have been granted a glimpse of that sacred enclosure.

Had I been born in the era of Temple worship, presumably I would have a different attitude. After all, for much of human history, the vast majority of women experienced a clear social and political disadvantage. Think of Virginia Woolf at Oxbridge, who was sternly reminded that "ladies are only admitted to the library if accompanied by a Fellow of the College or furnished with a letter of introduction."[2] When reciting the morning benedictions, I think about not just how grateful I am to have been spared the fate of being someone I am not, but also about how fortunate I am to have been spared the fate of being born a woman in virtually any other era. I am blessed to be a Jewish woman in the twenty-first century, when the texts I love studying and the religious roles that infuse my life with meaning are freely accessible to both men and women. Blessed are You, Lord our God, King of the Universe, who has made me a Jew, and a free person, and a woman of our time.

Mizmor Shir Chanukat HaBayit l'David

> A psalm of David . . . I will exalt You, Lord, for You have lifted me up, and not let my enemies rejoice over me. Lord, my God, I cried to You for help and You healed me. Lord, You lifted my soul from the grave, You spared me from going down to the pit. . . . At night there is weeping, but in the morning there is joy. . . . You have turned my sorrow into dancing. You have removed my sackcloth and clothed me with joy, so that my soul may sing to You and not be silent. (Psalm 30)

This psalm transports me to one of the darkest and bleakest moments in my life, when I was deep in the pit. Recently divorced at age twenty-six, I found my life had been completely derailed. I wasn't sure where

I should be living—on one side of the Atlantic, where I'd grown up, or on the other side, where I'd recently made my home—and I was in between jobs, trying to distract myself with freelance gigs while fretting about the future. Then one day I had coffee with a friend, who looked me squarely in the eye and told me something that has stayed with me. It was a platitude, and I'm almost ashamed to admit what an impact it had on me, despite my scorn for self-help literature and my snobbish insistence that the best advice for how to live one's life can be found in the novels of George Eliot. And yet there I was, profoundly shaken when my friend told me, quite simply, that the only constant in life is change.

My friend went on. Everything in life is in flux; our reality is never static and unchanging. And given how horrible I was feeling then, she said, chances were that with time I would feel better. She made me feel so much more hopeful. To be in the pit does not mean that we will forever be in the pit. If we are wearing sackcloth now—it was so hard, in those days, even to get dressed in the morning—there is always the hope, and possibility, that at some time in the future we will be clothed in joy. (I was glad, six years later, that I had saved my wedding dress.) And though every night I wept, perhaps at some point for me, as for the Psalmist, the morning would bring joy.

The sentiments expressed by the Psalmist are echoed in Shakespeare's Sonnet 29:

> When in disgrace with fortune and men's eyes,
> I all alone beweep my outcast state,
> And trouble deaf heaven with my bootless cries,
> And look upon myself and curse my fate.

The speaker is in distress and cries out to God, cursing his sorrowful fate. By the end of the poem, though, the thought of his beloved and her "sweet love" brings him such joy that he avows that he would "scorn to change my state with kings." Since that moment in the café with my friend, I have recited Psalm 30 thousands of times in my morning prayers. In moments of joy, it has served as a humbling reminder that surely there are others whose distress I can help alleviate; and in moments of sadness, it has reminded me that this too shall pass.

Ashrei Yoshvei Veitecha . . .

> Happy are those who dwell in Your House . . .
> The Lord is close to all who call on Him,
>   to all who call on Him in truth. (Psalms 84:5, 144:18)

I have a hard time making time for prayer. In the mornings I am always in a rush to start my day, and so generally I pray while walking to work. In the afternoons, when I am counting down the minutes until I have to pick up the kids, I am loath to interrupt my work to take a few minutes for *Minchah*. And at night, by the time the kids are in bed, I collapse in exhaustion and cannot imagine standing up before God in prayer.

Every so often, though, I am reminded of why it is so important to pray regularly, even when it is the last thing I want to do. When we pray regularly, we ensure that we have an open channel of communication with God. To invoke a modern metaphor, we might say that by engaging in daily prayer, we ensure that God is always at the top of our Contacts list, so that in moments of acute distress, when we need to cry out, we don't have to start searching for God's contact information. Nor do we have to start with a long and awkward preamble, the way we might if, say, we broke a bone and called a distant orthopedist friend: "Hi John, I know we haven't been in touch in decades, but we went to college together, you know, I was friends with Steve and Linda . . . Anyway, I'm calling because I think I have broken my arm, and I'm wondering if I could send you the x-ray." When we speak to God on a regular basis, God knows who we are and we know how to talk to God, and so God will be close when we cry out in our brokenness.

Over time I have developed a deep appreciation for the transformative power of prayer, and I rarely bring novels with me to synagogue anymore. But sometimes I simply do not want to confront my own inner demons and desires, and I'd rather lose myself in someone else's fictional world. Other times I am tired of reciting the same words day after day—I don't know what will happen on the next page of my novel, but in the siddur I don't expect to find surprises. And then suddenly I'll hear the prayer leader recite a phrase that jumps out at me, catches hold of me, and perhaps even takes my breath away, and I return to the siddur with renewed determination to lose myself—and ultimately find myself—in its pages. I surrender to the inevitable moments of monotony with the faith that in the boredom comes the unbidden. Perhaps the siddur will never have the same appeal as a novel, but I hold out hope that by integrating the person I am into the liturgy each day, I can find my own way to make the ancient prayers and blessings feel just a bit more novel.

יי שְׂפָתַי תִּפְתָּח ...

Adonai, s'fatai tiftach ...

Adonai, open up my lips ...

—Psalm 51:17

Notes

1. Richard Wilbur, "Love Calls Us to the Things of This World" from *Collected Poems 1943–2004* (New York: Houghton Mifflin Harcourt, 2004), 307.
2. Virginia Woolf, *A Room of One's Own and Other Essays* (London: Folio Society, 2000), 24.

CHAPTER 3

Experiencing God
While Studying Jewish Texts

RABBI MARC KATZ

FOR ALL OF JEWISH HISTORY, our ancestors have been painting their lives onto the canvas of our holiest texts. Engaged in the sacred task of marrying ancient words with modern needs, they mine our rich scriptural tradition for meaning, placing it in conversation with their lives. For them, study is an act of faith as they hope that a three-thousand-year-old verse or story might have something to teach them about their own world. More often than not, it does. Something in the text calls out from the distant past, a touch of the archaic, wrapped in relevance.

Of all the texts in our tradition, I have always found the story of the Tower of Babel to be a particularly useful starting point to explore the role of ancient Scripture in our modern world. Anyone who has studied the story knows that the Tower of Babel is one of the most theologically baffling texts in the Jewish canon. In it, a group of people, united by language, decide to build a tower up to God. "Come," they say, "let us build a city with a tower that reaches the sky, so that we can make a name for ourselves and not be scattered over all the earth!" (Genesis 11:4). However, during the project God confounds their speech. Unable to communicate, they are forced to abandon the project and populate the far-flung reaches of the earth. The story serves as an etiology to explain why different locales have different languages.

What makes the story so confusing is that God never fully explains why the people deserve this punishment. In fact, God's inner mono-logue makes little sense, "If, as one people with one language for all, this is how they have begun to act, then nothing that they may propose to do will be out of their reach" (Genesis 11:6).

For me, the ambiguity of the text is the reason for its beauty. One of the hallmarks of Jewish literature is that it understands that our need to interpret is insatiable. Accordingly, it does not try to tie up loose ends. Jewish writing is defined by its terseness, which allows space for interpretation. The literary critic Erich Auerbach famously observed that contrary to Greek literature that seeks to include every detail lest it leave unanswered questions, the Bible (and much subsequent Jewish literature) leaves open gaps in the text for us to insert our own interpretations. For him, our texts remain "mysterious and fraught with background."[1] Since our Scripture cannot possibly answer all our questions, it does not try to, thus opening the door for us to read what we need out of and into our texts.

Since my life is always changing, what I need from any given text is changing as well. In my earlier years, I found deep relevance in the quest for justice. Though I saw the world through varied lenses—theological, interpersonal, psychological—it was the ethical that animated me most. Early in my studies, I encountered the following midrash that explained why God brought punishment on the people:

> The tower was built with seven steps on the east side and seven steps on the west side, and it was seven miles high. It took a person one year to climb from the bottom to the top. The bricks were carried up from one side, and the line of workers went down on the other side. If a worker fell down and died, they paid no attention to him. But, if a brick fell, they would all sit and weep, "What a loss," they would say. "Look how long it will take until we can bring another brick to take its place." (*Pirkei D'Rabbi Eliezer* 24)

Suddenly the text was transformed. No longer was it situated in Mesopotamia. Instead, it was a proverb, a cautionary tale for my era. Each fall, as I reflected on the story as part of the weekly Torah portion, it affirmed one of my deepest held convictions: people are paramount, and no project or endeavor should ever supersede the individuals involved.

Years later, when I would change and the quest for justice would fall behind other needs of mine, the text would remain, still as relevant as the day I first studied it. When I turned thirty, for example, and I began realizing my own mortality, the tower would morph for me into the ultimate futile quest to outrun death. I began to see it as an effort, on the part of the ancients, to build something that would outlast them. They might leave this world, but their structure would endure.

Today, as a rabbi who has counseled many through trauma, as well as encountered some of my own, I have tended to read the story through the lens of the sixteenth-century scholar the Maharsha, who put the story in dialogue with the Torah's previous tale of Noah and the Flood. For him, the people building the tower had inherited a collective anxiety, being only a handful of generations after a flood destroyed the earth and all its inhabitants. I have imagined them looking up to the clouds, wondering if God would keep the divine promise never to destroy the earth again. Despite the occasional bow in the sky, each instance of rain must have been a triggering experience. So, instead of ceding to their fears, they develop a plan: they will build a tower to heaven so they might pierce the clouds, letting the water out slowly and ensuring they would control the elements. Their desire to keep the chaos of the universe at bay is a universal feeling. For anyone who has felt out of control, it is only natural to seek out order and agency, even if it means building a tower to heaven to puncture the sky.

For me, study is an act of faith. I wholeheartedly agree with Rabbi Ben Bag Bag, who famously quipped, "Turn it, turn it, for all is in it" (*Pirkei Avot* 5:22). Even while I believe in scholarship and know that our Bible is a product of human hands, a piece of me feels that there must be something Divine about it. In its words exists every world, every life, every question. Our ancient wisdom cannot not speak directly to the challenges of our hyperconnected, technologically saturated, globalized society. All our problems and our entire world are somehow embedded in the text. Our sacred literature may not speak explicitly about the twenty-first century, but it has something to teach us about that which is most pressing: the modern experience of divorce; the question of whether or not to place our parents in a nursing home; what to do about the immigration crisis on the border; and how to raise our children.

And even if I'm wrong, and God had no hand in the making of the texts I study, the complex act of making meaning out of ancient words is a master class in human ingenuity. If the miracle is not in the written words themselves, then we, the readers, are the miracle. One can only stand in wonder and awe at our capacity for imagination and insight when we engage in study. As we sit down with a text, we watch our God-given gifts in action.

Many throughout time have argued about exactly what the Torah means when it says that humanity is created *b'tzelem Elohim*, "in the image of God (Genesis 1:27)." Some have identified our divine spark as compassion, others as dignity; but perhaps the most famous definition was found in the twelfth century, when Maimonides wrote in the *Guide for the Perplexed* that our most divine attribute is our "intellect" (*seichel*).[2] Just as God is capable of real thinking, so are we. When we exercise our intellect, we tap into one of the most divine parts of ourselves.

I have always found the study of commentaries to be more meaningful than the original texts with which they are wrestling, in part because they give me a glimpse into our ancestor's divine intellectual mechanisms.

Again, take the Tower of Babel as an example. Just as I have sought throughout my life to make meaning out of the text, so, too, have our commentators. Watching them is a master class in the use of divinely imbued creativity.

Abraham Ibn Ezra, for example, links God's decision to confound the people's speech to the need to have multiple philosophical languages. How we speak often influences how we think; therefore, having different modes of speech might broaden our collective thinking, whereas speaking only one language would have limited us in our ability to think creatively together. Ovadia Seforno, on the other hand, saw a unified language as limiting in a different way. For him, speaking only one tongue would have meant that people tried to impose their own religious truth—their sacred language—on one another. Left without the choice to worship whomever we see fit, we could never have achieved credit for choosing the right path forward. God had to confound our speech in order to ensure that diversity in language would lead to diversity in religious outlook and that we would have that level of choice.

At face value, these two interpretations appear inventive; the Tower of Babel story says nothing about philosophy or religious tyranny. However, observing that Ibn Ezra was writing during the Golden Age of Spain in the twelfth century, when the cross-pollination of ideas between Jews and other faiths facilitated a blossoming in religious philosophy, art, and science, brings a whole new meaning to his words. They become more relevant and help us to situate ourselves in our globalized, open world. Similarly, Ovadiah Seforno, writing in Italy in the early sixteenth century, found himself in the shadow of the Inquisition. Born in 1475, he watched as his brethren were forced to leave Spain. His reading was colored entirely by the religious fanaticism and violence he observed in the wider world around him.

Both of these interpreters seamlessly integrated their world into the biblical text. In the same way that we can watch the Olympics and marvel at the strength of the weightlifter, the speed of the sprinter, or the grace of the pole vaulter, we encounter these commentators in their writings and stand in awe of their mental acuity and ingenuity. The primary role of a teacher is to be a translator: to take a text that speaks to them and show to the skeptic why that text mattered to them—and why it matter to us, too. Reading their words, I am transported back the palaces of Andalusia and the tribunals of Córdoba. I see myself standing beside the philosopher and poet and I too am affirmed through Ibn Ezra. I walk together with the Converso and the refugee and I feel seen by Seforno. Through their words, our commentators defy time and location—and I define myself as being on one map with them.

Any good book should transport you. That is the magic and miracle of literature. It allows you to visit distant lands, inhabit the lives of forgotten people, experience eras easily ignored. Jewish study does all of this for me. It gives me a taste of the pain and fear our ancestors felt after their Temple was destroyed. It situates me under a tree, at the foot of some of the most powerful minds in Jewish history, as I wrestle beside them, seeking to make the Torah speak in our respective ages. I begin to read, and suddenly I am there when Rabbi Akiva falls in love with his wife Rachel, or when Bruriah has to tell her husband Meir about the deaths of their sons, or even when Hillel, unable to afford the fees to attend school, crawled onto the building's roof, peering through the skylight so he could listen in.

Yet, the difference between Jewish study and reading great literature is that God dwells in our midst when we study, as noted first by the ancient sage Ravin bar Rav Adda (Babylonian Talmud, *B'rachot* 6a). Virginia Woolf famously described reading as "perpetual union with another mind."[3] What she likely meant was that as we read, we lose our sense of ego, fully inhabiting the characters and in a way becoming them. Study allows me to do this with the great characters of our history, with Moses and Miriam, David and Job. This act alone can be described as a spiritual experience, a sort of negation of the self that mystics called *bitul hayeish* ("the erasure of existence").[4] And since God is the central character in the Jewish story, then the greatest "union" we might achieve is to become one with—or at least a little closer to—God.

However, read in light of religious philosophy, our "union" may be something even greater. I have spent most hours of my learning in personal, private study. In fact, I prefer to learn alone. I remember where I was when I first realized this, tucked away in the corner in the library at Hebrew Union College–Jewish Institute of Religion in Jerusalem. Many of my classmates were traveling during our winter break, exploring far-flung places only a short plane ride from Israel. After a short holiday in Istanbul with friends, I had returned with a few days to kill before classes started back up, and I decided to spend it studying. That first semester I had gotten a taste of Jewish learning, and I wanted more.

I was the only student in the library. I found a cubicle in the corner of the second floor, and after taking two Talmudic translations off the shelf, I began to make my way through the texts. Without a teacher to guide me, I decided to start from the beginning. Since I wanted to know everything, looking up terms I did not know and making charts of arguments so I would not lose the thread, it took me a few days to reach page six and read the words of Ravin bar Rav Adda for the first time—but even before that, I had already had a nagging feeling that I was studying wrong. Every model of study I had ever seen was in community. The structure of Jewish study has changed throughout time, moving from disciple circles in early Palestine to Babylonian academies, from groups of mystics in sixteenth-century Safed to modern rabbinical seminaries. But one thing always seemed constant: for two thousand years, Jews have learned with others.

However, since there was no one with whom I could learn, I decided that I did not want to wait for others to study. Over the next few years, study became a constant companion. Rarely did I leave the house without a tractate of Talmud or a book of philosophy in my bag. My tomes show the evidence of private learning—dog-eared corners, cracked bindings, marinara stains caused by ill-wiped fingers vigorously turning pages, engrossed in that day's ancient argument. Even at my loneliest, I did not feel alone during private study. God was in the pages.

But where? Reflecting back on God's place in my learning, I often think about the teachings of Mordecai Kaplan, Abraham Joshua Heschel, and Martin Buber, perhaps Judaism's three greatest twentieth-century theologians. Though their philosophies are diverse, each tries to answer the fundamental question of how we encounter God in the world. For Kaplan, God is "the power that makes for salvation,"[5] an opaque term that explains God as the extra push that all of creation, including us, needs to reach its truest potential. For Heschel, God is found in moments of awe.[6] When we encounter the ineffable, those things that take our words away, we encounter God. For Buber, God is found in relationships, not just relationships to people but to anything with which we can be fully present.[7] This "I-Thou" encounter can be with another person, but also with a song, a vista, or a piece of art—and for me, it can be a relationship with a text.

My spiritual connection to study vacillates between each of these three approaches. When we study an insight from our ancestors, we glimpse the products of our ancestors' highest potential. As Kaplan teaches, they have tapped into the source for salvation, and their insights have poured forth on the page. In conversation with them, I seek out that same source, hoping that I might reach the peaks of my own intellectual understanding and encounter God.

At other times, I have encountered Heschel's sense of the ineffable. I sit in a cafe with a book before me, mouth agape at the beauty and wisdom of what I have just read. In fact, if awe is meant to silence us, giving us experiences that words cannot capture, then it is only natural that often after a session of study, the only appropriate response I can think of is to repeat what I have just read to another person, to teach that page's insights to another person—since the text must stand alone, and I cannot find better words for what it taught me.

And sometimes, I think of myself studying in the categories of Buber: If the I-Thou encounter is found in being fully present, then I personally feel it most during study. There are times when I am reading and the world around me disappears. I do not read a text for a specific purpose, only so that I can continue down the page. I stop worrying about how I might use a text, or if I will remember it, and instead simply embody it. Since God dwells in the I-Thou encounter, I look back at those moments of reading and remember the energy bouncing between me and the written page.

When I study together with someone else, these three spiritual experiences become magnified. I have watched a classmate find something deep within themselves and reach unexpected intellectual and creative heights. I have stood in awe, not just of our material, but of my partner's ability to engage with it. I have connected deeply with *chavruta* partners, no longer wanting to look smart or impress them with my textual prowess, but instead being fully present with them on our shared literary journey.

The more I learn, the more I realize that study is a paradox. My knowledge is wholly mine, and yet my intellect comes somehow from God. My learning is grounded in words but connects me to the cosmos. It opens a door to the past while speaking clearly to the present and guiding me toward the future. It leads me toward awe for others and toward wonder within myself.

That is not to say that every time I study, I notice these tensions. In fact, I often learn with a goal in mind ("I need to finish this tractate or that page by day's end"). However, there are those moments in which I am least expecting it to happen that I get lost in an argument or a story— while sitting in a bagel shop or bus depot, stealing some moments before I move on to what is next—when a text brings it all together for me. Suddenly, God is somewhere in the room, within and among me. In that moment, I have joined three thousand years of learners, wading in the sea of our sacred texts, held up by their collective wisdom.

When that happens, the only words I can offer is the blessing *Shechalak Meichochmato*. Traditionally recited when we encounter a great scholar and usually spoken when we are standing in their presence, I have often adapted it for my own use. If I am lucky, I learn with the great sages of my generation, but every day, by simply opening a book, I encounter other sets of teachers, like Ibn Ezra and Ovadia Seforno, who amaze and inspire me. Every day, I gain an insight from a friend or colleague. Every day, I surprise myself with my God-given ability to make meaning from ancient words. Then, sometimes in a gasp, some- times with a sigh, I find myself uttering the prayer:

בָּרוּךְ אַתָּה, יי אֱלֹהֵינוּ, מֶלֶךְ הָעוֹלָם,
שֶׁחָלַק מֵחָכְמָתוֹ לִירֵאָיו.

Baruch atah, Adonai Eloheinu, Melech haolam,
shechalak meichochmato lirei-av.

Blessed are You, Adonai our God, Sovereign of the universe, who gave a portion of Your wisdom to those who stand in awe (Babylonian Talmud, *B'rachot* 58b).

NOTES
1. Erich Auerbach and Willard R. Trask, *Mimesis: The Representation of Reality in Western Literature* (Princeton, NJ: Princeton University Press, 2013), 15.
2. Moses Maimonides, *Guide for the Perplexed* 1:1
3. Quote found in afterword to Rachel DeWoskin, *Someday We Will Fly* (New York: Penguin Books, 2020).
4. This concept is found throughout mystical literature.

5. Mordecai Menahem Kaplan, *The Meaning of God in Modern Jewish Religion* (New York: Reconstructionist Press, 1962), 40.

6. Abraham Joshua Heschel, *Man Is Not Alone: A Philosophy of Religion* (New York: Farrar, Straus and Giroux, 1951).

7. Martin Buber, *I and Thou* (1923; New York: Clydesdale Press, 2020).

CHAPTER 4

Experiencing God
While Making Jewish Food

Melanie Cole Goldberg, rje

Baking challah has become integral to my weekly Shabbat observance. If I'm not able to bake challah because I'm sick or away
from home, I feel like something is missing. I have come a long way,
because I used to think that challah was too hard to bake. I was afraid of
yeast for no apparent reason.

Fortunately, I found a mentor who allayed my fears. My friend Daniela Horn had the practice of baking homemade challah for her family,
and her challah was delicious. I became inspired by her example and use
of a bread machine to make the dough. What I thought of as being difficult became easy. I also found the incredible book by Maggie Glezer,
A Blessing of Bread,[1] which opened my eyes to the world of challah and
Jewish breads. After a summer of experimenting with Glezer's recipes,
I adapted one that has become my go-to, fail-safe dough. Each Shabbat
and holiday, baking challah brings such warmth, goodness, and amazing smells into my home. My family and friends at my table delight in
the special taste, and I take pride in being able to spread joy with my
skills as a challah baker.

Over a decade ago, I started bringing a challah loaf to my weekly
Shabbat minyan. Sometimes I would bring a plain challah; sometimes I
would bring challah topped with seeds or stuffed with raisins, chocolate
chips, or cinnamon sugar. Soon I was teaching classes in the synagogue
kitchen. From other challah bakers, I learned about the spiritual aspects
of making bread.

On a trip to the Negev, I had the wonderful opportunity to bake challah with Hadas Meir, who hosts classes at her bakery/shop in Mitzpe

Ramon. In an interview with *Tablet* online magazine, Meir talked about the spiritual connection with making bread: "I think bread is a blessed food. It is the most moving interpretation of combining matter and spirit. Even physically, bread is spiritual in essence. There is a mass of dough which is 100 percent matter, and then air enters it and makes it rise. The spirituality, the magic, and the beauty of bread is what I try to show other people."[2] I recall Hadas's delight when she showed our group the huge tub of dough ready to be turned into braided loaves, "alive" with the magical, stringy stretchiness of yeast meeting flour, water, and all the other yummy ingredients that make challah so delicious.

We then said the blessing for separating challah. Separating or "taking challah" is a halachic practice: When making a large batch of dough (using at least fourteen cups of one flour or a combination of five flours: wheat, spelt, rye, barley, or oats), a handful, or a minimum of the size of a large olive, is separated. Like the main dough, this small piece is also called "challah." The baker holds it up with his or her right hand, says a blessing for the separation of challah from the dough, and declares, "This is challah!" Hadas explained that this moment of separation is particularly spiritual, as we are believed to be especially close to God, and we may add prayers for family, community, and Israel. The small, separated "challah" is then burned, separate from the rest of the delicious dough. We observe this ritual in remembrance of the custom of donating portions of bread to the priests during biblical times.[3] Every time I teach challah baking to a larger group, using at least five pounds of flour, I incorporate the blessing for separating challah. I mention the custom of saying a private prayer at the time when common ingredients turn into bread. Those prayers add a sense of spirituality to our baking.

I know that by making challah I am helping myself, my family, and others to connect to Jewish tradition and life. Challah making has supported my efforts to engage in the mitzvah of hospitality and "welcoming guests" (*hachnasat orchim*). Welcoming guests has been an essential aspect of my life and the life of other Jews throughout time. The text that is used to teach the value of this mitzvah is the story of Abraham and Sarah in *Parashat Vayeira* (Genesis 18): They quickly prepare a meal for angelic guests who appear at their open tent. Although Abraham is still recovering from his circumcision and surely in pain, he and Sarah rush to make a sumptuous meal for the three strangers. Guests feel welcome and comfortable when the focus is on them and not you—when you consider what your guests can or cannot eat; when you create an atmosphere that is relaxed, open, and warm; and when you help your guests through the choreography of conversation, listening, and eating so that their visit seems effortless. Ironically, this takes much effort, but for me, the weekly practice of baking challah and sharing it with my community at the synagogue or with friends in my home has become a blessing. I am grateful for this enriching experience. It connects me to my mom, who was an amazing hostess, and I know I have passed down the value of welcoming guests to my sons as well, who now consult with me when planning a gathering at their respective homes. Food has become a conduit of Jewish values.

Recipes

I cannot help smiling with warm memories of the time my Bubbe Cole, in her small, white kitchen, grinned mischievously at my sisters and me. Whispering, she shared her secret ingredient for her delicious chicken soup with us. We were there to learn and inhale all the methods and aromas from the master herself. She was petite and elegant, with blondish silver hair, and may have been born in Russia but was proudly American and assimilated, without any accent whatsoever. Almost silently and with reverence, she looked deep into our eyes and said, "Sweet potato." The secret was now ours. What a gift!

Bubbe Cole's gift of teaching me how to make chicken soup is a good example of my Jewish culinary learning and my spiritual connection with food. There was also Bubbe Rivke's method of making matzah balls and sweet-and-sour meatballs for Rosh HaShanah; my mom's strudel, lovingly baked for Yom Kippur break fast; and my mother-in-law Reggie's plum *kuchen* from her native Germany. It may be a cliché, but having a culinary, spiritual connection to Judaism is real. For me, Jewish food feeds my soul. These recipes link me to past generations, and when I make the foods I learned to cook from my relatives, I feel a real connection to them. They are there with me, each time I prepare, taste, and critique the outcome of my labors. I think of them and what they meant to me, how they shaped my values and personality, and I remember how much I loved them, and they me. I imagine many people have similar feelings and thoughts when they are re-creating a beloved recipe they inherited from a family member or dear friend.

Deeply connecting with others is one way to experience the Divine, as Martin Buber has taught.[4] Food is one conduit to make those connections. We are hardwired to be social, to share meals for sustenance and pleasure. Jewish food's long history includes the development of kashrut, the rich cultural diversity of Diaspora communities, and the local tastes of Jewish geography. Thankfully, many of us today have access to a variety of Jewish delicacies. We travel the internet in search of recipes and investigate great Jewish cooks and cookbook authors such as Joan Nathan and Claudia Roden, who share the wealth of the Jewish culinary world in their work. We can also learn, step-by-step, many Jewish food skills, such as how to braid challah or make *charoset* in whatever style we want, by viewing videos online. So even if our relatives do not have a Jewish background or are inept in the kitchen, we can find role models of people who excel at being Jewish foodies, and if we want, we can make Jewish food a spiritual practice. My Jewish food life has shaped my spiritual life: I keep kosher, observe the Jewish calendar, and bake challah as a weekly activity.

Following the Jewish calendar is another way in which food helps me to create deep spirituality. Every Jewish holiday has food items and recipes connected to it. I love to prepare and serve special foods according to the holidays. For Rosh HaShanah I make sweet foods such as sweet-and-sour meatballs and honey cake to welcome the new year with sweetness. I have adapted the Sephardic tradition of a Rosh HaShanah seder with special blessings for foods like new fruits, dates, beets, leek, squash, and so on . . . although I have never actually put a real fish head on my table, just a photo of one. For Sukkot, I make foods showcasing the fall harvest and include the Seven Species listed in Deuteronomy 8:8 as growing in Israel, namely wheat, barley, grapes, figs, pomegranates, olives, and dates. For Chanukah, I make latkes or other foods made in oil. We celebrate Tu BiSh'vat with a *seder* of fruits, nuts, and wines from

Israel. For Purim, I make *hamantaschen*. For Passover, I make multiple versions of *charoset* from around the world and *kasher* our entire kitchen for the week. It is a huge undertaking, but one that gives me a great sense of accomplishment. We also incorporate the ritual of searching for *chameitz* and burning it before Passover starts.

Making Jewish food for holidays has been an important way for me to learn more about the Jewish calendar and practices. My library of Jewish cookbooks includes recipes from Italy, Iraq, India, and Israel. The books provide wonderful background information about the ways those Jewish communities eat on a particular holiday and what those foods symbolize to them. Being exposed to culinary traditions from various parts of the world makes me feel connected to other Jews and adds adventure to my table.

Kashrut

Keeping a kosher home was definitely an act of rebellion on my part. I grew up in a Reform household that did not observe kashrut and where food experimentation was highly valued. We ate whatever we wanted, whenever we wanted. I remember hearing complaints from my mom while I was growing up about the rules the Jewish Federation had about kosher food at their meetings. She was annoyed that she, as a committee or board member, was required to conform to the norms of the commu-nity and could not bring in non-kosher food. It felt like an unwarranted burden on her. I am sure it was quite a shock when I told her I planned to keep a kosher home after I was married. I had been studying and liv-ing in Jerusalem and was influenced by the Jewish Renewal Movement. As an avid reader of *The Jewish Catalog*,[5] I thought that keeping kosher would make me feel connected to other Jews and "the Jewish people." It was an adventure for me to learn about Jewish food laws, and I was excited to create my own variations on them. After thirty-two years of keeping kosher according to my liberal interpretation, I check all labels of foods but don't necessarily only buy foods that have a *hechsher* (kosher certification). If a product is labeled "vegan," it is parve to me. I wait only a short period of time between eating meat and dairy; instead of waiting six hours, I clear off my table, wash and remove any dishes, and then switch to the dairy course of my meal. It is personally meaningful to me to observe kashrut the way I do; it connects me to my faith and God and provides a daily spiritual practice. Modern philosophers such as Mordecai Kaplan, according to whom Jewish civilization and folkways are means of connecting to the Divine, drive my spiritual practice. The feeling of being connected to a Jewish peoplehood by learning and transmitting the traditions of our history is an essential aspect of my life.

Blessings

As a continuation of including Jewish customs into our daily life, my husband and I have adapted the practice of reciting blessings over our food before eating dinner. When our sons were young, we played a game with them to teach which blessing was correct for the type of food being eaten. I have found that pausing for a blessing is a good way to acknowledge my thankfulness for having something to eat. In a privileged life, it is very easy to take our food for granted, and the practices of saying a blessing and eating kosher foods help me to show gratitude.

Community

Over the years, I developed a practice of preparing Jewish holiday foods with friends. Daniela Horn would have me and my kids over every year to prepare *hamantaschen* for Purim. We would bake according to family recipes and invent new combinations of fillings. Dulce de leche and Nutella were popular with our children, while we liked the combination of melted dark chocolate and softened, cooked apricots. Before Passover, I prepared homemade gefilte fish with my friend Bonnie Aibel and her mom Teddi Robbins, with real stock made from fish bones and vegetables. Making foods like *hamantaschen* and gefilte fish together with friends was a wonderful way to connect to people who really treasured Jewish customs. Of course, during our preparation, we talked about the upcoming holidays and how we were going to update and make them extra special that year. We talked about our families and different tasks of the holiday. We reminisced about family members who were no longer alive. Additionally, preparing holiday foods with friends made the communal aspect of the holidays come into focus, such as creating packages of *mishlo-ach manot*, "gift sending," at Purim or helping the Jewish community with the delivery of Passover foods to Jews in need.

Sharing food with others adds to the joy of Shabbat and holidays and helps focus on the mitzvah of welcoming guests. The experience of eating is not just about taking in sustenance; rather, it emphasizes the joy of community, creativity, and connection. As a host, it is important to me to make my guests feel like they are a part of the creation of the atmosphere at the table. I invite each person to bring a special dish they would like to share if they are so inclined. They have the opportunity to proudly share a family food tradition or to showcase their culinary talents. When Fran Gaynor brought her special brisket to our home for seder, we all loved it, and it meant the world to her and her family. When Julie Lambert made her Passover brownies, which are, without a doubt, an amazing dessert, we shared love, just as we shared chocolate.

Didactics of Cooking

I have also used my love of Jewish food and holiday cooking as a teaching tool. Most recently, I have opened my home to people studying in an Introduction to Judaism program for sessions on Jewish cooking. Students learn to make five different varieties of *charoset*, *hamantaschen*, and challah. I have found that the technical aspects of making the food are secondary to the emotional connections people begin to develop with these new skills. My students are so proud they can make these foods; they share them with their partners and families and feel bonded to Jewish life. When someone is able to make holiday foods, that person develops a sense of true ownership and connection to the holidays. The connection to the greater Jewish community can also be strengthened, when those who are skilled enough in Jewish cooking share their dishes with others. Sharing food brings joy both to those who partake in the food and to the cooks who are sharing their special treats. Nearly every community has someone who is known for their special Jewish cooking skill. I think these people need to be acknowledged and offered as mentors to others. The person who makes the best cheesecake for Shavuot or the person whose homemade *kugel* everyone looks forward to for the break fast after Yom Kippur should be encouraged to share their techniques with others in the community, because it will help other people connect to Jewish culinary traditions. Teaching these recipes will spark discussions about the meaning of the upcoming holiday and the symbolism of specific foods. Cooking and baking can become openings to text study. Kaplan's explanation of the central importance of Jewish folkways for the spiritual identity and connection of a Jew to faith, community, and God are key to my Jewish life.[6] It is profoundly rewarding to know that my challah students of the past ten years continue to bake challah for themselves, their families, and their synagogues long after they learned from me how to make the beautiful loaves.

Tastes and Memories

I have already mentioned that the tastes of Jewish foods often trigger my memories of family members, friends, and special happy and sometimes sad occasions. I imagine that the reader of this essay can also recall a time when the smell or taste of a Jewish food transported them back in time. We are encouraged to refrain from eating matzah before Passover so that when we sit at the seder, our first bite takes us back not only to the story of our enslavement and the travails of our ancestors, but also to all the seders of the past. Eating matzah and all the other seder foods lets our minds wander to our first family seder or to the seder we had in another city while on a trip. We recall people who used to sit with us around the table and now are no longer here. The tastes help us connect to Jewish culture and history. It is not surprising that the power of the Passover meal is precisely to let food do what it does best: to connect us to each other and to connect us to the past.

Being a culinary Jew isn't something to chide or hide. Jewish food is a wonderful conduit to a Jewish life of spiritual exploration. Tastes and aromas of Jewish foods transport people to wonderful memories of their childhoods, of observance, and especially of beloved people. It helps new Jews feel they belong to the Jewish people when they explore and incorporate Jewish food into their lives. The intentions and interpretations we bring to food are what elevates Jewish food from something mundane to the holy.

בְּרוּכִים נִהְיֶה בְּעוֹדֵנוּ מְכִינִים, אוֹכְלִים, וְנֶהֱנִים מֵהָאוֹכֶל
שֶׁמָּסוֹרְתֵנוּ הֶעֱנִיקָה לָנוּ. מַתְכּוֹנִים אֵלוּ מְקָרְבִים אוֹתָנוּ
אַחַת לַשֵּׁנִי, לֶאֱמוּנָתֵנוּ וְלֵאלֹהֵינוּ. אָמֵן.

B'ruchim nih'yeih b'odenu m'chinim, ochlim, v'nehenim meiha-ochel
shemasorteinu he-enikah lanu. Matkonim eilu m'karvim otanu
achat lasheini, le-emunateinu v'l'Eloheinu. Amein.

May we be blessed to create and enjoy the foods of our tradition with others as a way to bring us nearer to each other, to
our faith, and to our God. Amen.

NOTES

1. Maggie Glezer, *A Blessing of Bread: The Many Rich Traditions of Jewish Bread Baking Around the World* (New York: Artisan, 2004).
2. Dana Kessler, "Baker Hadas Meir Makes Bread Come Alive in the Desert," *Tablet*, January 8, 2015. https://www.tabletmag.com/sections/food /articles/bread-comes-alive
3. Extensive information on how to separate challah can be found on the web or in Maggie Glezer's book (see note 1).
4. As outlined in Eugene B. Borowitz, *Choices in Modern Jewish Thought: A Partisan Guide* (New York: Behrman House, 1983), p. 147.
5. Richard Siegel, Michael Strassfeld, and Sharon Strassfeld, eds., *The First Jewish Catalog: A Do-It-Yourself Kit* (Philadelphia: Jewish Publication Society, 1965), https://jps.org/books/first-jewish-catalog/.
6. Noam Pianko, "Reconstructing Judaism, Reconstructing America: The Sources and Functions of Mordecai Kaplan's 'Civilization,'" *Jewish Social Studies*, n.s., 12, no. 2, (Winter 2006): 39–55.

CHAPTER 5

Experiencing God in Dialogue
with (Non-)Jewish Poetry

RABBI SUZIE JACOBSON

A good poem helps to change the shape and significance
of the universe, helps to extend everyone's knowledge of
himself and the world around him.
—*Dylan Thomas*

EACH FALL I ride the rabbi's exhilarating wave of spiritual creativity
and lived ritual. After a too-short summer I find myself sur-
rounded by a present and energized community. I fight the malaise
of the blinking cursor, endure noisy coffee shops and writer's block,
and eventually emerge triumphant, sermons and prayer book in hand,
ready to serve. Accompanying our community through another season
of *t'shuvah*, "repentance" and "renewal," is a blessing. The healing, gen-
erative, meaningful experience of the Jewish High Holy Days, Rosh
HaShanah and Yom Kippur, highlight for me the relevance and vibrancy
of our Jewish tradition. Judaism doesn't live on a dusty bookshelf. It
does not implore us to beat our chests and drown in our inadequacies
and our own sense of shame and guilt. Instead, we are invited to enter
into a season of possibility—a world where change is not only possible,
but expected. A living, rich tradition.

And of course, when I bring my tired body home, the baby is crying,
the kitchen is a mess, a sukkah needs to be built, and an email box is
overflowing. The shift back into mundane yet comforting realities is a
part of the cycle, too. Though I leave the holidays ready to begin anew
and armed with a commitment to change, I so often fall back into habits
and patterns. In a typical year, the magic of the holidays, the sense of

urgency that makes these holiest of days feel so important, fades after a few weeks. This is why the High Holy Days are necessary every year—as human beings, we cannot help but rack up a year's worth of mistakes and misdeeds, beginning often moments after the holiday has ended.

In the middle of Tishrei 5780 (October 2019), I emerged from these marathon holidays with the foreboding sense of "what now?" Something from those holy days continued to rattle around in my rib cage. I had the niggling feeling that something was left incomplete, like the worry that you left your car doors unlocked or the kettle on a low flame. You might desire to keep on going, but your own prescient anxiety wants you to go home and check the burners.

Something from the holidays stayed with me. It was not the holidays' theology of repentance, prayer, and charity that kept my attention. Nor was it the majestic theme of *Avinu Malkeinu*, of "God, our Sovereign." I certainly did not draw continued inspiration from my own sermons, and even the beautiful music already seemed distant. The meaningful thread that kept me spiritually engaged that fall was not even of Jewish origin. Like a skipping record, I kept hearing this line from a Mary Oliver poem on repeat in my head:

> "You must change your life."
> "You must change your life."
> "You must change your life."

In her poem "Invitation,"[1] Mary Oliver shares lessons learned from goldfinches, her delight and gratitude for a life lived in the present moment, and an invitation to join her in witnessing the honesty and majesty of the natural world. Oliver mirrors and overtly references Rainer Maria Rilke's poem "Archaic Torso of Apollo,"[2] and though I shared both that year in the Yom Kippur afternoon "Poetry as Prayer" session at Temple Israel of Boston, this is certainly not established Jewish liturgy. During the 5780 High Holy Day season, I was able to find God in that poem in the most powerful and poignant way—a beautiful, simple poem about goldfinches singing in a "field of thistles."

I do not credit Oliver with prophecy or any such divine intermediacy, and yet her poem lived in me for months. Carrying with it a spiritual resonance far beyond its simple frame, the poem served me as a *kavanah*, an "intention," toward positivity and growth. In moments when I face difficult decisions or challenging conflict, her words guide me. Used as a mantra, this simple poetic phrase calls to mind complex feelings and ideas. And since the poem was read on Yom Kippur, using it as part of my daily spiritual practice turns it into a continual link to the meaning of that day. "We must change our lives."

Mary Oliver might not be part of a traditional Jewish canon, but the use of poetry as prayer language is age-old. The historical, poetic expressions of the Jewish people are found on every page of the siddur (the "prayer book"). The devotional yearning and spiritual seeking of one generation becomes part of the fixed canon of the next generation. The siddur is filled with the poetic imagination and creativity of our biblical ancestors, the ancient Rabbis, and the medieval poets. Metaphors for God change and shift in each generation. Central themes of creation, revelation, and redemption find new voice and expression, depending on the authors' primary motivations. Jewish prayer is expressed in the poetic voice, culled, edited, and canonized through generations of human beings searching for God.

Until recently, Western culture has privileged seemingly objective theology and philosophy over poetry when searching for the Divine. The best example is Plato, who often wrote disparagingly about how his society used poetry to express what is best explored systematically through philosophy.[3] In *The Republic*, Plato says that "there is an old quarrel between philosophy and poetry."[4] Though he acknowledges the greatness of poets such as Homer, he believes that philosophy provides a society with greater stability and discipline. Poetry, on the other hand, is too emotional, too unpredictable. While philosophy uses logic to explore law, ethics, and theology, poetry uses metaphor, imagery, and subjective, emotional artistry to portray a single author's perception of the human and the Divine.

Some interpret Plato's debate to represent the growing rift between a burgeoning academy of philosophers and scholars and the popular culture of the masses. However, our Jewish ancestors preserved a "more is more" attitude regarding the creation and proliferation of texts. The Rabbis in particular freely explored God theologically, debated and decided on issues regarding Jewish halachah (law), while at the same time creating the imaginative world of midrash. They created systems of logic to frame their exploration of objective truth while also creating and sharing expressive, subjective poetry that became an integral part of the Jewish prayer service.

While Plato feared that the accessibility and subjectivity of poetry would render society both shallow and unstable, those who created Jewish poetic prayer made the Jewish service both more personal and more complex. The accessibility and subjectivity of poetry is exactly why it resonates so well with the more "theological" prose prayers.

Poetry is uniquely suited to lend itself to spirituality and devotion. Poetry is able to get to the heart of human experiences without being obtuse, because it explores human observations and relationships from the first-person perspective. A poem may explore an emotion, a theological concept, an experience, an observation—in a deeply personal and nuanced voice, and without trying to resolve all tensions. For example, the biblical authors write in the Song at the Sea (Exodus 15):

> *Mi chamochah ba-eilim, Adonai;*
> *Mi kamochah nedar bakodesh,*
> *Nora t'hilot, oseih fele!*
>
> Who is like You, Eternal One, among the celestials;
> Who is like You, majestic in holiness,
> Awesome in splendor, working wonders!
> (Exodus 15:11)

Here the rhetorical questions, the repetitive, melodic construction, and vivid adjectives allow the reader or person in prayer to express wonder, amazement, or gratitude. Each person who utters these words speaks in a unique context. In this way, a poet's voice is preserved on paper, but when the words are spoken or sung, chanted or whispered, the meaning and messages belong to the one who prays.

This is felt poignantly in poems such as Psalm 23, a text ubiquitous at funeral gatherings:

> *Adonai* is my shepherd, I shall not want. . . .
> Though I walk through a valley of the shadow of death,
> I fear no harm, for You are with me;
> Your rod and Your staff—they comfort me. (Psalm 23:1, 4)

Themes of comfort and accompaniment in the face of death and despair resonate deeply in gatherings of mourning and remembrance. Metaphors like "shadow of death" capture the experience of losing a loved one, and the comfort of God's shepherding—as expressed through the descriptions of God's "rod and staff"—honor our desire to be guided and cared for during moments of loss. Poignantly, the psalm is written from the first-person perspective. Even when we read or sing this psalm together, we each are expressing our individual grief. Such is the power of poetry.

However, despite this pluralism of ideas and modalities, it is often simply the age of a text that gives it its weight and authority. Over the millennia of Toraitic transmission, Jews have learned to view Jewish rhetoric and writing as not merely creative, but rather a part of the ongoing experience of revelation. As our mythology teaches, God gave the Torah on Mount Sinai not as a definitive course book, but as an ongoing experience of finding God in the wit and wisdom of human beings who speak, write, and importantly, read and teach. The Torah (its storytelling, law, and poetry) is considered the most important and authoritative. As more and more time passes since those ancient words were authored, we begin to feel inadequate in regard to the words of contemporary poetry: Does it merit a place alongside the Song at the Sea? And if it does, is the same true for poetry written by non-Jewish authors? For example, does Mary Oliver, a non-Jew, find a place in this chain of holy transmission?

Like all great sermons, prayer is always written in the language of the time. There is power and beauty in recalling the poetry of our ancestors, but we also need to find our own spiritual and emotional translations. It is clear to me why Oliver was a more poignant spiritual voice for me this High Holy Day season than *Avinu Malkeinu*—Oliver and I are part of the same cultural conversation; we are speaking the same language. Like many, I find it difficult to be inspired by the hierarchical images of a God who yearly leafs through a book of my deeds, ready to punish every misstep. Yet, when Oliver writes in her poem "The Invitation" that "it is a serious thing / just to be alive / on this fresh morning / in the broken world," I understand that my humanity ordains me to a higher purpose. This world may be broken, but I am alive and therefore responsible. Yom Kippur is our "fresh morning," our new chance, and Oliver writes the liturgy that serves as a potent spiritual tool.

Poets Oliver, Rainer Maria Rilke, Ada Limón, and Billy Collins will not likely be canonized as traditional liturgy. Neither will their Jewish poetic counterparts Marge Piercy, Adrienne Rich, and Yehuda Amichai. And yet all of these poets found their way into our 5780 "Poetry as Prayer" Yom Kippur service.

For the past four years, I have gathered with a few dozen congregants between the morning and afternoon services in our "poetry as spiritual practice lab." At the beginning, I introduce the structure and intentions. Our time together is a prayer service, not a discussion group or a work-shop. Everyone receives a packet of poems, each to be read sequentially by two different readers. Repetition is key, as poems are read differently by different individuals. Pace, tone, intonation, and emphasis all change meaning. Readers are not called upon or invited by the leader. Instead, individuals step forward to read when they are interested. There is no rush; I encourage space to be given between poems, even silence, so we can absorb and enjoy each poem separately. And though I serve as rabbi and facilitator of the ritual, after introducing the process, I sit back and remain silent throughout. The prayer experience is democratized; all voices have equal weight.

The order of the poems in the packet is intentional and follows a theme. Last year our theme was "difficulty making change." In prior years, themes included forgiveness, social change, and images of God. Sometimes two or more poems placed sequentially are in conversation with each other or contrast starkly in imagery or message. This is not an intellectual exercise, and most years we do not leave room for con-versation or group reflection. The poems are chosen and recited for the sake of personal meaning-making. The atmosphere is meditative and prayerful. The poetry is our shared language, but we each hear and absorb differently.

Just like in a more traditional prayer setting, the poetry service serves as a collective experience that opens up new worlds of personal meaning-making. Even when a poem is familiar, every recitation brings new insight, touches our hearts in new ways. The poem stays the same, but our lives are always changing. A poem is able to speak to us in clear, accessible spiritual language, a refreshing change from the ancient and medieval Hebrew language of the rest of Yom Kippur.

The introduction of secular poetry on Yom Kippur is not revolutionary; the Reform Movement *machzor* (High Holy Day prayer book), *Mishkan HaNefesh*, is full of poetry, particularly on the interpretive left-side page. The *machzor* incorporates poetry as an alternative or translation to traditional prayers and spiritual themes. The prayer leader can incorporate the poetry into the order of the service, and the prayer participant can always elect to read the poetry privately, instead of engaging in whatever is happening in the room. This poetry service is different: it does not follow a traditional order, there is no Hebrew (though I have sometimes included medieval poetry for the sake of contrast), and very few poems have overtly Jewish content.

One reads a poem differently when it is read in the final hours of a religious marathon, after we have spent a day fasting and steeped in the emotional and spiritual prompts of the holiday. When we read Mary Oliver's line "You must change your life" on Yom Kippur afternoon, knowing that *N'ilah*, the closing service approaches, the poem takes on a different sense of urgency. Poetry can provide us with the prayer language of our hearts.

Human beings search for God with every tool our hands can reach. On a day like Yom Kippur, our tradition encourages us to search by fasting, praying, singing, and Torah. But there are many spiritual tools at our disposal that day and every day. Reading poetry is the accessible, subjective, and transcendent spiritual device many need to open up their hearts and give language to the beauty and complexity of our lives.

May we each find language that moves us, inspires us, compels us to see this complicated world anew. May we have the bravery to seek out new words; may we make room in our hearts for new pathways toward the Divine. With these words in our mouths and these meditations in our hearts,

מִי יִתֵּן וְנִפְתַּח אֶת לִבֵּנוּ לְדַרְכֵי צְדָקָה, רַחֲמִים וְשָׁלוֹם.

Mi yitein v'niftach et libeinu l'darchei tzedakah, rachamim, v'shalom.
May we open ourselves up toward pathways of justice, compassion, and peace.

Notes

1. Mary Oliver, "Invitation," in *Devotions: The Selected Poems of Mary Oliver* (New York: Penguin Books, 2020), 107.
2. Rainer Maria Rilke, "Archaic Torso of Apollo," in *The Selected Poetry of Rainer Maria Rilke*, ed. Stephen Mitchell (New York: Vintage International, 1982), 61.
3. See Charles L. Griswold, "Plato on Rhetoric and Poetry," in *Stanford Encyclopedia of Philosophy* (Spring 2020 ed.), ed. Edward N. Zalta, https://plato.stanford.edu/archives/fall2016/entries/plato-rhetoric/.
4. Plato, *The Republic*, 607b 5–6.

CHAPTER 6

Experiencing God While Making (Jewish) Art: Glimpses of Splendor

Rabbi Hara E. Person

Awareness of the divine begins with wonder.
—Abraham Joshua Heschel, *God in Search of Man*

ONCE UPON A TIME, before my identity was intertwined with being a rabbi, I was a photographer. Everything I saw, every draping of light, every juxtaposition of one object against another, every interesting grouping, every contrast of the illuminated and the shadowed was a wonder, and a potential photograph. For many years, I breathed in the world through my eyes, composing and arranging what I saw even when the camera was not in my hands.

I became a photographer in high school, and photography remained at the center of my life throughout college as well. After college, I worked in a photography lab at an educational center in Jerusalem, teaching youth leaders from around the world how to use photography to teach about Israel when they got back to their home communities. After that, I studied photography in Tel Aviv. Though I had had stray thoughts about rabbinical school since age ten, I put that impulse on hold and returned to New York for graduate school in fine arts in a program specializing in photography.

For a long time, the world made more sense to me through the lens of a camera. I couldn't have said so at the time, but now I understand that the defined edges of the photograph helped me keep chaos at bay. There they were—four straight lines, four clear boundaries that defined the edges of the image. Whatever was going on inside the image—beauty, color, shadows, tension, joy, sorrow—was contained within the borders.

The ability to compose an image within those four edges was comforting. I could focus my view and my energy on that box and manage what went on within it. I was the storyteller, choosing how to tell the story. I moved one way or another to get the best angle. I was drawn to composition that set objects off from each other and that allowed contrast between the sky and whatever else was in the frame. Distinctions between foreground and background pulled at me. Although I wouldn't have said so at the time, when I look at my old photographs I see that there was often a tension between the eternality of the horizon and sky, and the human detritus that disrupt the clean, spacious lines of the heavens.

I preferred to shoot early in the morning or in the late afternoon, when the sun was softer and sculpted whatever it hit. When I studied in Tel Aviv, I would take an express bus early in the morning from Derech Beit Lechem in Jerusalem, leaving when it was still dark. I would arrive in Tel Aviv as the sun was spreading out across the city, golden and warm. Since my classes didn't start for a while yet, I would walk to the beach, sit and eat my breakfast of *leben* and a sesame roll, and watch Tel Aviv wake up. The contrast of the white buildings in the warm early-morning light against the turquoise of the sea and the cyan of the sky filled up my camera that year.

I loved printing almost as much as I loved photography itself: the smells, the equipment, the math, the artistry, the power to draw forth the story out of shadows and light. And I loved it equally—the hands-on aspect of black-and-white printing on rich, velvety, matte stock, and the more mechanized color printing, turning dials to achieve evocative, deeply saturated yellows and blues, magentas and greens, creating drama from shades and hues. I loved the microscopic brushes and the little gray bottles of tints used to touch up prints, and the unique ways that master printers could coax forth more variegated grays, more vivid color.

The program I was in offered only one class in digital photography, this being the early 1990s, and none of us took it seriously. We were studying with artists—digital photography seemed irrelevant, even boorish. But when I got pregnant with my first child, I stopped printing. Worried about the toxicity of the chemicals, I stepped out of the darkroom and never returned. At the same time, I made the decision to apply to rabbinical school. Photography receded into the background. Between school and parenting and work, I had little free time to begin with, and what spare time I had became devoted to writing. Writing required no equipment or chemicals and could be done at any hour of the day or night. It was a seamless transition into a professional life centered around words rather than visual images.

For years, my photography was limited to family pictures and utilitarian pictures that could be used in books I edited. Along the way, I began to play with digital photography. Not so silly after all, I realized, and I now have a phone that takes photos that are almost as good as my old Nikon FM. At my son's urging, I began to experiment with posting photographs on social media. It sounded like the ultimate time-waster—why in the world would I need one more form of social media? But it turns out he was on to something. Using my phone, I found a way, however circumscribed, to reconnect to photography.

The filters available through various apps give me some small amount of control over the image—different from what I used to be able to do in the darkroom, but not that far off. I can saturate the colors, I can make a photo warmer or colder, brighter or darker. One of the options is even a choice of borders, a simulation of what was possible with negative printing. And I've come to love the small square shape of photos online. The size and shape feel intimate, personal—small jewels encased in the black border. The square shape also hearkens back to photography's early days of square, large-format images, creating a bridge between the technology of the past and the present.

Some years back I hit a skid in my personal life. Though I knew objectively that I had much to be grateful for, it was hard to acknowledge a sense of gratitude. It was difficult to notice the positive that was out there beyond the slog of getting through every day. But now and then, I'd feel the impulse to take out my phone and capture a slice of beauty. These fleeting glimpses of splendor broke through my horizon of pain and lifted me up.

The photos I began taking at that time on my phone were quite different from what I had done in art school. They weren't gritty, documentary images. They weren't social commentary or insightful observations about relationships. These photos, taken on my way to the gym in the morning as the light was coming up over the F train overpass, or as the setting sun glinted through the trees above the electric wires at the end of the day, or as a shadow cut magnificently across a wall while I hurried to do an errand, were about stumbling upon unexpected splendor, savoring random moments of grace in the midst of an overfilled, overcomplicated life. These were moments to stop and actually see the wonder around me despite the swirl of so much else going on, time to stop and breathe and slow down.

These photos on my phone became a way of reclaiming my old practice of experiencing the world visually, while also enabling me to stop and savor the grandeur of the quotidian. The words in which I was immersed daily came from the head, but a photograph starts with a gift that the world offers up. In teaching that we are to say one hundred blessings a day, the Talmud encourages us to take notice and not simply lurch unseeingly through our days. "It is taught in a *baraita* that Rabbi Meir would say: 'A person is obligated to recite one hundred blessings every day'" (Babylonian Talmud, *M'nachot* 43b). Bringing photography back into my life was a visual version of this urging to truly perceive and experience the beauty of the world and not take any of it for granted. At a time when feeling grateful was difficult, when praying was a challenge, and when God felt distant, making these small photos on my phone and then sending them out into the universe helped me find my way back to gratitude and a connection to God.

> You have seen all that the Eternal did before your very eyes in the land of Egypt, to Pharaoh and to all his courtiers, and to his whole country: the wondrous feats that you saw with your own eyes, those prodigious signs and marvels. (Deuteronomy 29:1–2)

Our tradition teaches of miracles, such as those related to Passover, that happened in our mythic past. However, our lives are also full of signs and marvels, those gifts that not only arrive during miraculous and extraordinary times but happen to us every day if we take care to notice. I soon understood that through these photos, I had found my way back to gratitude. They became my *modah ani*—my daily reminder that life can be beautiful and sweet and that I had much to be thankful for, despite it all. Taking notice was what enabled me to grab onto gratitude and climb my way out of the darkness.

> God said, "Let there be light!"—and there was light. And when God saw how good the light was, God divided the light from the darkness. (Genesis 1:3–4)

When the world was created, on the very first day, light was created, along with darkness. From that very elemental, primal beginning the rest of Creation unfolded, swathed in light by day and covered by darkness at night. This image of God as artist, painting and sculpting the world into being, writing our lives through speech, is both powerful and empowering. Created in God's image, we, too, can be artists; we, too, can imagine worlds into being; we, too, can express our particular, unique visions through dance, song, stories, drawing, or photography, or any other infinite number of mediums. In so doing, we become God's partners in Creation, each of us in our own humble way echoing God's masterwork as we do what we can to explain, interpret, reflect, and even improve upon the world as we encounter it.

Abraham Joshua Heschel wrote:

> Radical amazement has a wider scope than any other act of man [*sic*]. While any act of perception or cognition has as its object a selected segment of reality, radical amazement refers to all of reality; not only to what we see, but also to the very act of seeing as well as to our own selves, to the selves that see and are amazed at their ability to see.[1]

The images created on my phone were my personal version of Heschel's radical amazement: they were an easy and doable way, within the realistic parameters of my daily life, to truly *see* the world around me. Wherever I am, and whatever I'm doing, if beauty or wonder jumps out at me, I can respond. These photos have become part of a spiritual practice that grounds me and reminds me that not all is difficult, not all is complicated—that joy and amazement exist—if I take a moment to look.

בָּרוּךְ אַתָּה, יי אֱלֹהֵינוּ, מֶלֶךְ הָעוֹלָם,
אֲשֶׁר מִלֵּא אוֹתָנוּ בְּרוּחַ אֱלֹהִים.

Baruch atah, Adonai Eloheinu, Melech haolam, asher milei otanu b'ruach Elohim.

Blessed are You, Adonai our God, Sovereign of the universe, who fills us with God's inspiration.

NOTE

1. Abraham Joshua Heschel, *God in Search of Man: A Philosophy of Judaism* (New York: Farrar, Straus and Giroux, 1955, 1983), 46.

CHAPTER 7

Experiencing God
While Leading Jewish Song

RABBI KEN CHASEN

I WAS TEN YEARS OLD when music moved into the center of my life. I had started taking guitar lessons, and while I quickly demonstrated ability, it was not matched with discipline. Once my parents figured out that I was talented enough to cram successfully for my next lesson after not practicing all week, they understandably decided the lessons were a poor investment and put an end to them. They likely assumed my guitar playing days were over. But almost immediately, being left alone with the instrument felt like liberation, and I spent day after day in my childhood basement, listening to my favorite Beatles albums and figuring out how to play along with them. Clearly, this was the way I was meant to learn to play.

By the time I first attended Goldman Union Camp Institute (GUCI), the Reform Movement summer camp in Indiana, I was nearing my twelfth birthday and was already a fairly accomplished guitarist. However, until then, my guitar had only summoned the songs I loved from my records and the radio. I didn't yet know that a new spiritual vernacular was already developing, one that was spoken by people like me: singers who could accompany themselves on the guitar. My first camp songbook in that summer of 1977 was dominated by the songs of Debbie Friedman, Jeff Klepper, and Danny Freelander, and it was their liturgical melodies that filled our daily worship services. For the first time, I discovered a language of prayer that felt native. I could do more than witness these prayers. I could offer them myself—and lead others to do so with me.

My home synagogue wasted no time in putting my newfound self-discovery as a prayer leader to work. In youth group services, in our Religious School, and sometimes even in our main sanctuary services, I was welcomed by our cantor, Paul Silbersher, to the front of the room with my guitar in hand. I also worked as a song leader at regional youth conclaves while attending as a participant, developing comfort and skills as a worship leader as my opportunities increased. By the time I graduated from high school, I was already one of the main music leaders at GUCI—and it was as that summer drew toward its end that a chance invitation changed the arc of my life.

One of the camp's unit heads, Bruce Lustig, was soon to head back to Cincinnati for his third year of rabbinical studies at the Hebrew Union College–Jewish Institute of Religion. Among his responsibilities that year would be making biweekly visits to serve as the Student Rabbi for the tiny congregation of Beth Boruk Temple in Richmond, Indiana. When Bruce figured out that his drive from Cincinnati to Richmond would take him along US Highway 27, straight through Oxford, Ohio, where I was to start my freshman year at Miami University, he made me an offer. He asked if I would be interested in serving as his cantorial soloist in Richmond for the High Holy Days.

I remember being equally flattered and flummoxed by this invitation. Being only seventeen years old, I certainly didn't know how to sing any of the traditional High Holy Day liturgy that his congregants would be expecting. Bruce already had an answer for that: he would send me a packet of all the sheet music for the Rosh HaShanah and Yom Kippur melodies, enabling me to learn them over the coming month before the holidays arrived. It was a daunting task, but I couldn't resist the honor and the challenge, and I began preparing to serve as the cantorial soloist of Beth Boruk Temple.

This assignment would afford me only a few opportunities to play and sing the music I had learned and come to love at camp. Most of the melodies Bruce sent me came from the traditional canon of Classical Reform synagogal music. As a child, I had heard many of these pieces sung by my temple's cantor and choir with organ accompaniment. I wondered if I could find an authentic voice for offering them—if, beyond the proficient delivery of the notes and words, I could infuse them with the profound spirit the season demands.

Filled with a mixture of earnestness and self-doubt, I stepped into the space before the open ark on Erev Rosh HaShanah to sing Max Janowski's majestic setting of *Avinu Malkeinu*. It was one of the pieces that had taken me the least time to prepare, for I already knew it well, having heard it annually ever since I could remember. What I was not prepared for, however, was the effect that singing it on behalf of a praying community on the High Holy Days would have on me. It is something that I still struggle to describe, even thirty-seven years after it happened. The closest I can come to finding words for the experience is: I felt God.

Until that moment, I would have considered myself one of the least likely people to say he had "felt God." It is not that I hadn't already been blessed to enjoy many wonderfully spiritual experiences in my young life. Certainly, the discovery of the music I learned at camp, and my many opportunities to share it with others, had inspired my soul deeply. But what I felt that evening on the *bimah* of a tiny synagogue in a small Indiana town was different. It was *physical*. A rush of spirit overcame me—a feeling of connection spanning centuries, a situating of myself across time and place. I was a part of a great oneness . . . the great Oneness our tradition teaches us to sense. I felt it in my body, in my breathing. I had to account for it in order to complete my singing of the piece. Don't ask me how I knew—but I knew it was God.

Of course, after experiencing this once, I hungered to experience it again. I discovered, though, that it was not something I could manufacture. The conditions had to be right, and even then, it would require a type of receptivity that had to be cultivated. I had to create an opening to let God in. And over time, I concluded that this was not something meant to happen routinely. The transcendence I felt in that moment is rooted in its very uncommonness. Just as our tradition teaches that *k'dushah* (holiness) can be identified by its juxtaposition to *chol* (the "ordinary"), I learned that my "God moments" in music would reside in the terrain of the extraordinary, predicated upon a combination of readiness and surprise.

That is not to say that they have been so extraordinary as to be entirely absent. I have felt God when singing in the widest variety of settings, from summer camp to the Western Wall to the bedsides of those about to die. It's not any sort of corporeal or providential God I am feeling. It's the bounty and purity in which everything aligns to reveal the great Oneness we pray about when singing *Sh'ma Yisrael, Adonai Eloheinu, Adonai Echad*—"Hear, O Israel . . . hear, in the wonderment of this sound, the Unity in all being, which binds all of creation as One."

I have also been blessed to witness others who have felt God through song, even some who did not see themselves as singers or musicians. Perhaps the most striking example occurred while I was working in my first job as a rabbi, as I came to know the Greenberg family.[1] They were a family of five that was highly engaged in temple life. The father, Matthew, was Jewish. The mother, Debbie, was not, but it did not take me long to discover the distinctiveness of Debbie's Jewish soul. She was clearly the driving force in raising her three children as Jews, but it was much more than that. She was a frequent Shabbat worshiper who sang the words of the siddur (prayer book) with joyous conviction. She was a regular student in our *parashat hashavua* (weekly Torah portion) class, where her comments were characteristically among the most incisive (and often echoed teachings of our greatest sages). She was wholly committed to synagogue volunteerism as well. Debbie was everything a rabbi could want in a congregant. She just happened not to be a Jew.

While Debbie and I were still in our early months of getting to know each other, we learned that her mother had died in the small southern town where Debbie had grown up. Very quickly, a spontaneous shivah gathering unfolded at the home of this Protestant woman who had lost her Protestant mother. The house was filled with leading members of our congregation, young and old, who came to fulfill the Jewish commandment of *nichum aveilim* (comforting the mourner). Transfixed by the beauty of this organic outpouring of sympathy, I remained in the house until the other visitors departed. With embers in the fireplace dying down, Debbie and I sat in the living room and talked about her childhood home, her mother's parenting, her small-town Christianity. And then, finally, I could no longer resist the obvious question.

"Debbie, do you ever think about converting to Judaism?" I asked.

"Not really," replied Debbie.

"I have to admit to being a bit surprised," I countered. "You're so deeply immersed in our Jewish community. Look at this turnout tonight from our temple. Do you ever feel like you just *ought* to be a Jew?"

"It's not that I wouldn't be honored to be a Jew," explained Debbie. "But it doesn't feel right to me. I hold the Jewish people in such high regard—almost in awe. It's such a remarkable heritage . . . such a deeply meaningful history. It doesn't feel to me like something one can rightly choose. I'm proud to live among the Jewish people and to bestow Jewish identity upon my children. I don't know, however, if I could ever imagine feeling as though I am, in fact, a Jew. Does that make sense?"

"Of course . . . that's fine," I said, not wanting to seem like a proselytizing bully, but wondering whether her statement actually did or did not make sense.

Four years passed before Debbie and I discussed her religious identity again. If anything, Debbie's "non-Jewishness" had come to seem more and more antithetical with every passing year, and yet I remained silent about it. Remembering her living room explanation years earlier, I concluded that it would be inappropriate for me to revisit the matter. However, one day, Debbie poked her head into my office doorway: "Rabbi, do you have a second? I'd like to know what's involved in the conversion process. I think I want to convert to Judaism."

I was stunned by the suddenness of her request. "When your mother died, you told me that conversion was really not an option for you. What changed?"

"It's kind of hard to describe," Debbie answered. "This past Friday night, when we were at services, a wonderful feeling of wholeness sort of washed over me. It was during the singing of the *L'chah Dodi* prayer . . . I looked over at Sally Millner [a past president of the congregation and also a regular Shabbat worshiper], and she was singing her heart out to welcome the Sabbath, just like me. We smiled warmly at one another, and I just had this compelling feeling: I am no longer *with* the Jews . . . I am now *of* the Jews. I can't really explain it. I just realized that Judaism isn't a choice for me to consider anymore. I have already chosen it—God, Torah, Israel . . . all of it. So what's the process for me to convert?"

I remember almost laughing at the idea of asking Debbie to start a conversion process: "I agree . . . you have already chosen Judaism. So, I'm not going to send you to a class or ask you to read some book that you've probably already read. What's the 'process' for you to convert? The past twenty years have been your process. Let's study Hebrew names together and make a good choice for you, and then let's book a date for *beit din* (a rabbinic conversion panel) and *mikveh* (ritual bath). But I want to talk with you more about this epiphany you had while singing *L'chah Dodi*—because I think you found your way to something more than just Jewish identity in that moment."

I told Debbie about my musical "God moments" over the years, and I watched as she nodded knowingly. She, too, knew what it felt like when everything lines up just right, enabling a soul to experience the feeling of being a part of the great Oneness.

As I prepared to be ordained as a rabbi in 1998, I began to turn my attention as a musician to composing original Jewish music for liturgical, educational, and camp settings. I was curious to see if I could feel God in the creative process and, in so doing, perhaps help to create the conditions for others to experience what can happen when soulful readiness meets spiritual surprise. Just as it is on the *bimah*, I cannot will a "God moment" into being when composing, but in those instances when I have been most honest and unguarded while working on a developing piece, I have on occasion found my way to the One.

Sometimes, it has happened while writing a new liturgical setting; I feel suddenly and unexpectedly tethered to other souls across centuries who have yearned as I do to give ancient words a new voice. Sometimes it has happened when I have trusted that my own profound experience in a life-cycle moment is not so unique to me, enabling me to write in anticipation of a warmly knowing reception in other hearts. Sometimes it happens because I am patient. Several years ago, I set out to compose a song built around the ancient Rabbinic blessing parents are to recite when their daughter reaches the age of bat mitzvah: *Baruch shep'tarani mei-onshah shel zot*, "Blessed is the One who has transferred religious responsibility for this child from me to her." My daughter was only turning ten years old when I started on this piece, and I would not finish it until just before her bat mitzvah day. It took time for me to get out of the way and allow the timeless truths about what was happening between my daughter and me to unspool in song. But once it did, both she and I were willing to take the chance of experiencing its rawness in front of our entire community from the *bimah*, and that familiar but never common rush of spirit returned . . . a kiss of blessing on a blessed day.

Of course, it has been especially fascinating to witness and participate in musical "God moments" occurring on online platforms during the coronavirus pandemic. Sometimes the hunger to experience human companionship at a time of such profound physical separation seems to have opened an even wider gateway to the experience of Oneness. The first shivah service I led in memory of a congregant who died from COVID-19 included over one hundred worshipers from three different continents. When we joined in singing the familiar setting composed by Nurit Hirsch for *Oseh Shalom* following the recitation of the Mourner's *Kaddish*, we all encountered something new—the experience of *seeing* ourselves engaged in collective song, not only hearing it. Our souls could suddenly "hear" voices joined with our own—in Los Angeles . . . in New York . . . in Paris . . . in Ethiopia. It was a sensation of soul unity unlike anything I had ever felt. Sometimes even physical impediments can open us to new spiritual surprise.

When I was first beginning to discover the spiritual power of Jewish music in my life, my childhood rabbi taught me a famous saying attributed to Saint Augustine: "To sing is to pray twice." I always loved that suggestion. It expressed very succinctly what I believed myself to be feeling—that something mysterious and unknowable . . . something "more than" . . . could happen when song became the vehicle for the soul. But it was only years later that I encountered the teaching that, for me, began to unlock the mystery of the "more than." It was written by Abraham Joshua Heschel, arguably the greatest of the twentieth century's Jewish thinkers. Heschel wrote, "When we begin to sing, we sing for all things. Essentially, music does not describe that which is; rather, it tries to convey that which reality stands for; the universe is a score of eternal music, and we are the cry; we are the voice. Reason explores the laws of nature, trying to decipher the scales without grasping the harmony; while, the sense of the ineffable is in search of the song."[2]

Much of my religious life has been spent in search of the song to cradle that sense of the ineffable. Every now and then, the two find each other—and holiness abounds.

בָּרוּךְ אַתָּה, יי, עוֹשֶׂה קוֹל אֶחָד.

Baruch atah, Adonai, oseh kol echad.

Blessed are You, Adonai, Maker of the One Voice.

NOTES

1. All of the names in this story have been changed for the preservation of privacy.
2. Abraham Joshua Heschel, *Man is Not Alone: A Philosophy of Religion* (New York: Farrar, Straus and Giroux, 1976), 41.

CHAPTER 8

Experiencing God
While Composing Music:
Listening for the Still, Small Voice

CANTOR JONATHAN COMISAR

THE FIRST SERIOUS PIECE of music I composed ended with the cry of a baby. Of course, this was unplanned and unscripted, nowhere written in the score.

It was a sunny September day in San Francisco on the holiest day of the Jewish calendar, the day of Yom Kippur, during the *Yizkor* (memorial) service for loved ones who had died. That baby was just being a baby and was probably hungry or tired or needed mom or dad. But if there is such a thing as a divine message, that was it. That baby had no idea that at that moment, it was standing in as my angel or oracle. It was delivering a poetic message about what composing music would mean for me from that point onward: listening to and trusting that pure inner voice, deep within me. I, as a composer, was born with that baby's cry.

At that time, I was a young twentysomething musician, finding my voice as an aspiring cantor and composer. My journey as a young, creative, gay, and Jewish man brought me to San Francisco and its LGBTQ synagogue, Congregation Sha'ar Zahav. We LGBTQ Jews from all over the country were creating something new together—with one foot anchored in the traditions we came from, and one foot taking bold new steps into the future. And amid that pioneering spirit, where creativity and new terrain were celebrated, my compositional voice was born.

One day I got a call from Sha'ar Zahav's Rabbi Yoel Kahn, a beloved mentor and someone who believed in my talent: "I have an unusual but exciting project for you."

A woman in the congregation wanted to honor the memory of her father with the composition of a new work—a setting of a Russian poem, "The Death of the Poet" by Anna Akhmatova. It would be premiered at the opening of the *Yizkor* service for Yom Kippur. I was thrilled to be asked to embark on my first music commission.

But then a shaky unease set in. I immediately felt the awesome weight of responsibility. The woman who commissioned the piece, her Russian father who had died, the poet Akhmatova, the poet Boris Pasternak (who was being eulogized in her poem), my mentor rabbi, the weeping congregants in the pews, and the Source of All who would be hovering over all souls in the sanctuary that day . . . How could I honor all the people that needed to be honored in the composing of this new work? Did I have it within me to do right by all of them? Talk about diving headfirst from a cliff into an untested ocean below.

However, I gathered up my passion, my music skills, and my chutzpah and took the first tentative steps. Fortunately, we had several talented instrumentalists among us, and I dared to dream big. The piece would be a cantata for bassoon, clarinet, violin, cello, piano, and two gifted singers.

And then the hard part. Starting. Really starting from nothing. Staring at a blank page. The choices are endless. Does the cello or bassoon make the first utterance? Will there be a compelling motif or theme? What is the prevailing mood or color? What kind of journey will I take the listener on? What will be the climactic moment of the text? Who will have the last word?

No matter how simple or complex the creative task is, the answers to all my creative questions are found in three words: *kol d'mamah dakah* (קוֹל דְּמָמָה דַקָּה), "the still, small voice" (I Kings 19:12). It is that voice inside that reaches for authenticity, that knows what honesty is. We hear these stirring words uttered by the cantor embedded into the liturgy of the High Holy Days: "The great shofar will be sounded. And a still, small voice will be heard." The services of Rosh HaShanah and Yom Kippur unfold like a powerful drama—a play with several acts, with courtroom deliberations, visitations by God, shepherds, angels, and ancestors.

There are vows made and broken, decrees on life and death announced by the authorities. The shofar summons the overarching message of repentance, return, and renewal. And yet, among all the pomp and weight of the High Holy Days, the greatest drama that takes place is that tiny flicker of awareness or awakening in the praying individual. That is the still, small voice. It is the inner voice that rises up to the surface and says, "I must change my life," or "This is the path I must take." It is as pure as a baby's cry. And it is from that very internal well—that place of inner knowing—that my inner artist knows how to choose the first and last notes of the score.

The *kol d'mamah dakah* is the inner compass that is always there to remind me to strive to tell the truth, to be real, to be authentic. My most influential teacher of music was my piano teacher Sophia Rosoff. She touched the lives of countless musicians all over the world and taught well into her nineties. For twelve years, I made pilgrimages to her East Side Manhattan apartment, where I learned as much about life as I did about Bach, Chopin, or Prokofiev. Each lesson started with establishing a physical relationship to the piano. Sophia instructed me to cozy up to the instrument, gently resting my head on the ebony and ivory keys to feel an affectionate connection to the Steinway piano in her living room. The piano lost its intimidating aura. It was not something to conquer, attack, or subdue—but rather a loving partner and friend to help bring out the deepest, truest, and most beautiful part of myself.

Sophia taught me about the "emotional rhythm" of a piece of music, which is different from simply the meter; for example, a dotted quarter note has three beats, and four sixteenths make up a quarter. No, emotional rhythm is a thread of sincerity and is felt as aliveness, humanity, and honesty. As I was learning complex works of music, she would say, "I don't care if you miss some of the notes, but don't lose the rhythm." She demanded that that thread be there, that *all* of me show up from the first note until the last of every piece of music. Those lessons were sacred study sessions. The piano provided a different page of Talmud each time. And my piano teacher rebbe just had another way of saying, "Don't forget the *kol d'mamah dakah*, and let it carry you through."

So, when I had that blank page staring back at me, my inner voice told me to learn all I could about the poet Anna Akhmatova, whose words I would be setting to music. Before I sat down to the piano or composed a single note, I needed to step into her world and live in it for a while. So, I stepped into the world of this Russian writer and the dark Stalinist purges under which she lived. I learned how Russians of her time looked to Akhmatova as a poet-warrior and conscience of her nation. She was grieving the death of a towering figure of Russian literature, Boris Pasternak, but also grieving a Mother Russia that had betrayed her people and her promise.

Then, slowly, the notes started coming to me. A craggy folk fragment, on a violin, emerged, almost out of tune—from the earth, sad, simple, evoking a peasant trying to eke out a living from a stubborn field. From there, a door was opened. The pastoral images from the poem found their voice through the wood of the clarinet and bassoon. Boris Pasternak turned into the rain or wheat that he had previously written about. This sweet lyricism took root in the music and all the instruments found their place in the storytelling.

Music composition is a series of revelations—similar to a birthing process. One can sketch and plan, but that inner compass keeps redirecting the path of the music. The first words of the poem were "Yesterday, an unrepeatable voice fell silent. . . ." The mezzo-soprano and baritone would have to be silent for a while. The first several minutes of the work emerged as an instrumental elegy made of earth, tears, and tattered pages of poetry volumes. When it was time to set the Russian text, Leo, my Russian immigrant friend, sat with me and helped me syllable by syllable with the words' meaning and pronunciation. I entered into the soundscape of the original poetry—a crucial map for navigating the words, along with their natural and emotional rhythms.

After months of chiseling away, agonizing, doubting, and having faith, the work was completed. The most terrifying and most exciting moment in a composer's life is the first rehearsal when the music is heard live for the first time. The great twentieth-century composer Arnold Schoenberg taught that composition includes a measure of faith. If composers do all their work in the intricate process of composition and work out all the challenges to the best of their ability, then the Almighty bestows upon the work an unforeseen gift. Something transcendent, something from beyond, appears in the music. One never sees or hears it during the pregnancy, the process of composing. It is only revealed with that first sound—that first cry of a baby. When I heard my setting of "The Death of the Poet" for the first time, I felt tears welling up in my eyes. The spark was there.

And then something even more unexpected happened. You could call it either a "spiritual experience" or a "good imagination." But I remember it happening. After that first hearing of the piece, I felt a brief visit from the poet herself, Anna Akhmatova. She was in the room with me. I felt like I had deeply connected with her after immersing myself in her work and story. I could feel her presence with me. She had just listened to my music, too. She closed her eyes and gave me a nod, a solemn assent. And then she vanished.

I closed my own eyes. And I nodded briefly to that still, small voice inside me that guided me from a blank page to a piece of music with thousands of notes—that brooded, and danced, and soared. And spoke a truth.

A baby cried when my first significant work of music was offered to the world. Two things became clear that Yom Kippur day: I knew that being a composer would be an agonizing yet miraculous journey. And I knew that I would be able to find my way.

בָּרוּךְ אַתָּה, יי, שֶׁהִשְׁמִיעַנִי קוֹל דְּמָמָה דַקָּה.

Baruch atah, Adonai, shehishmiani kol d'mamah dakah.

Blessed are You, Adonai, who lets me hear the still, small voice.

PART 3
Relationships

Ben Azzai used to say: Hold no one insignificant and
no thing improbable, for there is no one
who has not an hour and no thing
has not its place.
—*Pirkei Avot* 4:2

CHAPTER 9

Experiencing God in Community

RABBI NICOLE AUERBACH

וְעָשׂוּ לִי מִקְדָּשׁ וְשָׁכַנְתִּי בְּתוֹכָם.

V'asu li mikdash, v'shachanti b'tocham.
Let them make Me a sanctuary that I may dwell among them.
—Exodus 25:8

IN THE BOOK OF EXODUS, when the Israelites are wandering through the wilderness, God instructs them to build a *mishkan*, a "portable tent sanctuary" in which the Divine Presence might dwell (Exodus 25–31, 35–40). God, of course, does not require a physical resting place. So, what is it about building this communal space that will allow these wanderers to experience God's presence? The eighteenth-century commentator known as Or HaChayim notes that the text does not say that God will dwell *b'tocho*, "within *it* [the tent]," but rather *b'tocham*, "within" or "among *them* [the Israelites]."[1] God can be found, this commentary suggests, between and among those who have gathered in sacred community.

That is certainly my experience. I am a rabbi and a "director of congregational engagement." When asked to explain what my title means, I explain that it is my job to create opportunities for members of our community to build and deepen relationships with one another, with the synagogue community as a whole, with Jewish tradition, and yes, with God. It is my job to assist our members in creating intentional, sacred spaces in which they can experience God's presence, love, and compassion, with and through one another.

I am not talking about the "big tent," large-group experience of God that our members might seek when they come to Shabbat or High Holy

Day services, although there is certainly something to be said for the awe and communal resonance that we feel when we gather by the hundreds to raise our voices in prayer and song.[2] I am talking about a "small tent" experience—a personal and intimate experience of the Divine when we are in deep and covenantal relationship with one another.

What does that feel like? It feels like love.

When I began rabbinical school, I conceived of God in intellectual terms. For me, then, God was a name for the unexplainable creative force behind the Big Bang, or the moral imperative that calls on us to be our best selves. At that point, it didn't really matter to me whether God was something that genuinely existed or simply a metaphor that we used to justify our psychological needs or moral instincts. In fact, God-as-metaphor was convenient, as I was groping my way from my past career as an attorney toward life as a religious leader. If God was a metaphor, I could bridge the gap between my religious and my secular worlds.[3]

It was therefore surprising to me when I began to experience God firsthand, in quiet moments of connection with other people, during my chaplaincy training. I slowly became accustomed to the experience of time slowing down, of a calm settling in my gut and my chest, of a sense of being able to be fully present without judgment. One day I was sitting with a woman who had dementia and who, in our circular conversations, kept asking, "Am I ok? Is this good enough? Am I doing it right?" I found myself saying, "God loves you just the way you are." This did not feel like my language at all. But in that moment, I could feel a love bigger than me, a love that did not originate with me, flowing toward this person. Only afterward did I realize that I believed the words I had said, which left me to wrestle with how desperately I wanted to believe that God loved me, too. When my mentor Rabbi Mychal Springer asked me what this experience told me about the nature of God, I answered that God is present and does not judge us and that we can best access God's love in moments of deep connection with other people. And that even in a nursing home, if we pitch a tent together, we can feel God's presence dwelling between and among us.

Around this same time, I began to meet with a spiritual director.[4] In our sessions I began to reflect on how my experience as a mother could inform my understanding of a loving and compassionate God. When I became a mother, I learned that there are times during those early weeks and months when we cannot understand what is wrong with our children. Sometimes all we can do is to hold them and rock them and tell them it will all be okay—which is as much of a prayer for ourselves as it is for them. We know there are some things we cannot fix, but so long as our child is held and knows they are not alone, we are doing our job. When I think of God as parent, this is what I see: God holding me, letting me know I am not alone—perhaps unable to solve the immediate problem, but there, nonetheless, a source of comfort and unconditional love.

These one-on-one I-Thou[5] experiences of God led me not only to a commitment to building a "ministry of presence" as someone who offers pastoral care and spiritual direction, but also to dedicate myself to creating opportunities for others to experience those moments of connection in relationship with one another in the context of a covenantal community. At the heart of my "relational" work are questions like these: First, how can we create the conditions in which members of our community can be on both the giving and receiving ends of God's love? In other words, if we believe that at the heart of our yearning for God is the desire to feel seen, heard, and known, then how can we, as a sacred community, create that experience for one another? And second, if we believe that it is our role to make God's love, compassion, and justice manifest in this world, how can we create the structures that will allow us to gather together and harness the power to make it so?

Among the many answers to these questions, I will offer three: (1) encourage people to pitch "small tents" together within the larger community to create a sense of joint purpose and obligation; (2) allow time and space for people to see and hear one another as individuals; and (3) discern opportunities for collective action that allow us to respond to the world's brokenness from a place of love.

Small Tents

If we want to increase our opportunities to engage with one another, to share our stories, and to support one another in times of joy and hardship, then we cannot just wander the wilderness on our own, hoping to bump into a kindred spirit. Instead, we need to build intentional communities on a small enough scale that each person can be seen, heard, known, and loved. Just as God did not deliver the *Mishkan* fully formed, but instead instructed the Israelites to each bring their individual gifts in order to build their communal sanctuary, it is essential that members of these small-tent communities are invited to contribute their own gifts in the form of time, presence, and expertise and to take part in the construction of the community that will provide them shelter.

This small-tent approach to community can take a number of different shapes. While I am a proponent of creating formal, member-led small groups that meet regularly with the express goal of building relationships,[6] there are many different ways to encourage people to connect more deeply with one another. The key, in my experience, is to make sure that there is a sense of shared purpose and commitment, as well as regular opportunities for people to share their stories and experiences.

For example, a few years ago, I worked with a group of congregants and fellow clergy and prayer leaders to form a small, participatory service on Shabbat mornings called, not surprisingly, "The *Mishkan*." The shape and feel of the service grew out of the desires of its "regulars" to learn and pray in a more intimate space. Not only do they sing and pray, but half an hour is dedicated to Torah study, in which everyone is invited to bring their particular perspective and life experience to bear. Three years in, not only have these regulars built a regular practice of praying and studying on Saturday mornings, but they have begun to care for one another, calling to support one another when they are sick, and asking after each other when they notice someone has not come in a while. Like the original portable *Mishkan*, we pitch our *mishkan* at different locations—sometimes we are in the social hall and sometimes in the lobby. But wherever we are, God shows up.

Opportunity for Individual Connection

As any community organizer or Hillel employee will tell you, the key to bringing people together is to begin one-on-one, through conversations in which people are able to share their experiences, passions, and concerns. Taking time for one-on-one conversations is not just a good tool for organizing and community building. It is an opportunity for sacred encounter. As foreign as it might seem at first to sit with someone with no agenda other than getting to know them and learning how they see the world, doing so gives both people a chance to experience God's loving, compassionate presence.

This ministry of presence is too important to be reserved for clergy. Members can be encouraged to reach out to one another, whether as part of a caring committee, an organizing campaign, or even a new-member initiative. Additionally, frontal programs or classes can be reworked to allow more time for people to listen to one another, so that everyone has a chance to be seen and heard.

Collective Action

Years ago, when Hurricane Sandy hit New York, I heard that my rabbi at the time, Sari Laufer, was heading up a collection effort for cleaning supplies. As we were checking out at Costco, my young daughter asked me, "Mommy, why is the rabbi collecting garbage bags?" I told her that part of the rabbi's job was to figure out what God needed to happen in the world and to get people to do it. God wanted to help people who were suffering. But because God could not deliver garbage bags, God needed us to do it.

If we believe, as I do, in the presence of a loving, compassionate God who does not intervene in human affairs; if we believe that we have the capacity to be conduits of that love and compassion and to experience it through our encounters with others; if we believe that the response to suffering is loving, nonjudgmental presence, then we will find ourselves called to seek out relationships with those who are suffering, to accompany them, and to then act, if we can, to alleviate their pain. This may look like delivering garbage bags or stopping to speak to the person who asks for change on the street. It may look like building relationships with those most affected by systemic injustice and showing up to follow their lead in seeking a more just world. Ultimately, for me, the impetus for such action does not come from the God of the mighty hand and outstretched arm who brought us out of Egypt. It originates instead in those quiet encounters when I am sitting with another person, feeling a love that is bigger than me filling the space between us. The impetus of such work comes from the experience of pitching a tent together with someone, acknowledging its holiness, and allowing ourselves to feel God dwelling among us.

I believe that my purpose as a rabbi, a Jew, and a human being is to make God's love, compassion, and justice manifest in this world. I believe it is my job to look at the world with open eyes and an open heart, to discern through the lens of my inherited tradition what God demands, and then to take action to make it happen. And I believe that the best way to understand what God is and does in the world is to be in relationship with others, allow myself to love them, and act accordingly.

בָּרוּךְ אַתָּה, יי, הַשּׁוֹכֵן בִּקְהִלּוֹתֵינוּ.

Baruch atah, Adonai, hashochein bik'hiloteinu.
Praised are You, Eternal Source of Love, who dwells among us in community.

NOTES

1. Chayim ibn Atar (Or HaChayim) on Exodus 25:8: "That I may dwell among [within] them: It does not say 'within it,' which means that the place that God will sanctify to dwell there is within the Children of Israel that encircle the Tabernacle with four banners" (trans. Sefaria), https://www.sefaria.org/activity/Or_HaChaim_on_Exodus.25.8.17/en/Sefaria_Community_Translation).

2. This "big tent" spirituality was powerfully described by Rabbi Maya Glasser in an impromptu interview at a baseball game: "I even think that loving a baseball team can be a religious experience. I was here in 2012 when Santana pitched his no-hitter. Everyone in this stadium was holding their breath at the exact same time. And when the game ended, everyone screamed with the same joy. We all felt so connected at that moment. And I think that was

holy. That's the feeling I want to create in my synagogue" ("Humans of New York," October 20, 2015, Facebook, https://www.facebook.com/humansofnewyork/photos/a.102107073196735/1112401775500588/?type=3&theater). It was also my first experience of God, as a child. There was something about feeling everyone raising their voices in song and vibrating at the same frequency that allowed me to believe that there was something bigger than all of us.

3. Rabbi Danya Ruttenberg describes a similar evolution from an intellectual to an experiential understanding of spirituality in her beautiful memoir *Surprised by God: How I Learned to Stop Worrying and Love Religion* (Boston: Beacon Press, 2008). Confronted by her own experiences of God but afraid to name them as such, she writes, "I had at this point spent several years studying religious phenomenology from the perspective of an academic trying to understand what people *thought* they were experiencing when they talked about God, even if in reality it was just a neurological reaction or something similar. And yet . . . I knew I couldn't entertain the possibility that my midnight excursions might be connected to the word *spiritual* without extending the word to its logical extreme. And opening even the question of the concept of God made me a little bit nervous, a little bit jittery, and rather nauseous" (50).

4. Spiritual direction is the practice of acting as a companion and witness to a person's experience, as a way to allow them to access and understand their connection to the Divine.

5. Martin Buber, in *I and Thou* (written in 1923 and translated into English in 1937) famously considers how divine love is experienced—albeit fleetingly—in moments of deep mutual connection.

6. For an introduction into this relational approach to building community, see Ron Wolfson, Nicole Auerbach, and Lydia Medwin, *The Relational Judaism Handbook: How to Create a Relational Engagement Campaign to Build and Deepen Relationships in Your Community* (Encino, CA: Kripke Institute, 2018).

CHAPTER 10

Experiencing God While Looking at Others

RABBI REBECCA L. DUBOWE

PHILOSOPHER MARTIN BUBER believes that the relationship between two or more human beings reflects an experience of the Divine. He states, "Meet the world with the fullness of your being and you shall meet God."[1] Buber's philosophy describes a personal and intimate dialogue known as an "I-Thou relationship": two or more human beings begin a dialogue, bringing their unique and whole presence to this encounter.

When a child is born, something new begins. The baby's first silent gaze establishes the connection the parents seek so eagerly with their new child. This connection can be defined as the very first I-Thou encounter between the child and the parents. As Buber explains, it is in those encounters that we are fully present for others and witness the divinity within them. Can you imagine being busy with your daily interactions while being fully present to the Divine in all possible ways?

I can—because I have to.

As my parents' first child, I was perfect in their eyes. However, when I was eighteen months old, my grandmother sensed I did not fully live within the world of sound. Heavy moments of truth descended upon my family, moments in which they had to accept that I was different from them; yet at the same time, they also upheld their truth that all children, including their own, are created *b'tzelem Elohim*, "in God's image." My parents created an intentional practice for themselves. Whenever they wanted to speak with me, they waited patiently until I was looking into their faces so that I could read their lips. Only then would I be able to understand them.

This is true for me until this day. In every moment, in every single encounter with every single person, I have to look into their faces in order to understand them—in order to partake in life. In order to survive in life, I depend on looking into your faces. I have to look into your face, see all your thoughts and emotions, and show you all of mine.

In my early childhood, I had assumed this was the way all people communicated with one another. I experience one I-Thou moment after the next. However, as I was growing up, it became apparent to me that this was not entirely true. Not every human encounter is an I-Thou moment. The need to look into each other's faces is not a necessity for the general population. This was a startlingly revelation for me: Not everyone had to show themselves to their partner in conversation. Not everyone had to wait for eye contact in order to be heard. I became painfully aware that my way of communication was different from the ways of most others.

At the beginning of every school year, my mother would make an annual visit to my school. She would meet with all my teachers. She gave them specific instructions ensuring I would receive the same educational opportunities as all the other children.

Year after year my mother would say, "Always face Rebecca when you speak with her. If you are not facing Rebecca, she will not hear nor understand what you are saying. If she is not looking at you, she will not hear a word no matter how loud or soft your voice is. Please do not yell to get Rebecca's attention, just tap on her shoulder, and intentionally look at her, and then she will be able to connect and respond."

Daily face-to-face encounters are part of my life, no matter how I am feeling that day—if I am tired, I still need to look into your face. If I make a mistake, I still need to look into your face regardless of my embarrassment. There are times when I receive praise or a compliment and I feel uncomfortable or humbled, but of course, I still look into your face. No matter what you are thinking or feeling in that moment, I still need to look into your face. There were times when I wanted to pretend that I do not need to look into your face, and as a consequence, I would completely miss the message, miss the instruction, miss the compliment, or miss the question that required a response from me.

I am well aware that there are times when you can actively choose not to see face-to-face because it would be too painful to expose your ignorance or embarrassment. I know you are aware that each time when you do not look at a friend, stranger, or foe, much of your communication is lost. You too know that in order to hear everything that is said in a conversation, it is not enough to simply hear and understand the words that are spoken. Ironically, you not only need the ability to hear, but also the ability to listen in order to fully understand. Only when truly listening can we be fully present to the person we encounter. The willingness to be vulnerable, to pay attention to the speaker, requires an ongoing practice of humility and respect. The Torah identifies these interactions—being in the presence of others—as *panim el panim* (face-to-face) encounters; we call them, in the words of Buber, I-Thou encounters.

One profound example of a *panim el panim* encounter comes from the biblical story of Jacob preparing to meet his brother Esau after many years (Genesis 32–33). As a rabbi, I have thought and spoken about the many layers of this story many times.

The powerful image of Jacob wrestling with the angel reflects the human wrestling with the fear of rejection. To resist or surrender? Fear of rejection is the greatest obstacle we as humans build for ourselves and others. Why does fear of resistance prevent us from coming close to others? It is because of our instinct to protect our own fragile egos from humiliation and pain—because rejection hurts. Jacob eventually seizes his fear and crosses the river in order to encounter his brother. He could do so because he had first been willing to look into the face of his own fears. Only after having wrestled with his own shame and embarrassment is he able to look into the face of the man he hurt most in the world—and to show him the sense of guilt in his own eyes.

A fear with which I struggle daily is the potential breakdown of communication. I may have excellent lip-reading skills; however, like everyone else, I become impatient when I do not understand the other person. When this happens, it leaves me with a sense of failure, of being cut off and not able to connect. As Jacob struggles with the angel, he discovers two things: that he can survive turmoil and that during struggle one encounters God. I sense that when we look into our own faces and encounter our own struggles and fears, we truly encounter God. While struggling with looking into his own face, Jacob's looks into the face of God. He resolves his anxiety and fear—resulting in his becoming a stronger person. He and God meet *panim el panim*—"face-to-face"—both in each other's presence: "Jacob therefore named that place Peni'el, [thinking]—'For [here] I have seen *God face-to-face*'" (Genesis 32:31).

His *panim el panim* encounter transformed Jacob—and so do those encounters transform all of us. *Panim el panim* experiences are essential to discovering the Divine Presence. Recognizing God's presence in each person's face allows me to remain strong and not give up so easily. It is always possible to communicate with God, because all that conversation requires from us is to look into our own faces. If that is true, then it is the same with people. Sometimes we might need to be patient, but as long as we continue to show our faces and seek the gaze of our partners, there is a chance for us to truly see each other.

The idea of God existing in each and every one of us implies that when we turn our faces away from someone, we reject ourselves, others, and God's presence. When I make myself fully present to others, I can be in the presence of others and, ultimately, in the presence of the Divine, which establishes my role as God's partner in this world. At times those experiences can be quite empowering for me, and I can only imagine that they are empowering for others, too. Every fully present encounter invites compassion and greater openness to each other. It takes efforts and patience, but to me, this is holy work.

How do I listen to God's presence while desperately struggling to be like others? Desperately wanting to listen to a podcast, listen to the radio, and listen to all that is spoken without having to look into someone's face?

> As you taught Torah
> to those whose names I bear,
> teach me Torah too.
> Its mystery beckons,
> yet I struggle with its truth.
> You meant Torah for me:

did You mean the struggle for me, too?
Don't let me struggle alone;
help me
to understand,
to be wise, to listen, to know . . .
Lead me into the mystery.
  —Rabbi Richard Levy[2]

Why me? Why must I struggle with its truth? Why not others? Why did God create me as who I am? Who is this God—this well-known beloved creator of human beings? According to Rabbi Levy, the truth lies in accepting and believing that no one is alone, even as we embrace the mystery of life.

Truth is acceptance. Life is a struggle. Being in the presence of the Divine means to surrender.

Every day is a choice to resist or to surrender. When I resist—meaning when I erect barriers between me and others and decide not to look into their faces—I feel the lack of connection, purpose, and direction. Silence is not a real barrier, because God is never silent for me. Like everybody else, I selectively choose what I want to hear or experience: sometimes I resist, and sometimes I surrender. If God is everywhere, then I must recognize that even with my deafness I can hear God's voice. To turn away from the face of another decreases my likelihood of experiencing holiness. *Panim el panim*—to look into another's face—not only helps receiving or interpreting a message, but also opens us up to experience the kind of connection so many of us crave in our daily lives. Something ordinary such as having a conversation can be quite extraordinary if one intentionally makes an effort to be fully present to one another and to God. I constantly seek God's presence; as a deaf person, this is a very simple task. I am trained to look into your face—and that is all that it takes.

Some of the most powerful holy moments in my rabbinate have been the times when I have offered the *Birkat Kohanim*, the Priestly Benediction. I say, "May God bless you and keep you, may God's face shine upon you and be gracious with you, and may God grant you peace"

(Numbers 6:24–26). Intentionally, when I recite the *Birkat Kohanim*, I take a moment to look at the person who is receiving these blessings. That moment of connection is holy and beyond words—it is full of love and reassurance. We acknowledge that we are in this world together and that God is in our presence.

As a spiritual leader and as a human being, I strive to connect because I need to connect—and so do others. We yearn to feel a sense of belonging and connection within the Jewish community. The most powerful way to achieve this is to constantly offer *panim el panim* encounters to others. It may mean to hold a hand or give a comforting hug during a time of crisis or offering a blessing during a time of *simchah*. It can come in the form of a smile or friendly words during the course of a day. It may occur in moments of teaching when new ideas emerge. I reach out to others, encouraging them to ask questions, acknowledging who they are, and most importantly, reminding them that they are important to themselves, to others, and to God.

So, can we hear God? Does God speak? According to a Chasidic teaching, the only sound the Israelites heard at Mount Sinai was the first letter of the first word of the first commandment—*alef*—which happens to be a silent letter. Rabbi Larry Kushner teaches, "At Sinai all the people of Israel needed to hear was the sound of *alef*. It meant that God and human beings could have a conversation."[3] To have a conversation with God or with others is the essence of living a life filled with connection and purpose, with self-awareness and discovery of others, and even more so, with sound as well as with silence. To recognize the many faces of God in every single human being is the truth to living.

בָּרוּךְ אַתָּה, יי אֱלֹהֵינוּ, מֶלֶךְ הָעוֹלָם,
אֲשֶׁר רוֹאֶה אוֹתָנוּ – פָּנִים אֶל פָּנִים.

Baruch atah, Adonai Eloheinu, Melech haolam,
asher ro-eh otanu—panim el panim.

Blessed are You, Adonai our God, Sovereign of
the universe, who looks straight into our faces.

NOTES

1. As quoted in "Martin Buber: The Creation of a Jewish Existentialism—and a Jewish State," by Daniel Septimus and Rachel Sabath Beit-Halachmi, My Jewish Learning, accessed July 23, 2020, https://www.myjewishlearning.com/article/martin-buber/.

2. *Mishkan T'filah: A Reform Siddur* (New York: CCAR Press, 2005), 151.

3. Lawrence Kushner, "The Silent Alef," in *The Book of Miracles: A Young Person's Guide to Spirituality*, 10th anniversary ed. (Woodstock, VT: Jewish Lights, 1997), 35.

Experiencing God in the Midst of Conflict

Miriam Heller Stern, PhD

"You're a hypocrite!" My ten-year-old son's high-pitched shriek signals that there is a fight brewing with his older, teenage brother.

"Stop fighting," I passively call out from the other room, delaying intervention.

"But he's a hypocrite!" He doubles down on the accusation, launching into a familiar tirade about being at odds with his brother. "He's telling me to clean up, but he's leaving a mess!" or "He keeps saying I'm wrong and I'm not! HE is WRONG!" or my favorite all-encompassing complaint, "He's telling me to stop being annoying, but he's being so annoying!" With each phrase, his volume escalates, raising my blood pressure along with it.

Siblings. They seem so close and connected, but then they regularly and predictably send each other into disequilibrium. Why can't they just live with their differences? Take a break and a breath, accept that sometimes they won't align? Would it be so hard to make a little space for one another?

I attempt to engage my favorite middle child in some reflection. "What do you think a hypocrite is?" I ask. His unflinching response: "He's two-faced! He acts the opposite of what he says!"

Two faces. If only there were just two! I think of the classic Talmudic adage that the Torah has seventy faces, and this plurality of interpretations is presented as a gift, a wellspring of curiosity and an invitation to honor difference. But such multiplicity can also be overwhelming and disempowering. How do we live with so many faces staring back at us, without the dizzying effects of walking through life as if we are trapped in a hall of mirrors? What happens when these different ways of seeing point our gaze in quite opposite directions and leave us confused, invalidated, frustrated, or unfulfilled?

At an early age, we crave having everything in life line up neatly. When that's not the case, children ask the adults in their lives to intervene and make the situation go their way. My child wants there to be two clear choices: good or bad, right or wrong. He begs me to simplify the world for him into these neat categories (and declare him to be on the right side of every conflict). But, of course, it is not that simple. How do I teach my children the disposition of integration—holding opposing ideas, conflicting behaviors, values in tension, and the everyday misalignment of the world, so that they can live in a relative state of equilibrium?

The real question to explore first is, how do I do it for myself? What do I do when struggling not even with others, but with an internal contradiction within me, arguing with my own self? What happens when I am arguing with my Creator? In this chapter, I will explore a variety of stances and techniques at the nexus of the worlds of education, neuroscience, psychology, and Jewish wisdom that help us manage life's dilemmas and paradoxes.

Humility and Conviction in Creative Tension

Can two seemingly opposing values or views both be right? Can we make space within our own hearts for "two rights" to coexist, even in paradox?

A classic Talmudic tale provides an illustrative example. The Babylonian Talmud (*Eiruvin* 13b) recounts an epic three-year dispute between two major legal authorities—the House of Hillel and the House of Shammai. The two experts frequently debated and disagreed in their rationales and rulings. In this case, there was a complete deadlock. Finally, a *bat kol*, a "heavenly voice," proclaimed, *Eilu v'eilu divrei Elohim chayim!* "These words [of Hillel] and these words [of Shammai] are *both* the words of a living God!" It could have ended there, as a tie, but there is a further moral of the story. The heavenly voice says the equivalent of "You're both right, you are both presenting the words of a living God.

But actually, the House of Hillel is a little more right; the law is according to Hillel." How could they be so different and yet both be declared right in the eyes of God? Because both rationales reflected their divine source and the dynamism of that source. Why then did the heavenly voice rule in favor of Hillel? The text goes on to explain that the House of Hillel was kind and humble; they studied not just their own teachings but the teaching of their main intellectual adversary, Shammai. They even placed Shammai's words before their own.

The operative element of the story is the humble stance of the House of Hillel. What ultimately tips the scales in Hillel's favor is not the substance of the argument or who had more convincing rhetoric, nor was it their track record for "winning" cases or having status as the favorite. Rather, their commitment to considering their opponent's teachings seriously made them the model to follow.

This type of humble stance is not easy to adopt when we are dealing with matters of morality, belief, and conviction. After all, when our endgame is to champion a deeply held commitment and accomplish a moral agenda, it is hard to imagine making space for an opposing view! How can we assume a humble stance when we are so rightfully upset and full of conviction that we want to shake our first at our interlocutor, our opponent, or perhaps even our Creator, point a finger and cry out, "Hypocrite!" Whether the debate is internal within ourselves or happening in the public square or in the private quarters of a family, practicing humility and conviction simultaneously is not just an attitude; it is a skill.

The moral of the story of Hillel and Shammai illustrates a way in which we might think about practicing an *"Eilu v'eilu* stance" in our lives—strengthening our resilience when we confront and must live with views that are different from our own, and sometimes incorporating those views into our worldview or theology. A group of research scholars at the University of Connecticut who run the Intellectual Humility and Conviction in Public Discourse project are dedicated to improving civil discourse and community dialogue on issues of great moral concern. They posed a philosophical and practical question: "How does one remain loyal to personally held beliefs while being open to the possibility of being wrong?" They use the phrase "intellectual humility" to describe a desired stance in public discourse that could help us manage this tension. (I deliberately use the verb "manage" here, rather than "resolve," as the tensions will remain dynamic even in the moments when we temporarily put them aside.) Intellectual humility denotes "the owning of one's cognitive limitations, a healthy recognition of one's intellectual debts to others, and low concern for intellectual domination and certain kinds of social status. It is closely allied with traits such as open-mindedness, a sense of one's fallibility, and being responsive to reasons."[1]

Intellectual humility is predicated on two kinds of acceptance about ourselves and how humans think and feel. The first is accepting the limits of our knowledge—in other words, embracing our own ignorance. That ignorance should spur us to pursue curiosity, a desire to know more, a desire to learn about the opposing or misaligned belief that is nagging or challenging us. The second is accepting the role of emotions in the formulation of our beliefs. Overvaluing rational thought can lead to ignoring the emotional thought that is profoundly powerful in formulating people's opinions about moral issues. (Consider Jonathan Haidt's *The Righteous Mind: Why Good People Are Divided by Politics and Religion*,[2] where he discusses people's tendencies to employ reason to support their instincts, rather than to inform and determine their opinions.) Part of the problem is the fast pace of debate and knee-jerk responses. The scholars who lead the Intellectual Humility project argue that the introduction of a mindset of intellectual humility into deliberation has the potential to slow down the process of forging hard-and-fast opinions, allowing the self to integrate competing ideas.

Finally, one who is intellectually humble is able to forgo the social capital and power that comes with being right. Curiosity and empathy are celebrated instead. The competition to be recognized for being right reinforces hierarchies and binary categories, making it harder for people to appreciate the possibility of integrating multiple narratives into their psyche. A politician scores more points for a clear, strong message. That kind of grandstanding wins political debates but does not offer us a technique for considering opposing views carefully when nuances are poking at our souls. In schools and religious learning settings, the competition to be heard and validated by the teacher often prevails (and obscures learning). In the family scenario, the child has trouble letting go of his need for validation that "Mommy says I'm right (and you're wrong)." But perhaps there can be another way. The child, as a growing learner, inquisitive seeker, and citizen, can draw spiritual satisfaction from opening her heart to more mature, integrative thinking and nuanced beliefs.

When I approach conflict with both conviction and intellectual humility, the endgame is not to convince my adversary that I am right, and she should therefore abandon her own values and drop her opposing argument. John Sarrouf, Co-Executive Director of Essential Partners (an organization that facilitates dialogue groups on contentious issues), teaches that when I approach a conflict with conviction *and* humility, my goal is to gently move my adversary from a place of certainty about her own belief, to curiosity about mine, to caring about me and my moral stance. The endgame, in this scenario, is to gain an ally who will at the very least defend and protect my right to exist even in my otherness.[3] In this model, within my own belief system, I can hold two conflicting values: prioritizing one, and maintaining a curious, supportive stance about the other. We might apply this case to different views of God, beliefs about parenting, visions of justice, and opposing views on abortion, euthanasia, and many other issues that carry significant moral and political weight and impact our social fabric.

Perhaps the first step is to give ourselves permission to feel both certain and uncertain. When we leave the door open to the possibility that we have something to learn, the internal conflict becomes an invitation for us to beckon the wisdom that is waiting for us around the bend.

The Value of Otherness

Because conflict often manifests as something dangerous and painful, we tend to think of conflict as a state to avoid. What does it look like to embrace conflict as a value? It may sound counterintuitive, but in fact one could argue that conflict is divinely ordained. Consider this illustration shared by Rabbi Ariel Burger, PhD, citing the teaching of his mentor-teacher Professor Elie Wiesel, about the creation of Eve. God conceives of Eve as Adam's partner, to be *eizer k'negdo* (Genesis 2:18), which translates awkwardly as "a helper against him." What does it mean to help someone and yet be against him? God created Eve to challenge and support Adam. When we have a partner to hold up the mirror and help us see our own many faces, as others see us, we have the capacity to become smarter, more resilient, and prepared to confront and overcome our weaknesses.[4]

Mirrors are our friends and our worst enemies. It takes courage to hold up the mirror and show someone their pain, and it takes courage to stare back when the mirror is before us. But if we can learn to see and accept our own blemishes, our own internal contradictions, Burger suggests, perhaps we can be more compassionate and forgiving when our partners bear contradictions that get in our way. If we can embrace the "otherness" in our own selves, we might appreciate it more in other people.

Yet we shy away from seeking out otherness. How ironic that our quest for a single right answer might halt our quest for truth prematurely and prevent us from exploring and integrating, stretching and deepening. The calcifying polarity of our society and the media echo chambers that reinforce the divide threaten our ability to access the seventy faces. In search of community, people take comfort among the like-minded and seek to reduce differences, instead of facing them. Burger calls this "a subtle tyranny of sameness," when we are trapped in groupthink, under the guise of community and connection. On the level of individual social behavior, a related phenomenon has been similarly labeled "the tyranny of niceness": we are socially conditioned to be polite, give in, avoid conflict. But, as psychotherapist Evelyn Sommers, PhD, has argued, this stance of just "being nice" produces feelings of regret, dishonesty, and an inner world of unresolved contradictions.[5] We need more strategies for approaching our own inner world with courage and humility, so that we can continue to develop the human capacity for intellectual and emotional resilience.

Learning to Embrace and Integrate Seventy Faces

Now that we have established the value of integrating complexity and otherness into our worldview, how do we learn the practice of integration? How do we train our minds, hearts, and souls in this practice so that we will be ready to grab and examine conflict, rather than running away? One avenue is through designing learning as an intentional practice of exploring and holding complexity. The Jewish interpretive textual tradition of commentaries lends itself to this practice. Studying the tradition in its multiplicity, embracing its "seventy faces," conditions people to live with multiple, even opposing, interpretations. Educational researcher and classroom teacher Dr. Ziva Reimer Hassenfeld suggests we might call this stance "cognitive pluralism," which she defines as "the ability to hold two or more conflicting interpretations in mind without rushing to choose a 'right' one."[6] In her research on how children develop the skills of literary analysis in Bible study, Hassenfeld has observed that children do not need the material to be oversimplified. In fact, introducing the idea of multiple ways of interpreting the same text is an intellectual move they can handle, if it is properly introduced and guided (what we call "scaffolding" in education jargon).

This approach to learning transcends literary texts to include abstract concepts, ideas, and beliefs, political and religious. Education researcher Dr. Sivan Zakai makes a similar point in her studies of how American Jewish children think about Israel. Her research has shown that even kindergarteners express conflicting narratives; they at once may think of Israel as a safe haven and dangerous, as a home for Jews and a home for others, and as both unique and ordinary. Having followed a group of students for six years in a longitudinal study, she suggests that we move from a "multiple choice" approach to teaching Israel literacy, where students have to pick one answer, to a "multiple choices engagement with challenging, debatable questions."[7]

Both of these approaches suggest that we can teach and learn a kind of critical thinking interpretive stance that invites curiosity to dialogue with the seventy faces of our tradition, as opposed to choosing just one. These learning practices can help students at a young age begin to consider the multiple sides of God as well: compassionate and a judge;

merciful and angry; male, female, and non-gendered; close by and far removed; all-powerful and yet in need of human partnership.

Reflective Prayer: Strength-Training Our Brains

Thinking takes practice. Our brains, like other muscles in our body, need nutrients and training to help us feel emotionally, intellectually, and spiritually stable. Psychotherapist and clinical professor of psychiatry Dr. Daniel J. Siegel writes that when we are teens, we are just developing our capacity for integrating the brain's multiple functions. Various flows of information, opposing ideas, feelings, and beliefs begin to coordinate during adolescence. Teens are a study in what's hard about integration; as the brain is only in its developing stages, we see teens respond to certain stimuli with exaggerated emotion or heightened sensitivity. They are learning to find balance. "Integration is what creates the master functions of self-awareness, reflection, planning, decision making, empathy, and even morality—thinking about the larger social good."[8] While these are the basic skills of adulthood, even many adults struggle with finding and maintaining this type of integration in their lives.

It is fairly common in our culture to dismiss teens' behavior as crazy or a stage to just "get through" until they figure out how to "adult." But if we are willing to dig deeply, we can see that the work of training our brains in integration is a practice that just begins in that stage of life; we need to persist in building that practice throughout adulthood, when new complexities and experiences disrupt our equanimity. Siegel suggests that through a series of meditative and reflective practices that he terms "mindsight," such as taking time for reflection and examining our self-awareness, "we can cultivate the growth of the integrative fibers of the prefrontal cortex. Positive interactions with others and self-reflection are two ways to increase prefrontal integration."[9] What we have long suspected to be important spiritual work turns out to fill an essential neurobiological need as well.

We might view prayer, with its contemplation and connection with the Creator, as a unique opportunity for "strength-training" that very complex muscle that is the brain. The more we reflect and associate thoughts into patterns, the more we connect the circuits that enable our brain to do the hard work of integration. Leaders of prayer might design services with intention, to utilize the opportunities the liturgy provides for growing self-awareness. The abiding optimism offered by the liturgy of praise and blessing can be a reinforcement in our moments of doubt and cynicism.

Machloket L'shem Shamayim

Some disputes, even conflicts within our own hearts, remind us that we have divine purpose. In a complicated world, we need to train our minds and hearts in practices that allow us to hold distinctions and nuance in order to do a better job of being human. Our classrooms and worship spaces—be they in conventional institutions or in the learning and reflection spaces built into our everyday experience—can be sites for growing as intentional integrators. Difference can tear us apart, both interpersonally and within our own selves; but difference can also illuminate truth and the complex experiences of others, challenging us to be more empathetic and compassionate. Holding difference can make us more human, if we have the tools to look at ourselves and others with curiosity and wonder.

But conflict can be scary. Many of us are weary of conflict, weary of confrontation, ready to just avoid *machloket* (conflict) altogether, because why lock horns when you can disengage and stay disentangled? The rifts in our communities and in society are becoming deeper and more fractious. The rules of etiquette are breaking down, the attacks more personal. Let us remember, in those moments, our divine purpose. Let us remember that the Holy One created opposites for a reason, for balance, because life depends on having both: night and day, land and sea, sacred and mundane. In those moments where we are unsure if we have the strength to stare down those binaries and live in the gray, lean into the discomfort, and hold all of our feelings, we might invoke the daily blessing:

בָּרוּךְ אַתָּה, יי אֱלֹהֵינוּ, מֶלֶךְ הָעוֹלָם, הַנּוֹתֵן לַיָּעֵף כֹּחַ.

Baruch atah, Adonai Eloheinu, Melech haolam, hanotein laya-eif ko-ach.

Blessed are You, Adonai our God, Ruler of the universe, who gives strength to the weary.

May we garner the strength every day to perform our divinely inspired human purpose on this earth, to gather the complexity around us and hold it in our hands as a blessing of being human, and to make our communications and reflections a blessing.

NOTES

1. Readers may be interested in learning more about the Intellectual Humility and Conviction in Public Discourse project, a research and engagement initiative based at the University of Connecticut and funded by the John Templeton Foundation. A full literature review, "Intellectual Humility in Public Discourse," authored by Michael P. Lynch et al., is available at https://humilityandconviction.uconn.edu/blank/what-is-intellectual-humility/# (accessed July 10, 2019).

2. Jonathan Haidt, *The Righteous Mind: Why Good People Are Divided by Politics and Religion* (New York: Vintage, 2012)

3. I had the privilege of learning with John Sarrouf at a summit on civil discourse convened by the Wexner Foundation in October 2017 and November 2018. Essential Partners is a Boston-based organization that "fosters constructive dialogue wherever conflicts are driven by differences of identities, beliefs, and values" (https://www.whatisessential.org/; accessed July 10, 2019).

4. Ariel Burger, *Witness: Lessons from Elie Wiesel's Classroom* (Boston: Houghton Mifflin, 2018), 37.

5. Evelyn K. Sommers, *The Tyranny of Niceness* (Toronto: Dundurn Press, 2005).

6. Ziva T. Reimer, "Teaching the Seventy Faces of Torah," HaYidion, Summer 2012, https://prizmah.org/teaching-seventy-faces-torah.

7. Sivan Zakai, "'Israel Is Meant for Me': Kindergarteners' Conceptions of Israel," *Journal of Jewish Education* 81, no. 1 (2015): 4–34; and Zakai, "From Multiple Choice to Multiple Choices: Rethinking Israel Literacy in Our Schools," HaYidion, Spring 2016, https://www.prizmah.org/multiple-choice-multiple-choices-rethinking-israel-literacy-our-schools.

8. Daniel J. Siegel, *Brainstorm: The Power and Purpose of the Teenage Brain* (New York: Jeremy P. Tarcher/Penguin, 2015), 106.

9. Siegel, *Brainstorm*, 106.

CHAPTER 12

Experiencing God in Service to Others

RABBI GAYLE POMERANTZ

WITH RIVULETS OF SWEAT mixed with rain dripping down my face, I marched between Athens and Augusta, Georgia, on August 19, 2015, as part of the NAACP America's Journey for Justice, organized to restore voting rights and shed light on the continuing struggle for civil rights in the United States. Every day of the 860-mile journey from Selma, Alabama, to Washington, DC, at least one rabbi showed up to march. I was assigned that hot and humid day in August, almost a halfway point. There were hundreds at the beginning in Selma and would be hundreds at the end in DC, but on that ninety-six-degree day, we were only twenty-four people strong. We trudged for miles, sweltering in the heat and soaking in the rain. Cars and trucks whizzed by. Minutes ticked by, and still we marched, step-by-step, slowly, methodically, with great intention, moving forward.

Every day of the journey there were two visible symbols displayed, the American flag and the Torah, both symbols of liberty and justice. Carrying the (heavy!) Torah on that long stretch of highway was powerful, for while the Torah is traditionally housed in an *aron kodesh*, a synagogue ark, it is also meant to be lived in the world. It needs to walk with us wherever we go. The presence of the Torah transformed our march from a walk into a sacred mission. Carrying the Torah was our way of calling attention to God's ancient and ever-present call for justice. We carried it lovingly, protecting it from the rain with a specially designed pack, and passing it gently from person to person. Though weighty, it lifted us up as we marched forward.

Why did hundreds of Jews show up along the way to march for civil rights on that long, plodding journey? They showed up because so many others have before them, from civil rights protesters in Alabama to immigration justice advocates today. As Jews, we stand in a long line of Jews, from Abraham to Moses to Amos and Micah, who railed against injustice, who dared to challenge even God for the sake of justice and righteousness. From Herzl to Heschel, our leaders have not been content with the status quo if the status quo meant oppression. Shimon Peres even quipped that the greatest Jewish contribution to history is dissatisfaction. "We're a nation born to be discontented," Peres said. "Whatever exists we believe can be changed for the better."[1] Willful defiance against inequality is encoded in the Jewish soul.

Every Yom Kippur afternoon, Reform Jews choose to read a special portion containing the most central words of the Torah, the Holiness Code (Leviticus 19). Not only are these words located at the center of the Torah scroll; they are of central spiritual significance as well. At my synagogue in Miami Beach, it is our custom to read them from our most precious scroll, rescued from Prague when the Jewish community there stood in flames. This Torah scroll itself is a commanding reminder of what can happen when we live vacuous and selfish lives. And there, on that holy page, we chant: *Lo taamod al dam rei-echa*, "Do not stand by while your neighbor bleeds" (Leviticus 19:16); *V'ahavta l'rei-acha kamo-cha*, "Love your neighbor as you love yourself" (Leviticus 19:18).

These were the very words I was whispering as I held the heavy Torah in my arms, marching between Athens and Augusta, Georgia. I shared the feeling expressed by Rabbi Abraham Joshua Heschel, after marching with Rev. Martin Luther King Jr. across the Edmund Pettus Bridge in Selma, "I felt my legs were praying."[2] Heschel articulated how it feels to embody prayer through marching. Being part of a sacred community, working toward a common goal, creates not only a sense of purpose, but of transcendence. The lines between me and you, between me and God, between us and them, become blurred, and we connect in a mystical and meaningful way.

Whether it is marching for voting rights, protesting child separation, feeding the hungry, serving the disenfranchised, or organizing for justice, we manifest God's presence by making the words on the Torah's page come alive through our actions. I am grateful for the opportunities I have had to pray, sing, gather, and worship with others. But the place I feel most in relationship to God is that place where I am serving others. It is in living God's words through service that my beliefs and my practice are most integrated. In fact, the Hebrew word for "worship," *avodah*, also means "work" and "service." I believe this is to teach us that our worship should lead to the work of serving others.

Our traditional spiritual practices of prayer, chanting, and ritual, along with the alternative practices of yoga, meditation, and mindfulness, are ways to hear the still, small voice of God in our souls. God's voice is the voice of clarity, conscience, hope, and peace; it brings us inner calm and guidance.

Spiritual growth begins with turning inward, but its purpose is to turn us outward to the world surrounding us. Rabbi David Stern calls this "round-trip spirituality,"[3] explaining that the purpose of nurturing our inner lives is to then turn outward to those in need. Martin Buber taught that we put ourselves in order so that we can turn outward to the world.[4] This is also the message of the prophet Isaiah, who challenges us regarding the importance of the ritual fast: Yom Kippur is not a day to starve ourselves while conducting business as usual; rather, it is a day "to unlock the fetters of wickedness, and untie the cords of the yoke.... It is [a day] to share your bread with the hungry, and to take the wretched poor into your home" (Isaiah 58:6–7). Our prayers, rituals, and meditations are empty if they serve the purpose of self-growth or fulfillment only. They are meant inspire us to the service of God through serving others.

While prayer and ritual must lead us to service, true service makes our souls grow and flourish. When we do good in the world, pursue justice, care for the needy, mentor others, and answer the cry for help, we fan the embers of the soul, God's candle within us, creating "round-trip spirituality": God's candle inspires us to goodness, and our righteous acts swell the flame of God's candle within. We nurture our spiritual lives when we nurture and care for others.

Through service and activism, we act as God's hands in the world.

We taste the sanctity and the awesomeness of our responsibility to care for God's creatures. Knowing that we are not alone in this pursuit and that we are aligned with others adds heft and impact.

One of the reasons the March for Justice felt so significant was because each one of us played a small role in a large multiday action. Together, we created a movement, a wave of energy, that no single one of us could have created alone. Being part of a larger whole expanded our sense of connectivity to each other and to God. Though taking small steps, each individual played a significant role. One day of marching, serving one meal, writing one letter to a legislator, inviting one friend to an action, making masks to prevent contagion, extending yourself for one person—these are the ways we experience God through doing our work for social justice.

The work we do, day in and day out, to bring justice to our world cannot be compartmentalized into the category of "justice work," separate from "spiritual work." It is holy work. It is the way we walk, breathe, eat, pray, learn, and love in this world, in partnership with God, and in relationship with each other. Powered by text, prayer, and God, our mission as Jews is to bring holiness, healing, and hope to our world. Our theology demands that we take the Torah out of the sanctuary and into our lives. It is in living the words of Torah, in "not standing idly by" and in "loving your neighbor," that we live the essential Jewish life. This is the way we experience God in each deed.

While Judaism provides us with blessings for a myriad of life's experiences, from seeing rainbows to hearing good news, there is no specific blessing that is recited before performing a righteous act. Perhaps this is because the act in and of itself is the blessing. Rather than invoking God's presence through prayer, we manifest God's presence through service. This is the essence of Integrated Theology through social justice. It is a blessing in itself.

Notes

1. Shimon Peres in conversation with David Landau, *Ben-Gurion: A Political Life* (New York: Schocken Books, 2011), 14.

2. Rabbi Abraham Joshua Heschel's diary, as told by his daughter, Dr. Susannah Heschel, in "A Friendship in the Prophetic Tradition: Abraham Joshua Heschel and Martin Luther King Junior," *Telos* (April 2018): 67–84.

3. Rabbi David Stern, Tedx SMU, March 2011, https://www.youtube.com /watch?v=pvKdFnEMS8I.

4. Martin Buber, "The Human Way (Der Weg des Menschen)," a series of six lectures Buber delivered to a Dutch Quaker audience to share Chasidic thought and insights, 1940s. Published as *The Way of Man: According to the Teaching of Hasidism* (New York: Citadel Press, 1964).

CHAPTER 13

Experiencing God in Grief

RABBI ANNE BRENER, LCSW

W HEN MY GRANDFATHER had a stroke in his late sixties, I was
given the honor of feeding him. I stood by his bedside and
stretched my arms above my head. With painstaking care, I held aloft
a glass beaker, which contained his infusion of medicine and nourish-
ments. My eyes followed each drop of sustenance as it trickled through
a rubber tube to a needle and into a vein of his paralyzed right arm.
Grandpa, who had also lost his gift of speech, looked up at me from his
pillow. His eyes whispered gratitude and love. I returned his gaze. Pride
rose in my eight-year-old heart as my aching arms held their position
and my eyes returned to the next drop as it made its journey into his
immobilized body.

When the tube was drained of his provisions, his nurse, who had been
supervising my effort, discharged me from my duty. I left his bedroom
and wandered into his library, which was adjacent to the room where he
lay. I inhaled the musty aroma of his books. Written in Hebrew and Yiddish, many of them had been brought by him from the Bialystok of his
youth. I approached the shelves and extended my index finger to trace
the mysterious letters on their spines. My eyes followed that finger and
came to the end of one of the bookshelves. They landed on a plaque,
affixed to the wall above a desk. It read:

> If I forget thee O Jerusalem, may my right hand fail and my tongue
> cleave to the roof of my mouth. (Psalm 137:5–6)

I was shocked. I knew my grandfather, with his gray goatee and
black silk skullcap, had not forgotten Jerusalem. My grandfather had

brought a famous Hebraic poet to New Orleans to educate his three sons, four daughters, countless nieces and nephews, as well as the other children of the community. He traveled the Gulf South with a blue Jewish National Fund *pushke* to raise money to buy dunams of land for the nascent State of Israel. Near the end of the seder, as the family sang to welcome the prophet who would herald the Messiah, I peeked as my grandfather surreptitiously struck the table with his hands to punctuate the words that welcomed Elijah the Prophet. His subtle movements caused the wine he had piously prepared from his backyard vineyard to nearly overflow the rim of the large silver cup before him. I watched the sloshing wine and pictured a tipsy prophet who went from Jewish home to Jewish home, taking a sip from each glass of wine at each stop. At the end of the seder, Grandpa closed his eyes as tightly as he could. He *shukkeled* up and down in his seat at the head of the table and led the family in the chant *L'shanah habaah birushalayim*, "Next year in Jerusalem."

My grandfather had not forgotten Jerusalem. Yet there he was, suffering in the next room, separated from his precious books, unable to turn their pages or to recite the words of their prayers out loud. I wondered why. What had my grandfather done, or failed to do, to warrant his fate? I didn't understand.

That was it for me and God for a long while. The God that was spoken of in the synagogue and in Sunday school no longer spoke to me. The words of the prayers just did not seem true. I spent my hours in New Orleans's Touro Synagogue counting the electric light bulbs in its high dome. I was unable to imagine a connection to a heavenly light beyond.

I like to say that I was prematurely eldered. I learned early what many don't face until later in life: profound loss throws cold water on our belief system and shatters our faith in the simple justice promised in Deuteronomy:

> If, then, you obey the commandments that I enjoin upon you this day, loving the Eternal your God and serving [God] with all your heart and soul, I will grant the rain for your land in season. . . . You shall gather in your new grain and wine and oil—I will also provide grass in the fields for your cattle—and thus you shall eat your fill. Take care not to be lured away to serve other gods and bow to them. For the Eternal's

anger will flare up against you, shutting up the skies so that there will be no rain and the ground will not yield its produce; and you will soon perish from the good land that the Eternal is assigning to you. (Deuteronomy 11:13–17)

These words, which observant Jews such as my grandfather recite at least twice a day, are found in the third paragraph of the *Sh'ma*. They promise a reward for serving God with all one's heart, soul, and might (Deuteronomy 11:13) and for the fulfillment of mitzvot. They also warn of punishment for transgression. But I *knew* that my grandfather had not transgressed. My grandfather had not forgotten Jerusalem. So, I had to learn at a young age that the promise that good will be rewarded and evil will find punishment was false.

That moment of cognitive dissonance was my initiation. It shattered my unspoken assumptions about God, based as much on that Deuteronomic promise as on the needs of a child. When we are small, we assume that our parents are all-knowing and all-powerful. We need them to be. We project those same pediatric yearnings onto God. Just as at some point we must mourn the fact that our parents are not perfect humans, our shattered parallel projection onto God also must be grieved. Just as we respond to the imperfection of our parents with the tears and rage of grief, we must also mourn our pediatric understanding of God—a God created in *our* image. Some find a way of maintaining their childhood theology. By blaming themselves or others for the misfortunes that are the whims of personal and communal history, they remain frozen in their belief in a God that is a projection of judgmental and vindictive human reactions. For many, however, this grief ends their relationship with God.

I chose a third way, although I didn't know it at the time. For me, the shock that came with the recognition that the plaque did not tell the truth about my grandfather precipitated a first step onto my spiritual path. It was the beginning of a long process of bereavement as I journeyed from pediatric to mature spirituality. My painful learning process taught me to hold what Carl Jung called "the tension of opposites."[1] It helped me to make peace with life (in the words of early Chasidic rebbe Nachman of Bratzlav) on the "the narrow bridge."

I believe in the wisdom of Jewish mourning rituals anticipating the painful cognitive dissonance emerging in us when bad things happen to good people. They exempt those in early grief from some of the quotidian mitzvot that praise God:

> The following are the things forbidden to the mourners: to read the Pentateuch, to study Torah . . . to put on *t'fillin* the first day. . . . They are forbidden to study the Scriptures, the Mishnah, and the Talmud, including the laws and *aggadah* (*Shulchan Aruch, Yoreh Dei-ah* 339:340:2).

This reflects the understanding that the feelings of mourners are in strong contradiction to the belief system encountered in much of the Torah. Those who formulated the Jewish path of mourning knew that grief provokes a spiritual crisis. By excluding mourners from studying, they prevented too-painful encounters with texts that promised God's intervening presence, at a time in which mourners might feel abandoned by God. Kindly, they exempted mourners from reading and reciting texts in which God, whom they may have felt had let them down, would be praised.

Yet, the first ritual observed after a death seems designed to let the bereaved know that grief is a spiritual journey—one that may challenge their understanding of God. Upon hearing the news of the death, God is thrown in the mourner's face. Mourners are asked to affirm "God, the True Judge" as they rip their garment upon hearing the news of a death. This ritual act signifies the rupture that death causes in the lives of mourners. It can also signify another rupture: one between the mourner and God. Beliefs that may have worked before the experience of loss are replaced by death's painful initiation:

> Upon hearing the news of the death of someone for whom one must mourn, one must rend one's garment and pronounce the words (*Shulchan Aruch, Yoreh Dei-ah* 340:6).

The initial acts of tearing and praising affirm God's wisdom. This seems contrary to the instructions to the mourners during the early days of bereavement, which exempt them from many religious obligations but especially from praising God. They seem to ignore the challenges to the faith of mourners like my own questions in the face of my grandfather's infirmity. Instead, these words confront the mourners. They goad them to challenge the severe decree of the "True Judge." They catapult them onto the mourners' path and bid them to ask mourning's existential questions. They force them to begin their spiritual journey in order to forge a new relationship with and understanding of God.

That journey is intimated in the Book of Exodus. When God and Moses encounter each other at the Burning Bush, Moses asks for God's name. God reveals a new name by which the Holy One is to be known. God tells Moses that the name revealed to his ancestors, *El Shaddai*, was not God's true and eternal name: "*Ehyeh-Asher-Ehyeh . . . YHVH . . .* this shall be My name forever" (Exodus 3:14–15).

The name *YHVH* is different from the more descriptive and concrete name revealed to Moses's ancestor Abraham. *El Shaddai* can mean "the Nurturing One," "the Breasted One," or "the God of the Mountains," a name that speaks to the more childlike yearnings of humans for protection and nourishment. *El Shaddai* was an appropriate name for our people in its infancy. In contrast to that, *YHVH* carries a more mysterious and ambiguous meaning, one that calls for spiritual maturity. Unlike a breast or a mountain, *Ehyeh-Asher-Ehyeh* (*YHVH*) does not provide a concrete image. The ambiguity of the name *YHVH* provides a possible container for the ambiguous feelings of those who must learn to live with the Great Mystery of pain and loss while trying to make peace with life and its paradoxes and unpredictability. *YHVH* is translated variously as "I am what I am" or "I will be what I will be." It is a version of the verb "to be," often translated as "existence" or "isness." However, all of those translations merely point to the full Hebrew meaning of those four letters. They turn the Tetragrammaton *YHVH* into a noun, more often than not translated as "Lord." But *YHVH* is a verb. It might also be translated as "the Great Unfolding of the Mystery at the Core of Creation." *YHVH* is a movement, not unlike evolution, I once heard Rabbi Arthur Green say. It is something that can never be understood— however, it can be experienced.

Why do we serve round things such as peas and lentils in a house of mourning? Because like the pea, the mourner has no voice (*P'sikta Zutarta* [*Lekach Tov*]).

Those who have encountered loss certainly experience this Unfolding Whirlwind. Whether we mourn the loss of a beloved person or the shattered assumptions of safety and confidence in the future, experienced by many as they navigated experiences that accompanied the COVID-19 crisis, our world turns into a precarious place. Mourners need to learn a new way to walk in their radically altered world. Meanwhile, one word resonates in their hearts: "Why . . . why . . . why?" This "why?" may be expressed in unbearable sadness, confrontational rage, and limitless yearning. These emotions diminish and crescendo over and over, as mourners struggle to find words for their new and challenging truths. They must, literally, "come to terms" not just with the fact of their specific loss, but also the mysterious fact of impermanence itself. Things change. We live on a planet where living things die. When experiencing loss, we are face-to-face with our own mortality, and we must "come to terms" with the fact that our own mortality is a part of the Great Unfolding Mystery, too.

El Shaddai is a God for those of us in fear of the unknown; *YHVH* is a God for those of us who have been to hell and back. With curiosity and courage, we begin to tentatively make peace with the unpredictability of the Great Mysterious Unfolding.

YHVH was the name given to Moses, who was to bring a radical concept to the world: human beings do not have to be slaves. God wants us to courageously embrace our freedom. However, our freedom is limited. Another teaching from Deuteronomy demands that we walk in God's ways. The Talmud asks in the name of Rabbi Chama, son of Rabbi Chanina:

What does the text, "you shall walk after *YHVH*, your God" (Deuteronomy 13:5) mean? Is it possible for a human being to walk after the *Shechinah*? For it has been said that God is "a consuming fire" (Deuteronomy 4:24). But the meaning is to walk *after the attributes* of the Holy One of Blessing. As the Holy One clothes the naked, so should you. The Holy One visits the sick, and so should you. The Holy One comforts mourners, and so should you. The Holy One buries the dead, and so should you (Babylonian Talmud, *Sotah* 14a).

In the Book of Job, we witness a man struck with vast, unbearable grief caused by the Divine. In the preamble to the book, God makes a bet with the devil causing Job to experience loss after loss. He goes through many stages of grief and rage, challenging God to explain the injustice of his affliction. God responds to Job's challenge by revealing God's self to Job: Job experiences The Great Mystery at the Core of the Unfolding of Creation. While God does not really explain the hardship that struck Job, Job seems to be satisfied with the revelation of the awesome mystery that is God.

On the mourner's path, this moment marks our last step: we make peace with the lack of an answer to that simple, but existential question that Job asked of *YHVH*: "Why?" Like Job, most mourners never arrive at an answer. However, a new understanding is found. As the wife of a police captain who lost his life following the September 11 attacks said, with a strong Brooklyn accent, "Ya lose ya faith in God, but ya get a whole new religion."

That new religion begins as mourners approach the stage of spiritual maturity. But there is more. The Book of Job ends with an even greater mystery as God speaks to those who tried to stifle Job's angry determination to confront God directly, advocating that Job's suffering had to be merited because God was just. To them, God says, "You have not spoken the truth about Me, as did My servant Job" (Job 42:7). Rabbi Tamara Eskenazi, PhD, once taught in a classroom conversation that these are the last words in the Bible uttered directly by God. It is as if, after affirming the rationality of Job's rage and yearning, God hands the baton to us humans to fight for justice and "walk in God's ways." In part, walking in God's ways also means to walk in the ways of Job as he demanded justice and an explanation from God. We take our steps as mourners from the world of our grief back into the world we share with others. This is the mitzvah we fulfill as we take the existential leap from a belief in *El Shaddai* to faith in *YHVH*.

It took me a long time to come to this spiritual maturity. In the years following my grandfather's death, God was irrelevant. I didn't believe. I didn't ask questions. I saw the fight for social justice as my way of being Jewish in the world. But shortly after the tragic and unexpected losses of my mother and sister when I was twenty-four, I was apprehended by *YHVH*.

I was in a yoga class. I lay flat on the floor. I had just come down from a posture that required me to lie on my back and push my feet and hands into the floor until the trunk of my body rose in an arc, raising my heart toward heaven. I had thought that it was the shape of my elevated body that caused the instructor to call the posture "the Bridge." However, as I lay there, I suddenly had the sense that a curtain had been pulled aside. I peered into the world of the dead. My mother and my sister felt very close. I knew I had not lost them.

I began to weep more deeply than I had in the months since their deaths. Then, out of some distant, encrusted corner of my soul rose the words of the *Sh'ma*, words that my parents had sung into my ears as I drifted into sleep during my childhood. I had not recited those words in many years. Yet, as I lay there, I chanted its six words over and over again. I lingered, each time, on the word *Echad*. Each of my cells was tingling in the presence of the Oneness.

Shortly after that experience, I met Rabbi Zalman Schachter-Shalomi. Following his presentation, I approached him. I told him of my experience in the yoga class. "Could that experience of Oneness be what the *Sh'ma* is about?" I shyly asked. "Yes!" he exclaimed. "Like Job, you have known God in your flesh!" My tears had replaced the pediatric God of Deuteronomy and led me to the comfort and companionship of *YHVH*. My tears had given me God.

בָּרוּךְ אַתָּה, יי אֱלֹהֵינוּ, מֶלֶךְ הָעוֹלָם,
שֶׁהֶחֱיָנוּ וְקִיְּמָנוּ וְהִגִּיעָנוּ לַזְּמַן הַזֶּה.

Baruch atah, Adonai Eloheinu, Melech haolam, shehecheyanu v'kiy'manu v'higianu laz'man hazeh.

With the gratitude and awe of my ancestors, as they
wandered through the desert wilderness, came upon

a pool of water, and fell to their knees for drink and refreshment, I praise the Great Unfolding Mystery (the artist formerly known as God), who has sustained me on this journey.

NOTE

1. Barbara Hannah, *Jung: His Life and Work* (New York: Putnam, 1976), 129.

Experiencing God in Fear:
Confronting the Night

RABBI EDWIN C. GOLDBERG

POET ONCE WROTE:

> In the middle of our life journey, I found myself in a dark wood. I had
> wandered from the straight path. It isn't easy to talk about it: it was
> such a thick, wild, and rough forest that when I think of it, my fear
> returns. . . . I can't offer any good explanation for how I entered it. I
> was so sleepy at that point that I strayed from the right path.

These words, from Dante's *Inferno*, capture a fundamental human constant: the forest, the wilderness, the jungle is a metaphor for a formative place of fear. We all have had to embark on internal journeys that we dreaded. Countless books, movies, and fairy tales recount the adventures of the hero on his journey through the wilderness, or the dark night of the soul. Whether we call it sadness, loss, depression, anxiety, or anger, it is tempting to rush out of this place, if we can. But here is a great truth: ironically, it is only by learning to live in the darkness that we can find our true selves.

As Joseph Campbell wrote, every culture has a story of a hero who must find herself or himself only through travel in the dark woods.[1] Our lives are made up of darkness and light. Susan Sontag once wrote this of sickness, but it could also be any challenge: "Illness is the night side of life, a more onerous citizenship. Everyone who is born holds dual citizenship, in the kingdom of the well and in the kingdom of the sick. Although we all prefer to use the good passport, sooner or later each of us is obliged, at least for a spell, to identify ourselves as citizens of that other place."[2] Be it sickness, depression, frustration, failure, or anger, we all carry both passports.

As Americans, we are famous for solving problems. But not all problems can be solved. And in America, we are not always as good at solving problems as we would hope to be. Whether we like it or not, sometimes the wilderness is exactly where we need to be, because that's where we are and this is where our destined task is waiting for us. M. Scott Peck once defined mental health as "a dedication to reality at all costs," meaning we cannot heal ourselves until we are truthful about the world we inhabit.[3] I like to paraphrase and say that spirituality is also a dedication to reality at all costs. Pretense has no place in spiritual moments, in our brush with divinity. The fear we feel is as real as it gets, even if the fears are unjustified. A passenger frightened by turbulence on an airplane feels fear even if the facts don't support the feeling. Facing fear is always real. If we are lucky, we spend much of our time holding our passport of good health and life. We forget about that other passport. But eventually the fear, the anger, the anxiety come back to us. The darkness is visible. Those of us who reach a certain age have all faced trauma from health scares, the death of loved ones, and reversals in our careers. Even when things are going well, we have felt a shiver in the sunlight, knowing that the night is near. Maybe we feel betrayed by a friend, we sink back into a bad habit, or we are disappointed in the outcome of a project or the cruelty of a child.

I have a favorite poem by Carl Sandburg, entitled "Limited":

> I am riding on a limited express, one of the crack trains
>   of the nation.
> Hurtling across the prairie into blue haze and dark air
>   go fifteen all-steel coaches holding a thousand people.
> (All the coaches shall be scrap and rust and all the men
>   and women laughing in the diners and sleepers shall
>   pass to ashes.)
> I ask a man in the smoker where he is going and he
>   answers: "Omaha."[4]

How tempting it is to focus on "Omaha" when so much of life is about the fear, the darkness, and the ashes. The title of the Sandburg poem, "Limited," does not only refer to the name of the train. Life itself is limited—and often we, in our own limitations, miss what is crucial and focus instead on the next best aim to reach. The spring of 2020 has been a global workshop in fear, anxiety, and dislocation. The sadness is pervasive, as is the death. It is easy to feel lost—and it is easy to lose sight of the deeper meaning of the time, and the actual tasks at hand, while we struggle to simply get through the days and do our jobs.

And yet I wonder: Could this very sadness also be a way to experience God? Could our acknowledging the fissures in our lives be a path to holiness?

A teaching from the *Tanya* of Rabbi Shneur Zalman of Liadi:

> As you arouse your heart by facing your shadow you may find yourself engulfed in a deep and troubling sadness. If so, do not be alarmed. Such sadness arises from and operates within the shadow of self, yet it draws energy from your innate yet hidden desire for God and godliness and thus kindles your passion for self-transformation. To work with sadness, say to yourself: "I feel utterly removed from God, yet within me is the light of God desiring only to return to God. . . . Therefore, I will cry out to God and God will end the exile of my two related selves. Shalom will come."[5]

It is tempting to think that the last place to experience God is in our confused and anxious state of fear. We certainly would like God to come into our frightened lives like some *deus ex machina* and give us answers and certainty. God should be in the healing and not the hurting, in the answers and not the questions.

If only.

This past summer I took a trip on the Rhine River, and I learned an important lesson about God, the woods, and the darkness. In the eighteenth century, the shores and rocks along the Rhine River in Germany became a popular place for romantics to walk the trails, enjoy the river, and contemplate the meaning of life. One Rhine-obsessed count built a deep, dark cave with both an entrance and an exit. The idea was to go through the dark tunnel while thinking about your life and then step into the light and the gorgeous view of the hills around and the Rhine River below. The moral of that experience was to teach that the woods, the caves, and the darkness are scary but also life-affirming. I went into this cave, and I would be lying if I said that all my cares and fears disappeared when I exited the darkness. But when I saw the view and the light at the end, I felt truly moved and inspired. In the middle of the cave, there was a hint of the light to come with a singular rooftop opening. Amid total darkness, that light brought me comfort, even joy. That crazy count was onto something important! He knew that the light would inspire, but only because of the darkness surrounding it.

I do believe that the cave's message should not be lost on us: to be human is to know the darkness, but it's also to remember the light.

The ancient Rabbis rejected the popular theology of their day, Gnosticism, and its implicit belief in two deities, a god of goodness and a god of evil. For them, there could only be one God, and therefore darkness was also created by God. In creating a morning prayer for Creation, they cited Isaiah's declaration, "I form light and create darkness; / I make well-being and create calamity; / I am the Eternal, who does all these things" (Isaiah 45:7). Yet, they changed the word "calamity" and replaced it with the statement that God makes *all* things. They fudged. They believed that that calamity comes from God, but they did not want to say that boldly. Perhaps they did not want to blame God *for* calamity—while understanding that God could be known *in* calamity.

I am not speaking of the good people who rise up in crisis and give of themselves. This may be a proof of the godliness inside of us. I am referring to the experience of God when the world is falling apart. There is an old saying, "Religious people are scared of hell; spiritual people have actually been there." I would rephrase that to say that spiritual people have found even in their personal hell an intimation of the Divine, both paradoxical and precious. As a rabbi I am often called upon to counsel people in their darkest times. I am unable to heal them. However, I have learned to sit with them in their darkness and help them come to see the choices they have in whom to blame, when to be angry, and whether their suffering is existential—and therefore helpful—or neurotic and therefore worthy of letting go.

There is a midrash on the Book of Genesis that refers to the strange verse "When Joseph's brothers saw that their father was dead" (Genesis 50:15). Since Jacob had died well before this time and the brothers had already gone to Canaan to bury him, the verse seems misplaced. The midrash suggests that what they saw was not that Jacob was dead, but that Joseph was acting differently toward them. Moreover, he had disturbed them on the way home to Egypt when he insisted that they stop at the place where decades before they had sold him into slavery.[6]

To the brothers it must have seemed that Joseph was plotting his revenge. But maybe Joseph's behavior was because he had arrived at a place of deep spiritual gratitude, acceptance, and forgiveness: he had come far in his achievements, wealth, and power; in the pit of darkness and hopelessness into which his brothers had thrown him, he had come to experience and encounter God in a mature way for the first time; and maybe those experiences led him to look at his brothers with loving eyes.

The brothers chose to see Joseph's actions through the neurosis of their own guilt. Before them was another way, the genuine perspective, of existential wonder at the ways that life take us and surprise us. This is an art and opportunity for those who counsel those who sit in darkness.

When I think of the times in my life I have been most afraid (usually because of some health scare that my hypochondria made worse), I found my dialogues with God constant. There was more than the Kübler-Ross bargaining going on, however. There was also gratitude for the life I have been given along with the desperate plea for life and hope. Such moments are awful but also filled with the intensity of real life.

The great poet Aeschylus wrote:

> He who learns must suffer. And even in our sleep pain that cannot forget falls drop by drop upon the heart, and in our own despair, against our will, comes wisdom to us by the awful grace of God.[7]

These words, which Robert F. Kennedy famously quoted after the death of the Reverend Dr. Martin Luther King Jr., are important for me when confronting my fears. The awful grace of God is a contradiction and absolutely real. The world is scary, sometimes more scary than at other times, and I have found God just as much in the darkness as in the light. God is in the hospital, in the storm, in the wilderness, dark and thick. God is in the message from the doctor's office. God is in the uncertainty of tomorrow and in the fear of the outside, unfamiliar world of these days. God is in the text from a child. God is in the fear that visits me at three o'clock in the morning. And God is in the specter that awaits us all—the specter that awaits me.

How tempting it is to possess God! How frightening it is to know that, actually, God possesses us. And how paradoxically comforting for me as well.

To find God in fear ultimately is to find God in the mystery of life, in learning to live with uncertainty. I have found it a hard but rewarding discipline. I suspect it will only get harder but paradoxically more rewarding.

Finding God in whatever we are feeling and without judging our feelings will be a difficult practice for most of us. But it's the only way to comprehend the awful grace of God.

בָּרוּךְ אַתָּה, יי, יוֹצֵר אוֹר וּבוֹרֵא חֹשֶׁךְ.

Baruch atah, Adonai, yotzeir or uvorei choshech.

Blessed are You, *Adonai*, Creator of light and darkness.

NOTES
1. Joseph Campbell, *The Hero with a Thousand Faces* (New York: Pantheon Books, 1949).
2. Susan Sontag, *Illness as Metaphor* (New York: Picador, 1977).
3. M. Scott Peck, *Further Along the Road Less Traveled: The Unending Journey Toward Spiritual Growth* (New York: Simon and Schuster, 1993), 75.
4. Carl Sandburg, *Chicago Poems* (New York: Henry Holt, 1916), 40.
5. Rabbi Shneur Zalman of Liadi, *Tanya*, chap. 26.
6. Rabbi Yitzchak said, "He went and peered into that pit [while in Canaan to bury their father]" (*B'reishit Rabbah* 100:8).
7. Aeschylus, *Agamemnon*.

PART 4

Bodies

You surround everything and fill everything.
You are the reality of everything
and are in everything.
—Rabbi Samuel Kalonymous

CHAPTER 15

Experiencing God in the Fragility of My Body

CANTOR EVAN KENT

Scene 1: Early Morning—a Swimming Pool on the UCLA campus

ANYONE WHO SWIMS in an outdoor pool in the winter, even in Los Angeles, will tell you that the twenty-yard walk from the door of the locker room to the edge of the pool is one of the coldest short walks ever imagined. Barely awake, with bare legs and a towel wrapped around my shoulders like a cape, I run from the locker room to the pool deck, and I discard the towel and flip-flops on one of the painted benches lining the concrete deck. I place my fins, pull buoy, and goggles at the end of the lane and gladly jump into the water. In the winter, at the UCLA pool, the outside air is much colder than the water, and the chlorinated pool offers a bit of relief from the chilly late December air.

I'm not a great swimmer. I usually feel heavy in the water, and my strokes are inefficient. But I've joined the UCLA Master's swim team to get in the requisite practice before my first Olympic distance triathlon in the spring. At this early-morning practice just a few days before the end of the semester, I feel tired, winded, and never seem to warm up. The hour-long practice feels never-ending, and I can't wait for it to be over. On the way back to the locker room, I ask a teammate if this workout was harder than others. "Nah," he replies. "About the same."

On my way to the synagogue, I stop in at a local sporting goods store to buy a new ski hat in anticipation of a ski vacation during the winter break. As I'm standing in line waiting for the cashier, I run into a synagogue member with whom I've become very friendly. She's on the temple board and has children in the preschool.

"Will I see you at the Chanukah party later?" Janice asks.

"Sure—can't wait," I reply. "The kids are really well prepared. They have some terrific songs to sing for the parents."

"Are you okay?" she asks. "You look a little tired."

"Just the time of year," I reply.

I pull into the synagogue parking lot and walk up the stairs to my office. I put my briefcase in my office, and I'm getting ready to go to a meeting when Gloria, my longtime administrative assistant who is really like a West Coast mother to me, comes into my office.

"You look terrible," she says. "Your lips are blue, and your eyes are glassy. I think you have the flu. Maybe you should go home."

"No, I'm fine. Just a little tired. Maybe it was the swim practice. It was tough this morning."

Ellen Goldberg (of blessed memory), our Religious School Director, comes into the office. If Gloria is my West Coast mother, Ellen takes on the role of an older sister.

"You really should go home." She places a hand on my forehead. "Wow . . . you're burning up. And look at your fingernails—they're blue. I'll drive you home."

"No, really, I'll be fine. But maybe you're right. I'll go home."

"I'll cancel your appointments," Gloria says.

I drive home, take Advil, and collapse.

Scene 2: *A Hospital in Santa Monica, California*

I end up in the emergency room at St. John's Hospital in Santa Monica along with what seems to be the rest of Los Angeles. Flu is rampant. People are sitting in hallways. I'm sitting in a wheelchair, shaking uncontrollably with a blanket on my lap and another over my head. Out of the corner of my eye, I see a teenager from Temple Isaiah. She turns to her mother and says, "That old man over there in the wheelchair looks just like Cantor Kent."

I want to stand up and tell her she's wrong—that it's not an old man, but that it's really me. But I can't move. I can't stand up. And when I try to speak nothing comes out of my mouth.

A doctor examines me. My husband, Don, sits nearby a bit concerned.

I can hardly move, and everything hurts. I'm still in the wheelchair covered in blankets.

"Evan—Cantor Kent, you have bacterial pneumonia. We've started a wide-spectrum antibiotic, and we hope it will work."

I try to take a deep breath—a breath of appreciation—but I only cough.

"If the antibiotic doesn't work, however, the bacteria will travel through your bloodstream, into your kidneys, your heart, and brain, and you're going to die."

Ted Stein, a friend and my gastroenterologist, acts as my internist—my gatekeeper. He tells Don to tell my family to come in from New York. It looks bad. Really bad.

I'm transferred to a room.

Put on oxygen.

And the antibiotics sort of work. Except the pneumonia doesn't clear from my lungs.

Tests.

More tests.

Scans.

A few visitors.

A lot of people talking quietly, and I slip in and out of wakefulness.

Surgery is indicated.

It's Christmas. The surgeon tells me he wants to wait a day or so—everyone is on vacation.

An intern comes into my room and asks me for some tips for running his first marathon.

The surgeon meets with me and maybe my family—I'm not sure who is around and who isn't.

I remember telling the anesthesiologist I'm a singer—a cantor—and if they must intubate me to please be careful of my vocal cords. And then for good measure, I tell her she should make sure to give me enough anesthesia so I don't feel any pain.

Don holds my hand and says a prayer as I'm prepped for surgery.

Pulmonologists.

Infectious disease doctors.

Don limits hospital visits.

I'm in intensive care.

Like angels wearing white lab coats, the nurses and interns, the residents and specialists keep me comfortable.

Comfortable and alive.

The surgery is extensive. My back has been opened, my lungs examined and cleared and cleaned. Recovery will take time.

The surgeon visits me in ICU.

"I hear you're a singer—and a long-distance runner."

"Yeah," I answer.

"Your surgery was a success. But you know, you might not ever get full function back in your left lung. Singing might be difficult, and I'm not so sure of the running. I thought you should know this."

"I sort of assumed this," I reply. I expected this. But didn't really believe it. Who truly wants to believe that they won't be the same after surgery?

Scene 3: Our Home in Sherman Oaks, California

There's no day or night when you're in the hospital. Even when lights are off, there's always a light on somewhere, and one day blurs into the next. The fluorescent lights emanate a blue-gray glow, and in ICU there's a constant procession of doctors and nurses checking and prodding and charting, and I am continually physically entangled in a maddening web of sheets, drains, catheters, and oxygen masks.

Machinery and monitors continually hum and beep, indicating rising or falling blood pressure.

Respiration.

Blood oxygen.

I beg the nurses for more of whatever painkillers I'm on. I try my best negotiating skills. Sometimes it works; often it doesn't. In pain-reliever-drip-induced half-sleep, I try to watch television, but I hallucinate instead. I see television shows that don't exist. I claim that Kokomo, our kitten, has come to visit, and I see people on the TV screen who have been deceased for years. I babble incoherently, and I know those visiting me are humoring me.

I think if I could just get out of here, I'll be better—I'll return to life as normal: singing, sitting in my office at the synagogue with bar and bat mitzvah students, preparing for a concert with the adult choir. I want to return to "normal." I want to sleep in my own bed, and I want to be awakened a bit too early by our cats to be fed. I want to sit in our living room and stare into the distance over the Santa Monica Mountains and see the clouds pass on top of the entirety of the San Fernando Valley.

After almost three weeks in the hospital, the surgeons and doctors release me. The car ride home is excruciating, and the few steps up to the front door are halting and painful. My mother stays with us—like a visiting nurse and visiting angel. More people come to visit. Members of the synagogue choir bring over meals. Friends stop by with cards, balloons, cakes. Visits are kept short—I'm in a lot of pain and unable to concentrate for extended periods of time. My mother acts as time-keeper and referee and makes sure no one stays too long.

Rabbi Jan Offel, the synagogue's associate rabbi, comes and visits. Jan has become a good friend and is a good pastor; she's an empathetic listener, and she promotes a theology filled not only with the sacred and the spiritual, but also with pragmatism.

We're sitting in the living room talking. Small talk about work. The office. The congregation. And then I start sobbing.

"How did this happen? How could this happen? And now what? Now what?"

She stares at me and holds my hand.

"There's no reason . . . there's no reason . . . but you have survived . . . you're alive and you're healing."

"But if I can't sing . . ."

"Have you tried?"

"No—I can barely stand . . ."

"Let's give it time."

We look at each other. There's only silence and the motor-like hum of Kokomo, our cat, who sits on the couch next to me.

Jan takes a deep breath and asks, "Have you ever tried praying?"

"Praying?" I ask.

"Yeah—praying."

Honestly, through this entire episode, I haven't thought of praying. I know people have been praying for me—but what prayers can I utter? What prayers can I say to aid my healing? Throughout all my time in the hospital and now at home, I have been in too much pain, too confused by painkillers, too deprived of real sleep to think about praying. Prayer hasn't been a part of my convalescence.

"What do you want to pray for?" Jan asks.

"World peace? A cure for cancer? A new bicycle?" I'm trying to be funny.

"No, seriously," Jan responds somewhat sternly.

I start crying again.

"I want to pray to be like before. I want to turn the clock back and be whole again. I want the scars to vanish. I want the pain to disappear. I want to feel like before all of this happened."

"So, let's pray for that . . ."

"That's sort of selfish isn't it?" I ask.

And on the spot, I make up a prayer asking for healing. Asking for strength. Asking for the elimination of pain. Prayer is no longer abstract—it is real.

Scene 4: Integrating Theology

In *The Insecurity of Freedom*, Abraham Joshua Heschel reminds us that often we think of religious existence as comprising ritual, myth, sacrament, dogma, deed, and Scripture. However, according to Heschel, these components of religious life aren't enough. For Heschel, the missing ingredient is the "innerness of religion."[1] With that spontaneous prayer in my living room, with the cat purring next to me, tears rolling down my face, and Rabbi Offel holding my hand, I find that missing element and momentarily enter what Heschel refers to as the dimension of "depth theology."

Heschel states:

> The theme of depth theology is the act of believing, its purpose being to explore the depth of faith, the substratum out of which belief arises. It deals with acts which precede articulation and defy definition.[2]

All the theology I had studied, all the philosophy I had tried to decipher, all the blessings I had chanted from siddurim are coming to life in these prayers post-surgery. Theology is no longer reserved only for Shabbat or the High Holy Days. A search for the holy and immanent becomes a part of my daily life. I begin a process of integrating prayer into the everyday, beyond those moments standing on the bimah. If there is a solitary blessing in contracting pneumonia and the major surgery that followed, this is it. The disease, the bacteria speeding through my bloodstream, has opened my soul, my heart, my healing body to what a vibrant prayer life can be like. My personal path to a prayerful life didn't begin in the abundance of nature, the vastness of the universe and the heavenly bodies, or the birth of a child. My initiation into a life where prayer is real and formidable was initiated by microscopic bacteria invading my blood and lungs.

Scene 5: Return—Still at Home

I can't stop thinking that the surgeon said I might never really sing again. I call my voice teacher, and he tells me not to panic; he'll come to the house and we'll see what state my voice is in. While waiting for my teacher to arrive, I recall Rabbi Offel's words to find a moment for prayer. I walk to the piano, and for the first time in almost six weeks, I open the keyboard cover and sit down at the piano. But before I begin my first attempt at vocalizing, I softly sing the last verse of Psalm 150: *Kol han'shamah t'haleil Yah*, "Let everything that has breath praise God." My fingers find the keys and I begin playing and singing.

It hurts to take a breath.

My ribs ache; my back feels swollen.

Slowly over and over I sing the words *hal'lu, hal'lu, hal'lu* . . .

The word *hal'lu* becomes a vocal exercise. I sing the phrase over and over in ascending and descending keys. Louder. Softer.

Fred, my voice teacher, knocks on the door. He sits at the piano. I grab another chair—standing up is too uncomfortable. Slowly, like an athlete warming up, we go through a series of exercises.

"Not so bad," he says.

"What does not bad mean?"

"It means you're exhausted, you haven't sung, but your voice is still there. Still intact. And it'll all come back. So—let's sing something," he says.

"Like what?" I ask.

"Let's try an aria—maybe the one from *La Traviata*? We were working on it right before you went into the hospital."

I pull out the opera score, and Fred begins to play.

And I begin to sing. It's not great. But it's not terrible. In the aria, Alfredo declares his love for Violetta. Toward the end of the first section of the aria he sings, *Io vivo quasi in ciel*, "I live like one in heaven." The words fly out of my mouth and resonate around the living room, and I stop singing.

Io vivo . . .

"Yes—yes . . . *io vivo*," responds Fred.

"It's amazing how sometimes the words really speak to us, isn't it?"

He replies, "You should call your surgeon and pulmonologist and tell them they don't know what they're talking about. You're gonna be fine."

Scene 6: A Local Park

After being with me as nurse, caretaker, and cook, my mother goes back to New York. Don goes to work—but checks in on me a few times a day. I've mustered the courage to drive short distances—as I'm still in pain. Volunteers have driven me back and forth to the synagogue, but I tire easily and head home after just a couple of hours.

With Don at work and my mother back in New York, I decide I'm going to attempt running. If I can sing—why can't I run? As I'm dressing to go running, I again recall Rabbi Offel's message: find prayer, make each moment holy, encounter the sacred even if you think it's mundane, pray for something.

I begin to dress: the running socks, the shorts, the T-shirt, the cap. I've done this hundreds of times. But this time—as I prepare for the first steps, I sit and contemplate what I'm doing. I've run thousands of miles without giving my feet hitting the pavement much thought. But this morning, I slow down and offer a prayer of gratitude for my feet that touch the floor, the legs that propel me across the trails and streets.

Modeh ani l'fanecha: I offer a prayer of thanks for my body, for a body on a path to healing and wholeness.

Modeh ani l'fanecha: I offer a prayer of thanks for the miracle of modern medicine, the wisdom of doctors, the generosity and caring of nurses, the love of family and friends, and the eternal love of a devoted husband.

Modeh ani l'fanecha: I offer a prayer of thanks for those who toil to make my running shoes, the socks, the T-shirt.

Modeh ani l'fanecha: I offer a prayer of thanks and remind myself to never take any of this for granted, to appreciate the routine and the everyday.

I slowly back the car out of the driveway and head down the hill to a local park with a running trail. At first, I walk slowly. The walk transforms into a slow run. I have the odd sensation that my body's organs are settling into place, they they're shifting, finding places to rest and lean against each other.

I run about half a mile and walk a hundred yards or so. I run another mile, and I feel ecstatic. Running has never felt simultaneously so labored and so easy. Each step is pained, but each step is also a victory. These two miles are a triumph over illness, a conquest over surgery, and a defeat over death. I sit on a bench in the park and I sob quietly. The words of an anonymous child poet from the Terezin concentration camp come to mind:

> Open up your heart to beauty
> And go to the woods someday.
> And weave a wreath of memories there—
> and if the tears obscure your way—
> You will know how good it is to be alive.[3]

Sitting on that park bench, months after surgery, tears streaming down my face, I know how good it is to be truly alive. I've completed a dozen of marathons, more half marathons than I can count, but I feel like an Olympic champion when I have completed those slow mile runs around Sherman Oaks Park.

And walking back to the car with the February sun brighter than I could've ever imagined, I recite my own version of *Shehecheyanu*:

Blessed are You, Adonai our God,
Who gives us life
Sustains us—
Sustains our breath
Sustains our bodies
Sustains me
Truly sustains me!!
And enables us to reach this day.

Epilogue: Twenty Years Later

My lungs are healed. In fact, a visit to a pulmonologist before Don and I made *aliyah* in 2013 showed both lungs were working at capacity. But I remember the surgery each day. A result of the surgery was some nerve damage, and the back of my chest aches most of the time—sort of like when your foot falls asleep. It's a reminder—a remembrance—a physical manifestation of what was and, unfortunately, what always will be. It's a physical recollection reminding me to never take my physical body for granted. My illness and surgery gave life to prayers I had often recited by rote every morning and now are imbued with a deeper and richer relevance. It is this dull ache that is my personal *Bar'chu*—my call to prayer every morning as I put on my running shoes and shorts. The daily morning prayer changes. Sometimes it's a spontaneous, impromptu blessing:

Thank You, God—thank You . . . for all of this . . . all of this—and so much more.

Often, I recite words from the siddur:

Elohai, n'shamah shenatata bi . . . , "My God, the soul You have given me is a pure soul. . . ."

Sometimes my blessing is a pre-run cup of coffee sitting on the *mirpeset* (balcony), listening to the sounds of early-morning Jerusalem awaken. And quietly, I go down the stairs, stand on the street, put on my sunglasses and hat, turn on my GPS watch, and remember:

בָּרוּךְ אַתָּה, יי אֱלֹהֵינוּ, הַמֵּכִין מִצְעֲדֵי גָבֶר.

Baruch atah, Adonai Eloheinu, Melech haolam, hameichin mitzadei gaver.

Blessed are You, *Adonai* our God, Sovereign of the universe, who makes firm my steps.

NOTES

1. Abraham Joshua Heschel, *The Insecurity of Freedom: Essays on Human Existence* (New York: Farrar, Straus and Giroux, 1966), 116.
2. Heschel, *The Insecurity of Freedom*, 117–18.
3. "Birdsong," sheet music (Schaumburg, IL: Transcontinental Music Publications, 2001).

CHAPTER 16

Experiencing God While Moving My Body

SUSAN FREEMAN

I HAVE BEEN A DANCER and a mover for as long as I can remember. As a child, my father gave me the nickname "Monkey" because of my propensity to be in perpetual motion, which included climbing up the walls in the halls of my family home. While I would tremble backstage before elementary school performances in which I had a speaking part, I never had a problem with dancing in the living room at family gatherings or in front of anonymous audiences. I experienced dance as pure joy!

As I grew up and became more sophisticated in spiritual languages and theological frameworks, I remained enthusiastic about dance. During rabbinical school, I became a member of the Avodah Dance Ensemble, a modern dance group focused on Jewish themes, and performed with them for four years. Within this venue, I was able to synthesize the joy of dance and my love of Judaism into integrated spiritual expression.

Years after I had left the dance company, at a gathering celebrating Avodah's founding director JoAnne Tucker, I shared this memory of performing a piece about the biblical Rachel and Leah:

> I often think of the awe-inspiring moments of holding a pose in "Sisters" at a synagogue in suburban Detroit—with the sanctuary in the style of an enormous tent. Any gaze extended into the "folds" of this amazing architecture. I felt so alive—spiritually, intellectually, emotionally, socially, aesthetically. It was one of those unique experiences of being wholly present—when the immediate moment becomes aligned with the eternal moment.

As my performing days waned, I have grown into an avid yoga

practitioner. Additionally, outdoor walks and runs, hiking, biking, and rollerblading have been significant and steadfast companions in my embrace of movement as expressing and reflecting the vitality of my soul/breath/spiritual essence, or *n'shamah* (breath, soul, or soul-breath), and the sacredness of this embodied life.

For the purposes of this chapter, I use the term "Engaged Somatic Experiences" as an umbrella concept to encompass a breadth of bodily felt (somatic) sensations that include and go beyond the choreographed or improvised movement phrases associated with artistic dance performance or with the dances of spontaneous movement at a life-cycle celebration or club. Moreover, I consider as Engaged Somatic Experiences any movement expressions infused with a conscious, or even subconscious, awareness of our human embodied condition, such as yoga, running, hiking, mindful walking, martial arts, biking, rowing, swimming, and so on. As Martha Graham (1894–1991), a well-known modern dance choreographer, stated, "The body is a sacred garment."[1]

Adamah, N'shamah, and B'tzelem Elohim: Body and Soul Created in the Image of God

Judaism points to foundational concepts at play in our human experience of God. The first books of our sacred literature teach that we are formed from the earth and infused with divine breath:

> God Eternal fashioned the human—dust from the soil—and breathed into his nostrils the breath of life, and the human became a living being (Genesis 2:7).

The Hebrew word for "human" (or "man") is *adam*, created from the "earth," *adamah*—words also resonant with the word *dam*, meaning "blood." These words point to our earthy physicality, our intimate connection with the material world. The word *n'shamah* hints at the more spiritual and soulful dimensions of our being. Toward the end of the Torah scroll, a potent allusion to *n'shamah* appears within the description of Moses's final moments:

> So Moses the servant of the Eternal died there, in the land of Moab, at the command of the Eternal (Deuteronomy 34:5).

The literal Hebrew for "at the command of" is "at the mouth of." Accordingly, Jewish tradition teaches that the greatest spiritual leader in Israel's history died by God's divine kiss.

Thus, the idea that we are created through divine breath comes from the Book of Genesis; and from the death of Moses in the final chapter of the Torah, we are to understand that with our last breath, our "soul-breath" returns to God.[2]

Also from the very beginning of our Torah, we learn that we are created *b'tzelem Elohim*, "in God's image":

> God now said, "Let us make human beings in our image, after our likeness. . . ." So God created the human beings in [the divine] image, creating [them] in the image of God, creating them male and female (Genesis 1:26–27).

Our entire being—our body/breath/soul/spirit—mirrors God. Maimonides, the medieval Jewish philosopher, associates *tzelem* with cognitive qualities; that is, "intellectual apprehension, not the shape and configuration" of physical form.[3] Maimonides emphasizes that humans emulate God more qualitatively, rather than materially or physically. I associate *n'shamah*, our "soul-breath," with qualities extending beyond the intellectual to include our emotional and spiritual lives, as well as our aptitude for connectedness. With Engaged Somatic Experiences, we can experience our God-given body and soul-breath in harmony with our nature as creatures created in the image of God. The awareness that our physical bodies are infused with divine soul-breath and imprinted with godliness grants us access to an intimate relationship with the Holy One: we are able to perceive all of life as sacred.

Walking in God's Ways

In the Genesis story, humankind's first experience of God begins with God "walking in the Garden" (Genesis 3:8). Later in Genesis, walking with God becomes associated with faithfulness. Noah, "a righteous man . . . walked with God" (Genesis 6:9), and God called to Abram to "walk before Me and be pure of heart" (Genesis 17:1). The Israelites walked and wandered forty years in the desert before they were spiritually ready to enter the Promised Land. We call the Jewish system for structuring our lives *halachah*, which comes from the verbal root "to walk." Effectively, many Jewish sources guide us to appreciate how our very walking has the potential to shape us and bring us into closer relationship with God.

When I was a camp counselor leading an optional day hike from an overnight campsite, there were only a few takers. When we arrived at the hike's summit, the three 10-year-old boys were overcome with awe. One of them happily chirped on the way down that when the others asked him how the hike was, he would say, "Nothing special," but then would surprise the sedentary campers with the follow-up barb, "We just saw God!" Closer to four hours than forty years, the hiking experience nurtured, in both the campers and the counselors, a felt sense of being close to the Holy One.

God's Name in the Human Body

Beyond the active "moves"—the deeds and mitzvot to which we are obligated—the idea of *b'tzelem Elohim* points to the very physicality of the human body. A Jewish mystical (kabbalistic) teaching suggests that God's unpronounceable name, *YHVH*, is literally the image of God that humans physically emulate. This is Rabbi Zalman Schachter-Shalomi's explanation of God's creation of humankind:

> So first I [God] will make Earth. Then I will form the Person out of My Name, *Yud-Heh-Vav-Heh*. I will make *Yud* [י] the head, *Heh* [ה] the shoulders and arms, *Vav* [ו] the spine, and *Heh* [ה] the pelvis and legs. And then I will blow into its nostrils and it will become conscious.[4]

At times we may experience God as emanant, as "out there," imbuing the world and the cosmos. To complement the idea of the emanant God, Schachter-Shalomi brings home the experience of God's immanence, which he defines as the God "within us." As alluded to in this chapter's opening vignette, in dance and other Engaged Somatic Experiences, we have unique entree to experiencing both the "out there" and "in here" dimensions of the Eternal One, at one and the same time. When we engage breath consciously and tune into Engaged Somatic Experiences, we tap into our nature as divine-infused beings. When we walk, sway, twist, reach, bend, and stretch, we engage our heads (*Yod*), our shoulders and arms (*Hei*), our spines (*Vav*), and our pelvis and legs (*Hei*). Doing so gives us an opportunity to connect with the Divine within ourselves, as we literally activate God's very name. The letters of God's unpronounceable name are resonant with the Hebrew word for "being." One way of translating *Yod-Hei-Vav-Hei* could be "Was-Is-Will Be." Movement engages experience in multiple time dimensions— past, present, and future.

In the summer of 2018, I hiked to the summits of several four-teen-thousand-foot peaks in the Colorado Rockies. In the present moment, I felt the earth beneath my feet, with each step. Connecting to the past, I was attuned with my historical experience of walking, having done so throughout the decades of my life. At the same time, I excitedly anticipated arriving at the "top of the world." Concurrently, I experienced the sacredness of these three "was-is-will be" dimensions of time, alongside an intent awareness of gravity and space.

Beyond Bodily Movement

Beyond the nuances of imperceptible breath, we can consider movement on a more subtle, exclusively energetic level. Jewish mysticism includes teachings about various realms of existence, also called "worlds." These realms range from the very material and concrete to worlds that are more ephemeral, mystical, energetic, spiritual. Each world has a role in God's creation, as well as in human experience. A common denominator traveling throughout and inhabiting the worlds are what the scholar Rabbi Adin Steinsaltz describes as "angels," which we might understand to be projections of human thoughts, emotions, and behaviors. According to Steinsaltz, "angels" are not tangible beings; rather, they are metaphoric energies that reverberate throughout the worlds.[5] Relating these Jewish mystical ideas to Engaged Somatic Experience, we can "feel" on levels that go beyond the material existence of our bodies. Potentially we can attune ourselves to an awareness of "invisible energy bundles" or "angels" that move beyond the concrete and embodied existence and guide us into other spiritual realms.

Not long after my father died, I had an especially potent Hatha yoga experience at the end of a practice. Participants lie still on their backs in Savasana, a final resting posture. I am not one to cry easily in my typical day-to-day life routine, but surrendering fully in the moments of stillness allowed my grief to "move" and the tears to flow. Lying on the ground with tears rolling down my cheeks felt sacred. This movement deep inside myself reminded me that God—and God's "angels"— invites me into full expression of myself. As it says in Psalm 118:5, *Min hameitzar karati Yah anani vamerchav Yah*, "From the narrow place I called out to God, who answered me in all of God's expansiveness."

Moving Within and Beyond the Limits of Our Body

My hunch is that most people identify with this notion: that a primal force makes us strive for knowledge of ourselves and for the realization of our full potentials. We seek to move, to change, and to grow. Some may say this force comes from God; others may say it is a product of human evolution. I relate to the language of Process Theology, according to which God "lures" us to become wholly who we are, to become the best selves we can be. As "images of God," the more fully and authentically we express ourselves, the more we connect with our divine nature, and the closer we are to God. Openness to movement and change within and beyond the limits of our bodies presents us with opportunities to connect with our own godliness and to fully experience the Holy One's love.

In his book *The Art of Somatic Coaching*, Richard Strozzi Heckler writes, "The further that we descend into the body, the less we are attached to it." He describes the paradox that the more connected we are to our bodies—the more we give in to gravity and the more aware we become of our breath—the less attached we become to them. Instead, we develop a sense of deep connectedness with other bodies and beings:

> My speculation is that by allowing myself to feel more deeply, it eclipses this notion of an "I," because it actually connects us to a greater field of energy. Where do I experience life? I experience life in this shape, in this soma, in this body. The more that I allow myself to experience life, what begins to happen is that the form, or the vehicle for the experience, begins to evaporate more. And what begins to show up is . . . deep interconnectedness between all forms of life.[6]

The Interconnectedness Between All Forms of Life: Adonai Is Echad, "God" Is "One"

While improvising, rehearsing, and performing with an ensemble of dancers, I developed a deep sense of interconnectedness. Dancing together, we were aware of each other's bodies, breath, and energy and were attuned with each other's thoughts and emotions. The need to be fully present in time, space, and intention bonded the group members together and gave us a sense of expansive vitality.

I also experienced profound interconnectedness when my sister died suddenly and under tragic circumstances. At the exact moment in which her death occurred, I experienced a physical reaction resonant with what I imagine she experienced.

There is a Oneness undergirding all earthly experience, congruent with the words of the *Sh'ma:* "Hear, O Israel, *Adonai* is our God, *Adonai* is One." While I may call this out-there/in-here Oneness "God," others may not, though their *experience* may be similar to mine. Feeling connected to a Oneness beyond the boundaries of our own physical and conscious self, we are able to experience spiritual "worlds"; we have a sense of interconnectedness, of unity with. We may even get a sense of the physical experience of a loved one—perhaps concurrent with their death—revealing interconnectedness with others on a purely energetic, metaphysical level.

In a study of nearly one thousand people, researchers exploring the varieties of spiritual experience concluded:

> The bottom line in understanding the phenomenology of subjective religious experience is this: Nearly every spiritual experience, in some small way, changes our sense of reality and relationship we have with the world. Generally, it increases our sense of unity and wholeness, not just in a metaphoric sense, but in the way we conduct our lives. In fact, almost three-quarters of our respondents indicated that they felt a sense of oneness with the universe or a unity with all of life. These feelings are also associated with a greater sense of purpose and meaning in one's life.[7]

Engaged Somatic Experiences offer the framework for integrating dichotomous experiences. Within our moving bodies, we can feel two (or more) things at the same time. We can feel our right arm, our left arm, then both arms together; we can feel fatigue in one part of our body and invigoration in another, then both at the same time; we can feel anger in our chest, forgiveness between our brows, then both anger and forgiveness at the same time. Our bodies can support all kinds of opposites, while we yet intuit an underlying recognition that *Adonai Echad*, God's Oneness, underlies, frames, and encompasses all who we are, within ourselves, and between us and all of existence.[8]

Radiating as Reflections of the One God

This chapter has focused on the human experience of God in dance and movement. Expanding on these explorations, we might consider how God experiences *us* through dance and movement. In a review of *Plain of Prayer*, choreographer Martha Graham invites us to contemplate this option:

> Although [the dance] is open to a multitude of interpretations, it did appear significant that at various points, one of the two protagonists dominated the stage like a divinity while the other was a suppliant; in other scenes these roles were reversed. The dance thereby suggested that whereas one always needs someone to love, the beloved, in turn, requires a lover. Similarly, the dance implied, some people are fated to seek and, because of their questing, never find rest. However, the object of the search is also never at rest, for such a being requires a searcher.[9]

Life invites us into a vast array of travails and celebrations. One of life's most potent experiences is grief. With our bodies and beings, we are called upon to be with grief as it periodically meanders or surges into our daily lives. Among life's experiences is joy and sweetness, as well.

> A season is set for everything . . .
> A time for weeping and a time for laughing;
> A time for wailing, and a time for dancing.
> (Ecclesiastes 3:1,4)

Engaged Somatic Experiences help us to draw upon the full expression of our humanity as we move through life's vicissitudes. Through Engaged Somatic Experiences, we live fully as both body and spirit, "image" and "soul-breath," as reflections of the One God. As we walk and wander through deserts and promised lands, we learn to integrate the grief and the joy, the mourning and the dancing. We learn to embrace the sacredness of human experience. As the Psalmist reminds us:

[God], You turned my lament into dancing;
You undid my sackcloth and girded me with joy.
(Psalm 30:12)

In gratitude for the Holy One's invitation to know and experience the sacred through the fullness of our bodies and beings, I offer this blessing:

בָּרוּךְ אַתָּה, יי, יוֹצֵר תֹּף וּמָחוֹל, שֶׁבָּרָא אוֹתִי בְּצַלְמוֹ
וּבֵרַךְ אוֹתִי בְּגוּף זֶה וְנָפַח בְּאַפִּי נִשְׁמַת חַיִּים.

Baruch atah, Adonai, yotzeir tof umachol, shebara oti b'tzalmo uveirach oti b'guf zeh v'nafach b'api nishmat chayim.

Praised are You, Creator of tambourine and dance,[10] who has made me in Your image—blessing me with this body and breathing into me Your sustaining spirit.

NOTES

1. Martha Graham, "I Am a Dancer," written for the radio program *This I Believe*, published in *This I Believe*, vol. 2, by Edward R. Murrow (New York: Simon and Schuster, 1952); also in *The Routledge Dance Studies Reader*, by Alexandra Carter and Janet O'Shea (London: Routledge, 1998), 96. Full quote: "The body is a sacred garment: it is what you enter life in and what you depart life with, and it should be treated with honour, and with joy and with fear as well. But always, though, with blessing."

2. In many Eastern spiritual traditions, parallel concepts to *n'shamah* are core to spiritual practice. *Prana*, a Sanskrit word for "breath," also means "life force" or "vital energy." In Hindu and Taoist traditions, *prana* can be a metaphor for "spirit" or "soul." Buddhism devised breathing meditations to give greater control over mental and emotional states. These traditions involve various spiritual practices in which adherents regulate the breath. Christianity, too, has a word for "breath," *pneuma*, which comes from ancient Greek and also is associated with spirit or soul.

3. Moses Maimonides, *The Guide of the Perplexed*, vol. 1, translated by Shlomo Pines (Chicago and London: University of Chicago Press, 1963), 22.

4. Ron H. Feldman, *Fundamentals of Jewish Mysticism and Kabbalah*

(Freedom, CA: Crossing Press, 1999), 100–101. Feldman references Zalman Schachter-Shalomi's book *Paradigm Shift* (Lanham, MD: Jason Aronson, 1993), 302.

5. Adin Steinsaltz, "Worlds," chap. 1 in *The Thirteen Petalled Rose* (Jerusalem: Maggid Books, 1980).

6. Richard Strozzi-Heckler, "Somatic Transformation," podcast interview by Tami Simon, *Insights at the Edge*, August 20, 2019, Sounds True, https://www.resources.soundstrue.com/podcast/richard-strozzi-heckler-somatic-transformation/. The interview references Strozzi-Heckler's book, *The Art of Somatic Coaching: Embodying Skillful Action, Wisdom, and Compassion* (Berkeley, CA: North Atlantic Books, 2014).

7. Andrew Newberg and Mark Robert Waldman, *How God Changes Your Brain* (New York: Ballantine, 2010), 81.

8. See Richard C. Miller's work on iRest. Specific exercises for working with opposites can be found in his book *The iRest Program for Healing PTSD: A Proven-Effective Approach to Using Yoga Nidra Meditation & Deep Relaxation Techniques to Overcome Trauma* (Oakland, CA: New Harbinger, 2015); e.g., chap. 7, "Welcoming Opposites of Feeling and Emotion," and chap. 8, "Welcoming Opposites of Thought."

9. Jack Anderson, "Dance: Martha Graham Revives 'Plain of Prayer,'" *New York Times*, June 4, 1986.

10. See Psalm 150:4.

CHAPTER 17

Experiencing God While
Using My Body to Create Order

Rabbi Sonja K. Pilz, PhD

W HEN SAD OR CONFUSED or exhausted, or all three together, many people seek solace in meditation, prayer, exercise, or entertainment. Me, I clean my apartment.

I like putting things in order. I love taking my dishes and cutlery out of the dishwasher and putting them back into their shelves; I love alphabetizing my books and lining them up with their backs right next to each other; I love to arrange my flowerpots, the stones and seashells and pieces of wood I have collected; I love folding, hanging, and sorting out my clothes; love doing my hair, love brushing my teeth; love rearranging the tubes and jars in my bathroom closet; love sorting pictures and my writing into folders on my computer; even love putting my dairy, ready-made food, and vegetables in separate spaces in my fridge . . . Don't get me wrong; I am not a neat freak. I love spending time at places that look messier and fuller than mine; I love hosting visitors for days and sometimes weeks at a time, and I love the many traces they leave in my apartment. And yet, I have learned that making order is, for me, a way to make myself at home in the world.

While my hands, and sometimes my entire body, sort, move, carry, lift, reach beyond and behind, scrub, fold, touch, sense, push, and bend my objects, my eyes measure, judge, and often enjoy the beauty I am creating. Sometimes I take a short break and just look at what I just cleaned or rearranged. I feel grateful for the things I own, and their beauty makes me happy. I feel happy about being able to live in a place of beauty. I am proud whenever I discover that I am able to put something up, fix or lift something that had looked too heavy, tricky, or broken for my humble technical abilities. I love to feel the strength of my fingers, arms, and back, and I love to touch the wood, glass, metal, wool, and ceramics that make up my home. Some years ago I read Mark Johnson's *The Meaning of the Body: Aesthetics of Human Understanding*.[1] Johnson is a philosopher of learning; his earlier book, a shared project with his colleague George Lakoff, analyzes how the metaphors we use ("up is happy") provide insight into the experiential categories in which we understand the world. His second book *The Meaning of the Body*, expands on his initial research and investigates the processes of human spatial learning.

What Johnson learned is fascinating. While still safe in the uterus of our biological mothers, our bodies begin to move. With these movements we develop a sense of space: up/down. Once we enter the world, we begin to dedicate a significant amount of time to exploring both our bodies and the spaces surrounding us: source/path/goal, up/down, into/out of, toward/away from, straight/curved — but also before/now/after! We learn to move our limbs and heads, and we learn to predict the movement of objects surrounding us. We learn to recognize others and ourselves in the mirror, and we learn to assume that an object temporarily hidden from sight still exists on the other side of the couch (object permanence). We learn about speeds, sizes, and weights of different materials (inertial motion); we learn about temperature and to anticipate pain or pleasure (causation; emotion); we make our first associations with familiar smells and tastes (intimacy is physical closeness; affection is warmth); we learn the flow and quality of music mirrored in the reactions of our bodies: heartbeat, muscle tone, and breathing (chapters 1, 2, and 3). In short, we learn to "organize" our world.

While we are busy doing all this, Johnson says, we are laying the basic foundations of our future linguistic, emotional (chapters 4 and 9), and logical (chapters 5 and 9) reasoning. We learn that one box fits into the other and will later on be able to grasp the logical "containment" of one category within another (chapter 9); we learn to differentiate between visual, tactile, olfactory, and kinesthetic images and will later learn to quickly grasp structural features (chapter 10); we learn to listen to music, and will therefore develop concepts of change over time (chapters 9 and 11). Through conceptual metaphors, our brains move from embodied meanings to abstract thought.

To summarize Jonson's findings: Through our bodily interaction with the world, we learn to move, feel, and think. That means that our bodies are not only the vehicles of our brains, but integrated parts of their development—our learning about the world. Ultimately, it is through our bodies that we experience the world; and it is through our bodies that we give, take, rise, fall, feel, think, connect, and die.

Those findings are highly interesting to developmental psychologists, therapists, artists, and philosophers—but they are equally insightful for theologians. Quite obviously, Johnson's research stands in stark contrast to dualistic concepts of bodies versus minds[2] and to kabbalistic categories of body, *ruach* (mind), *nefesh* (life-force), and *n'shamah* (godly breath/soul;) (*Zohar* 3:152b, based on Genesis 2:7). Johnson's findings deconstruct those carefully drawn medieval categories for the sake of a holistic image of the human being, of the "embodied mind": a breathing, moving, thinking, sensing, and feeling creature—all at the same time and place.

The image of the moving, touching, and learning human has accompanied me for the last several years—and at some point, I connected it to another image of a moving, touching, and learning being: the God of Creation.

The first two chapters of our Torah (Genesis 1 and 2) contain two Creation myths: the first, a metric composition with a clear poetic and developmental structure in which our world was created in a strongly choreographed chain of activities by God; and the second, in which, as an act of care for God's Creation, God forms the human out of mud and then—again as an act of care—forms the human's companion, upon which a tale of curiosity, passion, shame, fear, anger, and distancing unfolds.[3] Many of our liturgical texts—especially for the High Holy Days, commemorating Creation and the theological structure and mechanisms of our world—and Rabbinic stories riff on those biblical stories: metaphors of God as the worker of clay, forming us human beings; metaphors of God as a shepherd, watching over us like sheep; and metaphors of God as a parent, looking for us in the garden.[4] It is in those acts of ultimate power described in biblical, Rabbinic, and liturgical texts that we see God described as a maker and creator, making and creating us, but also making and creating the world.

The biblical wording of those Creation myths does not imply, as traditional commentators believed, a creation *ex nihilo* (from nothing). Instead, the first biblical narrative seems to assume the existence of a dark convolution of water and matter (the *tovu vavohu*), in which God, through separating the waters, concentrating the matter, and separating light from darkness, created order. God, in the purest meaning of the first narrative, did not "create" the world, but "ordered" it.

When I imagine God in the flow of the task, I imagine God's joy over the beauty and majesty of the emerging patterns of the large and small, intertwined in the new order. I imagine a sense of care for the vulnerable balance of life, of pride in the sheer beauty (movements, shapes, colors, smells) of Creation, of anxious hope for its well-being, of connection . . . I imagine God to have similar emotions to mine when I am ordering my apartment. I care, I create beauty, I am proud . . . I love to think that God loved touching the matter; I love to think that God loved seeing the patterns of beauty unfolding.

An attentive reader will have already noticed my careful formulations: "I imagine," "I love to think," "we see God described as," and so on. The reason for those careful formulations is, of course, that I am reading biblical texts as metaphors—human-made metaphors, based on our physical experiences of the world, pointing toward something else beyond our bodily, emotional, and cognitive experiences, approaching the tacit (an inner truth, a vague sense of a pattern, a "gut feeling").

My sense of an only tacitly experienceable God, approached through human metaphor, is in interesting dialogue with some of the work of another philosopher, Elaine Scarry. In her book *Bodies in Pain: The Making and Unmaking of the World*, Scarry describes the inherent tension in some of our most prominent theological metaphors and ethics:[5]

- Humans experience themselves in their bodily experience as deeply vulnerable in this world. Our bodies are subject to pain, age, and death. Therefore, we imagine God as a being without a body.
- We humans experience our lives (our physical existence) as beyond our control. Therefore, much of religious tradition imagines God as being in total control.
- We as human beings experience the limited power we hold in creating our own world. Therefore, we imagine God as the ultimate creator.

The God-Creator imagery of many of our biblical stories holds the unpredictable, painful, and passive human experience; it provides a sense of safety, protection, and relationship with a world that does not seems to care. On the other hand, the image of the ultimately powerful God becomes dangerous, because it is only from this God, from this only existing Ruler of the universe, that pain can come. In the framework of those theological metaphors, God is not only the protector, but also the ultimate source of pain. Therefore, the promise of safety and protection has to always be conditional ("if you do . . . , then I will . . ."), in order to provide a minimal sense of predictability. Embedded within the Creation myth is the notion that the beautiful order of Creation is vulnerable, that chaos is an integral and threatening part of the world in which we live, and that our lives are prone to fall back into pain and chaos at any moment.[6]

According to Scarry, the most central problem inherent to religion is that it depicts God as a maker—and ourselves as "non-makers" (her explanation of the fact that we are called upon to rest on God's day countless times but never asked explicitly to work on the other six days of the week); that it depicts God as the sole possible protection from chaos and pain—while keeping us humans in anxious suspense, waiting for the next wound.

I began to understand that while ordering my things and cleaning my apartment, I am experiencing myself as being in control. I create order out of chaos, I separate light from darkness, heal what is broken, and sort everything into my own categories. I am powerful and caring, giving and loving, and all of this to myself. I am protecting myself from chaos, darkness, and anxiety—by means of putting my books in alphabetical order. This experience is wholesome, not only in times of actual turmoil, but as a regular practice through which I am learning about the world and experiencing myself as a maker and creator.

As a scholar of ritual, I am aware that it is entirely possible to describe much of day-to-day Jewish ritual and halachah as such a practice. Our texts and practices provide the scripts to turn almost every daily experience (from waking up to eating to going to bed) as a consciously shaped practice of human creation (in the name of God). Ritualized behavior provides predictability and safety; it provides peace of mind and frees us from the insecurity of doubt, cluelessness, and worry.

At this point, I want to introduce one last philosopher, Emmanuel Levinas. Levinas is often placed somewhere between the categories of philosopher and theologian—which, I often think, is exactly the category of a Jewish theologian. Having accessed the Jewish sea of ink at an older age and after much philosophical training, Levinas made sense of Jewish myth and ritual by putting them in dialogue with what he had previously learned. He insisted that Western philosophy leave space for the possibility of God and that the idea of God is an integral part of being human.[7] He himself became a practicing Jew, in spite of being a doubter who wrote openly about his lack of faith, not only but especially after Auschwitz.

Explaining his own adherence to Jewish law, Levinas stated that by behaving and acting in the Jewish way, he was creating a physical space for the possibility of God in this world. By spending time and space on Jewish ritual and learning—in his deeds and in his thinking and writing—Levinas made sure that his life and work became a testimony of an order that places God first (or, in Johnson's words, "highest").[8] When Levinas took stock of his own life, measuring how much time and space he spent on his different interests, he wanted to make sure that it was clear to every observer that the highest priority in his life—his object of greatest interest—was God: because what else would you want to have in that position?

Levinas reordered his life after changing his priorities. He made space for a new category of "God." Speaking in Levinas's terms: When I am standing in front of the refrigerator in my kitchen, making space for the dairy, the vegan, and the ready-to-eat food items in my fridge (consciously omitting the category of meat), the object of my fridge turns into a testimony of faith. When Levinas spends his days studying Talmud with the mysterious Monsieur, he makes sure that his schedule becomes a testimony for his conscious decision to live with the possibility of God—and the way he makes space for that possibility is the way provided by tradition.

Many years ago, at a class at the Hartman Institute, I was asked why I wanted to become a rabbi. I answered with Levinas, saying that I wanted to make sure that my life would be a testimony that there is nothing more important than God by dedicating my life to the rabbinate.

I still think that's true. The order and patterns we create in the time and space surrounding us send messages both to ourselves and to others; in a way, we become messengers of our Torah in the ways we pick and shape our careers, friendships, and relationships, by the way we decorate our homes, open or close our doors for visitors, or walk down a pathway in a park. The amount of time we spend reading, speaking, thinking, or "doing" about God, in our very physical existence, is a witness to how we experience God—and how much space we make for the possibility of that experience. We order our lives according to our own categories.

Me, I move around my apartment, ordering sheet music, notes, books, and computer folders; folding laundry; sorting plates and cups; watering my plants; crossing things off my continuous to-do lists. I keep my world in order. At the same time, I am creating the image of a God who created and ordered a world in ways similar to mine. At the same time, my embodied experience helps me to overcome the passivity embedded in that image; it gives me a feeling of safety, control, and predictability. And yet at the same time, I am conscious of the fact that the very act of creating order (of creating and attributing space and time) hints to a tacit truth that I sometimes sense when I, once again, managed to create order, wholeness, and clarity: כִּי־טוֹב—*ki tov*, "and it was good" (Genesis 1).

While I am cleaning, ordering, and organizing, I am learning to care. While I am ordering, I am imitating God. While I am ordering, I am making space for God.

> *A blessing before creating order:*
>
> בָּרוּךְ אַתָּה, יי, הַמְסַדֵּר אֶת הַכּוֹכָבִים.
>
> *Baruch atah, Adonai, ham'sadeir et hakochavim.*
>
> Blessed are You, Adonai, who orders the stars.

NOTES

1. Mark Johnson, *The Meaning of the Body: Aesthetics of Human Understanding* (Chicago: University of Chicago Press, 2007).

2. Johnson is, of course, not the first to develop anti-dualist theories. Already the early phenomenologists focused on our body experience and learning of the world—in the United States, for example, John Dewey, whose continuity thesis is the basis for any further thinking.

3. Joan O'Brien and Wilfred Major, *In the Beginning: Creation Myths from Ancient Mesopotamia, Israel, and Greece* (Chico, CA: Scholars Press, 1982), chaps. 2 and 3; Oren Hayon, "Cosmic Disorder," in *Seven Days, Many Voices: Insights into the Biblical Story of Creation*, ed. Benjamin David (New York: CCAR Press, 2017).

4. See, for example, *Ki Anu Amecha*, in *Mishkan HaNefesh*, vol. 2, *Yom Kippur*, ed. Edwin Goldberg, Janet Marder, Sheldon Marder, and Leon Morris (New York: CCAR Press, 2015), 310.

5. Elaine Scarry, *The Body in Pain: The Making and Unmaking of the World* (New York: Oxford University Press, 1985), chap. 4.

6. A sense of the world that is reflected in Rabbinic midrashim of both Creation and the structure of the world (*B'reishit Rabbah* 2).

7. Emmanuel Levinas, "God and Philosophy," in *The Levinas Reader*, ed. Sean Hand (Cambridge: Basil Blackwell, 1989), 166–89.

8. Emmanuel Levinas, "Revelation in Jewish Tradition," in *The Levinas Reader*, ed. Sean Hand (Cambridge: Basil Blackwell, 1989), 190–210.

CHAPTER 18

Experiencing God While Loving My Body

RABBI EFRAT ROTEM

DURING MY FIRST YEAR of rabbinical studies, I would return to Tel Aviv after a day of classes at Hebrew Union College–Jewish Institute of Religion in Jerusalem with my head spinning with new words, melodies, ideas, questions, reflections, and sometimes feelings of both initial rejection and then again excitement over new insights. Each time, transitioning back to Tel Aviv from Jerusalem felt abrupt, and the contrast between my studies and the religious intensity brought by them and my life in Tel Aviv with my family, my queer community, and my work with Hoshen[1] felt like a simple fact of my life with which I had to make due.

Over time, however, and because I could not stop my mind from thinking, I began to notice quiet moments of an emerging integration between those two worlds. One night, I was lying in bed and looked at the body of the woman I was with. I was full of love, affection, and passion. I touched her body at three different places and spoke the words *kadosh, kadosh, kadosh* (holy, holy, holy) each time I touched her skin. I took this formula from the third blessing of the *Amidah* prayer, the *K'dushah*, which is traditionally said out loud only when there is minyan. Each time we pray the *K'dushah*, we rise to the tip of our toes three times as we speak those three words: *kadosh, kadosh, kadosh*. We imagine being part of an assembly of angels, praising God in the world above: "Each called upon the other: Holy, holy, holy is the God of all Creation; the whole earth is full of God's glory!" (Isaiah 6:3). At that very moment, I could sense that our closeness, love, and intimacy were filled with holiness. The *K'dushah* itself, with its embodied prayerful motions, merges the language of the body (when we rise to the tip of our toes in an attempt to stretch ourselves toward heaven, toward to the holiness of angels or maybe of God's self) and the holiness of human community (as we gather in a group to pray those words).

Rabbi David Dunn Bauer, gay, ordained by the Reconstructionist Movement, who served as a congregational rabbi at Congregation Beit Simchat Torah in Manhattan, also wrote about the words of the *K'dushah*, describing the moment of both great physical and spiritual intimacy. He imagines the angels of the *K'dushah* meeting at a kink party and writes about this party: "For me . . . [it's] community giving its members permission to praise God as who they are."[2]

I think of myself as a progressive Jew who belongs to a community of Jews from different movements: Reform, Renewal, Reconstructionist, and Conservative Judaism. When I began my rabbinical studies in 2011, the reality of women and LGBTQ Jews in the rabbinate was fully established in this community. Yet, because of the overall patriarchal structures of society and of Jewish tradition, this reality has remained contested.

It is impossible to speak about the juxtapositing of body and spirituality, of LGBTQ and queer identities, and of LGBTQ identities and the rabbinate, without looking back to the beginnings of feminism. The early feminists changed the public conversation, those changes led to many actual societal changes, and those societal changes helped the LGBTQ community to reimagine the role of the rabbinate to the point where it could include themselves. In 1983 lesbian Jewish theologian Dr. Judith Plaskow published an essay on the importance of a deep change within Judaism in an important anthology, *On Being a Jewish Feminist*, edited by Dr. Susannah Heschel.[3] Plaskow compares the status of women in Jewish thought to the status of Jews in the broader non-Jewish society. She explains that the role subordinate Jewish men had to play in non-Jewish societies was reproduced in the role of the subordinate Jewish women within Jewish society. Both the Jew within non-Jewish societies and the Jewish woman within patriarchal Jewish societies were declared to be other, different, demonic, and second-class humans—humans that were lacking.

Today, feminists and feminism itself still have to navigate those intersecting and hybrid identities. Before the founding of the State of Israel, Judaism had been the patriarchal religion of a minority. As such, on the one hand, Jewish cultures evolved as reinforcing the traditional patriarchal categories of men versus women, Jews versus non-Jews, the religiously privileged versus the religiously non-privileged, the old versus the young—while, on the other hand, they created textual traditions that speak extensively about otherness as the foundation of universal ethics, social justice, and shared responsibilities, embracing ambiguity, and critiquing the establishment of the notion of one singular truth and institutionalized power. Plaskow acknowledges that the creation of a gender-inclusive Jewish prayer language is an important endeavor. However, she emphasizes that a much more important effort would be the creation of a different kind of Judaism. This can only happen if the effort is carried out by all of us together. Plaskow writes:

> Feminism demands a new understanding of Torah, God, and Israel: an understanding of Torah that begins with acknowledgment of the profound injustice of Torah itself. The assumption of the lesser humanity of women has poisoned the context and structure of the law. . . . Feminism demands a new understanding of God that reflects and supports the redefinition of Jewish humanity.[4]

Feminist and queer philosopher Judith Butler adds to the notion of the subaltern as defined by their gender the notion of the subaltern as defined by their sexuality. She points out that in hegemonic conversations, the other is depicted as not fully human. The vulnerability of the other is not recognized and considered. Therefore, they face a much higher risk of getting wounded.[5]

Of course, when LGBTQ Jews in Israel began to enter the synagogues, it did not happen because of the feminist conversation. Many factors contributed to this development, among them the activism of American lesbians and bisexual women who had combined their efforts to open the gates of the synagogues for themselves and their families. In a groundbreaking publication in 1989, *Twice Blessed*, Plaskow continued to develop her feminist theology by adding the lens of sexuality:

> Our sexuality is fundamentally about moving out beyond ourselves. The connecting, communicative nature of sexuality is not something we can experience or look for only in sexual encounters narrowly defined, but in all real relationships in our lives. As Audre Lorde argues, our sexuality is a current that flows through all activities that are important to us, in which we invest ourselves. . . . From a feminist perspective, however, the power and the danger of the erotic are not reasons to fear and suppress it. . . . If we repress this knowledge because it also makes us sexually alive, then we repress the clarity and creative energy that is the basis of our capacity to envision and work toward a more just social order. . . . Can we stop evicting our sexuality from the synagogue . . . and instead bring it in, offering it to God in the experience of full spiritual/physical connection?[6]

It is interesting to put Plaskow's work, which has long become a vital part of feminist theological writing, in conversation with the broader societal conversation about gender and sexual equality, social justice, and, in religious terms, *tikkun olam*. The historian David Schneer writes that from the end of the nineteenth century to the beginning of the twentieth century, Jewish intellectuals of different ideological backgrounds perceived of a clear connection between the weakening of religious authority and the improvement of the state of society.[7] From this perspective, religions are means of oppression that have to be overcome as a society becomes more just. It was at this point in history that Christian and Jewish theologians began to draw connections between institutionalized religion and a movement toward social justice, among them the Reverend Dr. Martin Luther King Jr. and Rabbi Abraham Joshua Heschel. Those theologians saw their religions as inseparable from the ideal of social justice and established a tradition of biblical exegesis that reads the Bible as a means to liberation instead of oppression. However, it was the feminist movement that led to the radical new readings of biblical Scriptures of the twentieth and twenty-first centuries. Moreover, just as those gay, lesbian, and bisexual theologians and activists called for a new conceptualization of Judaism that would include different concepts of gender and sexuality, sexual and erotic energy, and power, today's trans Jews call for a different conceptualization, too: a conceptualization of Judaism that includes a definition of gender that reaches beyond the binary role models of the past.

In 1989 Plaskow described how human sexuality has shaped the reality of Jewish communities and theologies, and her work has continued to challenge us to this day. It has been expanded on by Rabbi David Dunn Bauer, whom I mentioned at the beginning of this essay. Rabbi Bauer is a sex-positive activist. He adds an important notion to Plaskow's theology:

> I actively work against the idea that you have to check your religiosity at the door of the bedroom, bar, or bathhouse, and that you have to check your sexualities at the door of the church or the synagogue.[8]

In my rabbinical studies, I was told to do the opposite of what Rabbi Bauer is advocating. I was told that I had be to a rabbi—just a rabbi, not a lesbian rabbi. In a conversation at the end of my first year at school, I was told that on my s'michah would be written not "ordained as a rabbi to the lesbian-gay community," but "ordained as a rabbi in the community of Israel." I was asked to stop my self-limiting and to reach out to the broader Jewish community. I learned from this conversation that apparently, in the eyes of my teachers, there was an inherent contradiction between my gender and sexual identity and the rabbinic work I had chosen for myself, and that my gender and sexual identity would significantly limit my professional options.

However, from my perspective, my identity broadens and deepens my perspective and helps me to integrate my seemingly diverging worlds. What did this process of integration look like? How could I turn the different parts of me into one whole me?

Twenty years ago, I came out as a lesbian, and I have been living my life as a proud butch for more than twelve years. A large portion of those years was dedicated to the psychological work of integration. At the beginning, I tried to separate my body's sexuality from my soul's spirituality. When I was a teenager, I decided if I had to be stuck in my body, I would not allow it to define me; its desires, needs, and looks were not really "me." In certain ways, this idea of a separation between "my real self" and my body has continued to this day, and I think it might accompany me for the rest of my life. When I finally came out and every time I come out again, I bring my whole self; I am integrating the seemingly contradictory parts of my self, and I engage in an act of refusal to hide and suppress my gender and sexuality. My life, my body, my spirituality—they are legitimate. Queer theory has taught me the extent to which queer existence in this world is important. Due to people with queer identities, all of us—queer and not-queer—learn about transformativity: the fact that all of us, and the world itself, are constantly in a process of change and transformation.

At some point, I decided to think about becoming a rabbi. In truth, I only began to imagine this possibility after my American roommate had hosted five queer American rabbinical students in our living room, and for the entire evening I had been unable to stop myself from asking them questions about their career choice—questions that I am getting asked every day now, too. That was the first time that I personally witnessed the integration of a queer gender and sexual identity with deep spirituality. This integration did not only take place in a critical reading of biblical or Rabbinic sources; no, this integration had taken the form of a life's dedication! Those American rabbinical students had dedicated their lives to the integration of Jewish tradition and contemporary queer gender and sexual identities.

Years later, I decided to follow in their footsteps—and while I am writing this I fully recognize that the danger inherent to this narrative is the same danger that is inherent to every coming-out narrative: just as a coming-out story never lives up to the ideal of total resolution, peace, and tranquility, so is my journey toward the integration of my queer identity and Jewish thought and tradition marked by recurring times of crises, moments of reconsideration and self-doubt, and difficult reactions from my surroundings. The Lutheran minister Nadia Bolz-Weber writes in her book *Pastrix* about a moment of shock and surprise she experienced one day during her studies at the theological seminary of Denver, Colorado:

> What the hell am I doing? Seminary? Seriously? With a universe this vast and unknowable, what are the odds that this story of Jesus is true? Come on, Nadia, it's a fucking fairy tale.[9]

When I read her description of this moment, I understood exactly what Bolz-Weber was talking about. To me, it was so important to read those words of a feminist Lutheran minister, covered in tattoos and a recovering alcoholic, who had found her way to lead a religious community without betraying her radical politics. In addition to the sudden sense of legitimacy of self, she also gave me a deep sense of the solidarity between women of different religious backgrounds. I, too, have lived through moments in which I asked myself, "What am I doing here? And why I am doing this here?"

When I began my rabbinical studies, I exchanged the relatively sheltered world of my work from home, my volunteer work at Hoshen, my more or less strong sense of belonging to my queer and lesbian community, for a world that was highly critical, very political, and strongly rooted in political liberalism. As a butch who looked different from the normative gender roles, who often passes as a man, I have often experienced that others have a sense of confusion about my body. After a session on LGBTQ Jews I led at the Reform Conference in Israel, one of the participants approached and told me, "If you want us to refer to you as a woman, you need to look more like one." Of course, I was thrilled to see how well the message of my session had been understood! In the liberal atmosphere of the Reform Movement in Israel, which ordains LGBTQ Jews and performs their weddings, there seems to be no more problems. Therefore, when I began to speak about my sense of lack and yearning, it was my sole responsibility to find the right words to describe why it mattered that I am a lesbian and a butch—and soon-to-be rabbi.

Judith Plaskow, Rabbi Bauer, and queer Jewish liturgy have helped me to find the words I need. My life as a queer person has taught me to bring my whole self, to develop and integrate all the different parts of my identity—those parts that are continuously changing, and those that remain relatively constant—to celebrate and enjoy them, and to acknowledge the price I pay for them—all the while continuing to live my life, day after day, as who I am. To me, this is a spiritual awareness that the queer community can share with the non-queer surroundings. My spiritual growth takes place when I work to fill the gaps between the worlds I inhabit. It takes place when I learn to live in the present. It takes place when I do not give in to the weight of the made-up stereotypes with which society burdens me, my friends, and my loved ones. It takes place when I do not accept the boundaries set before me.

When I recognize the challenges put in front of me as opportunities to grow spiritually and to connect to my resources of love and abundant care, I find the strength to blur those boundaries and to break with those stereotypes. If gender is a social construct, being queer has taught me not to believe in it, and my Judaism has taught me how to live as someone who does not adhere to it. When I was the leader of a congregation in the center of Tel Aviv, I began our *Kabbalat Shabbat* services with a few verses not from the evening prayers, but instead from the morning prayers: *Elohai, n'shamah shenatata bi t'horah hi*, "My God, the soul You have given me is pure." I think we can both believe and not believe at the same time. We can believe that our lives are whole and accepted, and that we will not live through further inner struggles. We can believe this while we live in a society in which homophobia and racism prevail, that wants to erase our yearnings, that does not accept our definitions of ourselves, that constantly attempts to belittle us and declare us unimportant, that does not want to give us space, that does not want us to speak, does not want to hear us, does not want to recognize our hurt and our anger, does not want us to voice our demands—and still join our communities, every Friday night, and sing together of our pure souls. To me, this is an experience of healing. It is an experience of healing of both mind and body. It is an experience of integration—of the integration of queer theology and Judaism.

To me, Judaism offers an ethics deriving from its many years as a minority religion. If those parts of Judaism will take center stage again, it can offer, in Israel, a true alternative for the form of dangerous Jewish racism developing here. As I understand it, in a true multicultural society, as we are being more particular, we are creating an alternative to the all-out identity wars raging right now. As soon as I deeply know who I am, no one will be able to undermine me. I don't need to tear apart and nullify the other in order to build my identity out of its remains. Our gift to the world, as queer people, is to always be the other, and Judaism adds to that the responsibilities the other invokes in me, challenging me to take upon myself.

The integration of Judaism and sexuality, spirituality and body, social otherness and shared activism, does not automatically lead to a peaceful utopia free from tensions and conflicts. Yet, I believe that if we make an effort to overcome and live through those tensions and conflicts, such integration will create the capacity for change and growth. In my former congregation in Tel Aviv, people of all ages, genders, sexualities, and statuses prayed together. I often wondered what connected all of them and what led so many to their devotion to this religious community. I think the answer lies in their shared spirituality—in the moments of deep spirituality that they experience in this community, and not in other settings of their lives.

It often seems like the aim of a feminist and LGBTQ movement is to open the world for women and LGBTQ people. I often think that an aim no less important is to open ourselves and our spiritual riches to the world. We have so much to share; as Joan Nestle wrote in *A Restricted Country*, "Being a sexual people is our gift to the world."[10] The integration of mind and body, sexuality and ethics, gender and liberation is by itself a radical act in a world that so often acts in oppressive and categorizing ways, telling us who we are. If we tell and listen more often to the experiences of queer Jews, we can tap into the full spiritual potential they bring with them.

There is a tradition of saying the *Sh'ma* at the bedside, a prayer that asks for God's protection throughout the night and a peaceful sleep. I wrote an additional prayer, meant for going to bed after a night of lovemaking. For this prayer, I integrated pieces of many other prayers, creating a religious language to speak about love and sexuality—moments many of us know ourselves, in which we experience a temporary union, in which no single word could capture the richness of our emotions and physical experiences. Those are the moments in which there is no more separation between our minds and our bodies; in which we live and breathe in a state of peaceful integration.

בְּרוּכָה אַתְּ יָהּ, רוּחַ הָעוֹלָם, הַמַּפְלִיאָה לַעֲשׂוֹת, אֲשֶׁר יָצְרָה
אוֹתִי כְּגוּפִי בְּדִבּוּר אֶחָד, הַבּוֹסֶכֶת שַׁלְוָה בְּנַפְשִׁי וְעֹז בְּלִבִּי.
כַּפָּנִים הַגְּדוֹלוֹת הַמְּאִירוֹת אֶת הָעוֹלָם, יָאֵר ה' פָּנָיו אֵלֵינוּ

וְיִחְנֵּנּוּ. בְּפָנִים אוֹהֲבוֹת אֵדַע כִּי מָצָאתִי חֵן בְּעֵינֶיךָ לְהַכִּירֵנִי. גּוּף הָאָדָם פָּנִים וְאָחוֹר יָמִין וּשְׂמֹאל, כְּנֶגֶד אַרְבַּע רוּחוֹת עוֹלָם, שָׁט עַל יַמִּים, מַרְחִיק עַד כּוֹכָבִים, מִתְקַיֵּם בָּרֶגַע וּבְאֵין-זְמַן, כְּרֶמֶז לְעוֹלָמוֹת עֶלְיוֹנִים. מוֹדֶה אֲנִי לָךְ, הַטּוֹבָה וְהַמֵּיטִיבָה, אֲשֶׁר יָצְרָה אֶת הָאָדָם וְהָאִשָּׁה בְּחֶמְלָה, רַבַּת פְּגִיעוּת, שׁוֹתֶתֶת אַהֲבָה, טְהוֹרַת נְשָׁמָה. בָּרוּךְ אַתָּה ה', הַשֵּׁם שָׁלוֹם בְּלֵילוֹתֵינוּ.

Praised are You, Spirit of the world, working wondrously, who created me as one whole body with one whole word, who pours peace into my mind and power into my body. Let Your face shine on this world, and be gracious to us. In the face of Your love, I will know that I please You and that You recognize me. My body is made of right and left, front and back, like a map of this world. It sails on water, it stretches to the stars, it lives in the moment and will remain forever—an unalterable part of the worlds above. Thank You, who blesses the world with abundance and wonders; who created the human body with mercy, vulnerability, overflowing love, and purity of soul.

בָּרוּךְ אַתָּה, יי, הַשֵּׁם שָׁלוֹם בְּלֵילוֹתֵינוּ.

Baruch atah, Adonai, hasam shalom b'leiloteinu.
Praised are You, Eternal, who gives us peace at night.[11]

NOTES

1. Hoshen is an Israeli nonprofit LGBT organization, which is listed by the International Lesbian, Gay, Bisexual, Trans, and Intersex Association as the largest such organization in Israel. Hoshen is the Hebrew acronym for "Education and Change." For more information, visit http://www.hoshen.org/Hoshen.

2. Merissa Nathan Gerson, "So, a Rabbi Walks into a Bar: It's Not the Beginning of a Joke, but of a Spiritual Journey," *Tablet*, November 7, 2013, https://www.tabletmag.com/jewish-life-and-religion/149663/rabbi-david-dunn-bauer/2.

3. *On Being a Jewish Feminist*, ed. Susannah Heschel (New York: Schocken Books, 1983).

4. Judith Plaskow, "The Right Question Is Theological," in *On Being a Jewish*

Feminist, ed. Susannah Heschel (New York: Schocken Books, 1983), 223–33.

5. Judith Butler, *Undoing Gender* (New York: Routledge, 2004), 17–40.

6. Judith Plaskow, "Towards a New Theology of Sexuality," in *Twice Blessed*, ed. Christie Balka and Andy Rose (Boston: Beacon Press, 1989), 141–51.

7. David Shneer, introduction to *Torah Queeries*, ed. Gregg Drinkwater and Joshua Lesser (New York: New York University Press, 2009), 1–8.

8. Gerson, "So, a Rabbi Walks into a Bar."

9. Nadia Bolz-Weber, *Pastrix: The Cranky, Beautiful Faith of a Sinner and Saint* (New York: Jericho Books, 2014), xvi.

10. Joan Nestle, *A Restricted Country* (San Francisco: Cleis Press, 1987), xvii.

11. In *Mishkan Ga'avah: Where Pride Dwells*, ed. Denise Eger (New York: CCAR Press, 2020), 40.

CHAPTER 19

Experiencing God While Listening to the Silence of My Body

Rabbi Myriam Klotz

W HILE A GRADUATE STUDENT at NYU in the 1980s, I was transitioning out of an Orthodox practice I had maintained for several years. I had been entrained with the daily rhythms of Jewish life, from daily prayer to kashrut to being *shomeret Shabbat*. I had loved studying Chasidic and Rabbinic texts and observing holy days. Still, my life eventually fell apart both in theology and practice. The serious spiritual practices I felt so aligned with had always seemed fulfilling by themselves. However, having been queer long before I became religious, I could not align my self with the basic rules of the game. The playbook, if I surrendered to it, left me cold and alien either to myself or to God.

When I engaged in daily morning prayer on my own, I felt an intimate relationship to the God of the (traditional) prayer book, a relationship that only deepened over time. When praying, even if in very loud environments, I felt a deep connection and quiet concentration. The bone-colored cover of my pocket siddur grew over time to have two dark gray thumbprints imprinted on it from my daily use. I would hold that siddur in my hands when on the New York City subway from Brooklyn to Manhattan many mornings, praying, a profound quiet enveloping me amid the jostles, screeches, and hums of the subway trains making their way underground. I loved those prayers, and I loved praying.

Also when I attended Shabbat morning services in my community, I was deeply engaged in the making of prayer. However, there was a *m'chitzah* separating the praying men and women. In a confusing, yet clearly deadening way, the *m'chitzah* felt like a splitting barrier right down the center of my self. Being gender queer (not conforming to conventional female or male gender identities), while having such a central and active relationship to my own personal prayer life, I felt a kind of vertigo being put in my assumed female and heterosexual place on the "other" side of the barrier. I wanted to be with the men on the other side, in their active engagement in Torah reading, service leading, and praying. I did not relate to the dresses and wigs that the women wore, not only on theological grounds, but also because I did not relate to being a woman in that binary way, religious or not. It was quite painful to experience the silencing both of my passionate prayer and my identity as queer. In this community of practice, the sweet silence in which I connected to God so deeply each morning on my own was thrust to some "other" place on the other side of the *m'chitzah*. This sense of alienation and displacement was amplified each time a young man peered at me from the other side of the *m'chitzah* or when I was urged by the women to date one of those men.

The *Bahir*, a twelfth-century work of Jewish mysticism, notes that the Torah ends with the letter *lamed*. The first letter of the Torah is a *bet*, or *vet*. *Lamed-vet* spells *lev*, "heart." The whole of the Torah narrative might just be summarized as "instructions from the heart [that is Torah]"—a heart that is often split by the endings of beginnings and the beginnings of endings; split down the middle; broken in its physical form; separated from what it loves by the layers of air, space, and nothingness between the scroll and us readers. Yet, Torah is also a great heart of compassion; a vast heart capable of holding within it rupture as well as continuity; silence as well as sound; emptiness as well as fullness; contradiction and paradox; being both this, yet that; being other, yet intrinsically one; holding death, as well as life; eternally birthing itself afresh from seeming finalities.

The reflections in this chapter reflect my relationship to God, which over the past five decades has both evolved and stayed the same, has been broken and gone mute, yet never has ceased in its somatic, nonverbal presence. I hope to share something about my sense of experiencing God as the God who holds all hearts in an unceasing flow of compassionate love, even as the journey toward knowing this love is a circuitous journey in silence, sometimes deafening and difficult to bear, even as silence is the great expanse within which and through which I experience God's presence, as intimately as each breath I breathe in or release.

M'chitzah and Marriage: Divided at the Silent Root

When I was still seeking to live an Orthodox life, I lived in Israel for several months. Personally and communally, those months were a fruitful and volatile time. During the winter of 1988, the Women of the Wall began to gather. I had been studying in Safed that fall, but a male friend who knew of my passion for *chasidut*, prayer, and Jewish learning, and also of my sexuality and feminist identity, urged me to come to Jerusalem, where I might find like-minded companions. I did find my community in the women, and supportive men, of Women of the Wall. I became actively involved in that struggle during those months of 1989. In some sense, I was externalizing my resistance against the many ways I felt repressed in a normative Jewish environment as someone other than a white, heterosexual male. To me, women, straight or otherwise, were all in a bind, and we were striving for religious equality of expression at the sacred site of the Kotel.

At the same time, I knew that I was looking for something different than most of the magnificent women leaders and community members in Jerusalem who could read themselves into straight relationships, family structures, and community roles. I continued to listen for the *kol d'mamah dakah* ("still, small voice" [I Kings 19:12]) inside me, seeking advice and answers from Orthodox teachers I respected and trusted. I asked them how one might find a place as oneself in the Orthodox world. It was a sincere and searing question for me. Time after time, sadly, I left those meetings disappointed. The most empathic and honest response came from Avivah Zornberg (then teaching weekly *parashat hashavua* classes at Pardes). She simply expressed her sadness and acknowledged that in truth, there was no place for a homosexual lifestyle in the Orthodox world (as we knew it then in Jerusalem). She did not heal or belittle my pain, but she stayed in deep and empathic conversation with me. By acknowledging and listening to my truth, she softened my growing cynicism. Yet, several male teachers responded in ways I found damaging and distorted and in whose presence I was left feeling at once invisible and very visible to myself in the intensity of my anger, outrage, and grief. One rabbinic authority I had sought advice from told me to marry a man and have a lover on the side if I must. It felt hurtful and callous, unethical and destructive, to pass as straight. It felt misogynist to be told I had to marry and have children, because, after all, "we are a post-Holocaust generation and I must do my part to grow our people again by bearing Jewish progeny." It did not make sense to belong to a practicing community anymore because even though my personal practice felt fulfilling, the only future that community could offer to me would be a life in hiding, split from my essence, repressing or disassociating from my self in the most painful way. I found that I could not surrender to humans telling me what rules I needed to obey if I wanted to remain on "God's team."

Even more salient, I found that I could not abide the presumption of those I queried that a normative heterosexual life trajectory was the only theologically "correct" choice one could make. I could not surrender to a God who would create me—whole, intrinsically and innately innocent, and sound in gender and sexual identity—and at the same time make those central aspects of my being somehow a deficit, a problem, something to be fixed. However, even then my anger was soothed by the words of the traditional verses from the Book Psalms or phrases from the siddur: *Lo ira ra ki atah imadi,* "I will not fear evil because You are with me" (Psalm 23:4); *Elohai, n'shamah shenatata bi t'horah hi,* "My God, the soul that You have gifted me is pure" (morning prayers). I was not truly alone, for God was with me. Me, a human with as pure a soul as any other human, devoted to cultivating the closeness between myself, a gender queer person, and God.

The Still, Small Voice: For You, Silence Is Praise (and Salve)

I found myself in a spiritual crisis. The Orthodox words and regulations that pointed toward a God to whom I could return were intellectually not sound and psychologically destructive. Somatically—on a preverbal, physical level—those halachic and theological norms were simply traumatic. Yet, miraculously, the brash and loud bluster of those violent preachings—not unlike a fire, an earthquake, a great wind—were not able to destroy my connection to myself or to God. They failed to touch the *n'shamah t'horah*, the "pure soul within me" that is beyond judgment, even my own judgments, and simply, silently, in its own still place, *is*. At root, I was guided by that *kol d'mamah dakah*, perhaps the *Bat Kol*, perhaps *Shechinah* Herself. In I Kings 19:11–12, we read of this still, small voice:

> And lo, the Eternal passed by. There was a great and mighty wind, splitting mountains and shattering rocks by the power of the Eternal; but the Eternal was not in the wind. And after the wind—an earthquake; but the Eternal was not in the earthquake. After the earthquake—fire; but the Eternal was not in the fire. And after the fire—a still, small voice.

Deep inside me, the seed of my soul was silently, potently, persistently, speaking. By grace, temperament, and my stubborn intellect and makeup, I persisted in listening for the *kol d'mamah dakah*.

Later that summer of 1989, I would live very quietly in Mitzpe Ramon, a small town in the Negev at the lip of a very large desert crater. I had received an artist's grant to write. After the loud and harsh months of fighting the misogynist rulings governing prayer at the Kotel and questioning the practices that shaped sexuality, gender, and spirituality in the Orthodox world, and after seeing that my efforts were in vain, I got quiet. I spent hours in the quiet of the desert, the only sounds being the clicking of my fingers on the typewriter or the lizards, ibex, or birds cutting wind or rock beneath their wings, hooves, and claws. Each evening I would sit on my patio and watch the moon move in the clear dark sky from one end of my vision to the other. Slowly, I healed.

The sacred silence inside me merged with the great silence of the life of the natural world. I would find words and could craft poems and narratives that insisted on the fact that *I was here. We were here. We were here, mysterious, flowing, vast, and unconditioned.* Looking back, that time was sacred time: I lived in dialogue, contemplatively, mostly silently, and in an intimate relationship with what I have referred to as the *Bat Kol*.

Never Ceasing: The Silent Voice of the Bat Kol

The S'fat Emet, a Chasidic master from the late nineteenth century, teaches (Shavuot 5657/1897) on the following verse from the Mishnah: "Rabbi Y'hoshua ben Levi said: Every day a Heavenly Voice (*Bat Kol*) is heard from Mount Horeb proclaiming: 'Woe to those creatures who have contempt for the Torah'" (*Pirkei Avot* 6:2). This *Bat Kol*, the S'fat Emet writes, derives from the "sound" (*kol*) of Torah when it was given, as it says, "a great sound (*kol*) that did not stop" (Deuteronomy 5:19)—for each and every day some new revelation occurs from this sound.

My own reading of this teaching, informed by my experience of living that summer in Mitzpe Ramon, is that the *Bat Kol*—that constantly speaking, silent voice that renews Creation in alignment with the Creator—is bringing new revelation every day. That voice, heard sometimes as a quiver in our gut, can easily be repressed or simply overheard. It is at once subversive and devotional; normative and disruptive; it instructs us to listen for what is flowing from Creation, moment after quiet moment, underneath the loud narratives of habit.

In the Torah, we find yet another aspect of the *Bat Kol*. In the Book of Exodus (3:1–17), Moses asks God by what name he should refer to God when speaking to the people. At this moment of revelation, Moses is barefoot. He has left the paths of habit, tending his sheep. Instead, he stands before the *s'neh*, the Burning Bush. In this moment of intimate encounter, God tells Moses to tell the people that *Ehyeh-Asher-Ehyeh* sent him. *Ehyeh-Asher-Ehyeh* means both "I Am That I Am" and "I Am Ever Becoming."[1]

The *Bat Kol* emanates from that which is *Ehyeh-Asher-Ehyeh*, both being now and ever unfolding. I know for myself that imagining God in those two ways has helped me stay attuned both to the integrity of my being and to that aspect of me that is ever becoming. The *Bat Kol* makes Her Self known to me in silence, somatic sensations, thoughts, ideas, and flashes of insight. Those flashes mark moments of my awareness of the divine becoming. I am a receiver; all of who I am is necessary to receive the silent voice in which the *Bat Kol* speaks.

Kol Han'shamah T'haleil Yah: All of My Soul (Body and Breath) Praises God

This unconditionally loving, knowing, and wise Presence somewhere in my being eventually gave me the strength to trust my self, to love myself, and to know that God, *Ehyeh-Asher-Ehyeh*, *is*. God does not distinguish and separate between the different parts of our selves, because this God is who I am, who you are, who we all are; this God is all there is.

> *In the surrender to the silence around, underneath, before, the words, there is awareness itself. Listen . . . get quiet, get curious, get kind, and listen.*

During a spring in New York, after I had returned from that formative year in Israel, I was in my Brooklyn apartment, preparing for Shabbat on a Friday afternoon. I was not partnered, and I felt isolated. I prayed to God, that tiny eternal quiet voice deep inside . . . I prayed with frustration, anger, confusion, I cried my tears, and I prayed for guidance. I got very quiet . . . And eventually, in my listening, I heard a very small, terse answer. "You don't have to do it anymore. You're okay. *It* is okay." Really? Really??

And then I knew. I knew it to be true.

I knew, not from words but from listening in silence for something deep inside me, that I was loved. God was revealing God's Self to my conscious being. I did not have to keep trying so hard to be religious for God to love me. I could let go. With tears of relief and some grief for the way of life I was about to tear myself from, I breathed out, and I knew I was free. It was that *kol d'mamah dakah* that brought me home to my self. With great intention, I turned on a light switch that Shabbat. It was the first time I had used electricity on Shabbat in several years. I illuminated a dark, silent part of my soul where the *Shechinah* had been in exile with me all along.

Some months after that Shabbat, I was finding my way. My religious practice ground to a halt as I was exploring New York City's LGBTQ communities. I was honoring my self, healing aspects of myself from which I had become distant in order to live a religious life. Yet, I also felt the void left by the absence of both personal and communal spiritual practices. My gender and sexual identities were aspects of my self, but they were not everything that was "me." I quietly yearned for a way to express my spiritual life without betraying my self.

On a mild April afternoon, I was walking along Fourteenth Street and came upon the Sivananda Yoga Center. Curious, I stopped to look at the yoga class schedule posted in the window. I had never done yoga before. As fate would have it, a class was starting shortly. I decided to give it a try, and I walked in. A few minutes later, I was given a yoga mat and a spot on the floor. The carpet smelled slightly musty, and I was wearing jeans that were a little restrictive, but those things did not matter. After fifteen minutes, I had come home to myself, safely in my body, dedicating my attention to the life force coursing through me.

> *Inhale, and slowly exhale. Place your hands . . . strengthen your thighs . . . soften your shoulders . . . close your eyes, and bring attention to the sensations in the chest . . . come to your knees, and bow your forehead onto your mat . . . bring your palms together, fingertips pointing toward the sky . . . let the breath move through you, and in these postures, free your self to align with the divinity inside your being as it courses through your veins.*

There was plenty of space between the words of the instructions. Each of the words was tethered to practice. Not talk about an abstract deity, but rather an invitation to come home to the sacred nature of being alive among all living beings: sacred practice. Sacred, safe, and devotional. An invitation to enter deeply into the miracle of my body, just as I was. This was an in-body way of praying, of reaching toward that deeply interior seed of sacred knowing. As Mary Oliver has written in her well-known poem "Wild Geese":

> You do not have to be good.
> You do not have to walk on your knees
> for a hundred miles through the desert repenting.
> You only have to let the soft animal of your body
> love what it loves.[2]

Or, as the Psalmist wrote, *Kol han'shamah t'haleil Yah, hal'luyah*, "With my entire soul, with each and every breath, I praise God. *Hal'luyah.*" Truly, fully, and lovingly.

In the silence between the words, in the silence born of all that was my being, in the present moment, I had come home to the God who yearned for me as I yearned for God. That day, I knew that I had found a home for my spiritual yearning that was loving, unconditionally and innocently. The answer had not come through disembodied words or abstract principles. It came through the invitation to find, in the quiet gentleness of breath and movement within the boundaries of a seven-by-three-foot rubber mat, the voice of the *Bat Kol* inviting me to life. Life. Love this life! With every breath. *Hal'luyah*, truly.

Almost thirty years later, I am grateful for the richness I have found in a Jewish spiritual practice that is premised upon self-reflection; that is invitational, not doctrinal; that integrates words of guidance and teaching; that integrates silence and experiential practice; that creates communities of practice that are truly experiential and truly inclusive.

I became a rabbi, a teacher of yoga and embodied spiritual practices, and a spiritual director. These days I find great joy in helping others to cultivate deep listening for their own inner voices and to trust in their inherent dignity, authenticity, and power.

I also continue to practice this way personally. When I rise, I pray silently. I meditate. In yoga or other forms of physical practices, I listen through and to my body. In spiritual direction, I listen for the experience of the sacred within others, and within myself, and for that sacredness resonating between us. When I teach Torah Yoga, I hope to transmit the invitation that participants can land in the truth of their own bodies, breath by breath, and cultivate the capacity to quiet the loud voices that usually speak first. Instead, I invite my students to listen to the soma, the voices of sensation, breath, and movement.

These practices help to cultivate our capacity to come present to our lives in this very moment. And this is where God can be revealed—not yesterday, not tomorrow, and not in a distant part of this world or any other world. Right now. Right here. It sounds so simple. Yet, to say, *Hineini*, "Here I *am*," right now, fully present to this moment within and around me, is to invite a spaciousness of being that is quiet, open, vulnerable, and beyond control to enter into our lives. With practice, it becomes possible to stand in the light of presence: embodied, silent, and whole.

Kol Tzedek: The Safety to Speak, in Silence and Song

Recently, I attended Shabbat morning services at Kol Tzedek, a congregation in Philadelphia. Kol Tzedek meets in an urban church. The rabbi, Ari Lev Fornari, is a transgender man. Many of the congregational members are people of many fluid gender and sexual identities. Each person is welcomed, however they understand themselves to be, and whatever is their way of becoming. While simple, this is a profound statement: *I am willing to listen to the truth of your experience and to honor the sacredness of these truths.* When we start with deep listening; when we are willing to sit in the silence of possibility; when we honor the reflection of God's limitless diversity and ever-evolving nature in our own bodies—then the softness and openness that allow for relationship can enter. Theology is based upon experience, allowance, and silence and is grounded in the sacred nature of embodied experience. It is "beyond words," even if we consider the liberating power some words have as they break a repressive silence.

That Shabbat morning, we prayed from the siddur together: from *Birchot HaShachar* (the early morning prayers), through the Torah service, and ultimately through Mourner's *Kaddish* and *Aleinu*. What moved me utterly was not that the sounds and the words were a continuation of centuries of Jewish religious expression. But it wasn't not that, either. It was that, just as in the *Sivananda* yoga class almost thirty years ago, each soul gathered felt honored, dignified, and sweetly encouraged to express itself as a being that can love, be loved, simply be wholly itself. No *m'chitzah* was necessary to protect human beings from one another on the basis of their gender and sexual identities. Rather, our humanly divine and diverse natures could dance with the *Bat Kol*, present and revealed. I felt safe in community; safe to declare my love for the Ineffable, the Non-binary, the All-Knowing *Ehyeh-Asher-Ehyeh*. Tears ran down my cheeks as I witnessed people being themselves in a world in which it is not yet always safe to be oneself.

What is it that enables someone to risk, to dare, to listen deeply to the "whispers of the soul," as Rav Kook suggests, and to cultivate a life of being and practice that honors the *Shechinah*, the aspect of God that never parts from us, which is, perhaps, our Soul itself, embedded in our bodily selves?

For me, this ability is rooted in the voice that speaks in silence, the silence of my being's depths. When I practice yoga and drop into my body's sensations and breath . . . when I sit in silent meditation . . . or silent prayer . . . or communal prayer, as at Kol Tzedek . . . when I sit with another in spiritual direction and listen in spacious silence for the movement of that sacred knowing . . . when I am in nature . . . Silence stirs Soul. Egoic chattering recedes, at least for some time. Then, I can hear it. I am called forth into Being. I am Inviolate, Becoming, Whole. I am standing on *admat kodesh*, "holy ground."

בָּרוּךְ אַתָּה, אֶהְיֶה אֲשֶׁר אֶהְיֶה, רוּחַ הָעוֹלָם,
רוֹקַע הָאָרֶץ עַל הַמָּיִם.

Baruch atah, Ehyeh-Asher-Ehyeh, Ruach haolam, roka haaretz al hamayim.

Praised are You, *Ehyeh-Asher-Ehyeh*, who invites me to find grounding in my ever-becoming.

Notes

1. I am grateful to Joy Ladin (*The Soul of the Stranger: Reading God and Torah from a Transgender Perspective* [Waltham, MA: Brandeis University Press, 2018]) for her teaching about being that is always just as it is and always evolving and on the cusp of becoming, too.

2. Mary Oliver, "Wild Geese," in *Devotions: The Selected Poems of Mary Oliver* (New York: Penguin, 2020), 347.

PART 5

Beyond Body, Soul, and Mind

The world was created with the breath of God. . . .
If breath is lacking, life is lacking.
—Nachman of Bratzlav

CHAPTER 20

Experiencing God by Simply Sitting with God

RHONDA KARLTON ROSEN

IN MY FIRST JOB out of graduate school I was working for Rabbi Abe Twerski, MD, psychiatrist, healer, and lover of addicts, who has a wondrous combination of lightness and gravity to his presence. For me, this combination is a marker of deep connection to the flow of one's soul and one's roots in the collective.[1] It was evident that Dr. Twerski was touched by holiness. I had been hanging out with Buddhists the previous six years and came to Gateway Drug and Alcohol to run their biofeedback program. My job was to teach combined meditative skills and physiological self-awareness in an AA-oriented drug and alcohol rehab center.

The biofeedback devices bring into awareness states of arousal and relaxation. When we are aroused, our hands and feet get cold, and our muscles tighten, including our diaphragm. Simple enough. In order to bring skills of self-regulation to vulnerable addicts in their first twenty-eight days of sobriety, when they are fragile and trying to navigate the liminal state between living and dying, we clinicians helped them to make use of all their resources.

Built right into the program was a necessity of operationalizing the residents' spiritual lives. Whatever its expression, their spirituality became a healing possibility. "Let go, and let God"; all the bumper stickers slogans were pointing toward choosing life. But in Pittsburgh in 1979, I was not allowed to use the word "meditation." I would have been mistaken for dealing with the occult. Consequently, I had to figure out how to teach nimbly, without jargon, meeting the residents' worldviews and theologies, in order to facilitate their individual journeys.

We worked on our mutual trust enough to learn to relax and let go. We examined the obstacles that got in the way. For those of us dominated by a harshly judgmental mind with a limited capacity for tolerating mercy, the obstacles become the path.

There is a fairly predictable emotional and spiritual path to walk. We have well-honed defenses against feeling vulnerable, feeling pain, or feeling anything at all. Receptivity to intimacy and love can be cultivated as a newly learned skill.

When I started having kids—four total—I left the rehab center and moved into private practice, working with folks with psychosomatic and anxiety-related disorders. I work and have worked with Catholic nuns, Chasidic women, and addicts in committed recovery. I work with tall people and short people. I work with all the genders. If my clients have an explicit or implicit spiritual life, I want to bring in that spirituality for their healing. And if they don't, we work with different metaphors and language.

I have been refining this work for many years. When people ask me what I do, I usually tell them that I am a therapist, social worker, clinical supervisor, and meditation teacher. With this chapter, I want to give a deeper and fuller answer: I am Jewish, I am moved by the writings of our Jewish mystics, and I want to continue to explore Judaism as a wisdom tradition. I use Buddhist meditative practices to cultivate and heal my own being, and I walk with my clients on their own journeys of healing. My practice utilizes the Buddhist understanding of the refinement of attention, helps me to illuminate my Jewish soul, and enlivens my reading of Jewish texts.

The Mishnah describes the early Hasidim as sitting for an hour before praying in order to prepare themselves.[2] However, if we are drawn to this suggestion, I do know that if I put an average, in-the-pew Jew next to a Buddhist-trained meditator and ask them to sit quietly for an hour, it will be the meditator who will be capable of just sitting there without running out of the room screaming or devising something more important he or she needs to be doing.

It seems to me now that all those years of sitting in silence have given me some access to the stirrings of my soul. After many years of doing this emotional and spiritual work outside of Judaism, I returned to Judaism because my soul would not let me do otherwise. My eyes would become wet with tears whenever I entered a synagogue and heard Hebrew chanted. I cried, embarrassingly and uncontrollably, on my first retreat with Jonathan Omer-Man whenever we met one-on-one. The book *Conscious Community* by Rabbi Kalonymus Kalman Shapira[3] vibrated in my hands when I picked it up from Special Orders at Barnes and Noble. I cannot explain why I was so moved by my Jewish roots. I cannot explain why I responded to the internal urging the way I did. Why do we ask God to "open my lips so I can pray" (at the beginning of the *Amidah*)? What even moves us to ask this?

I found that Buddhist meditative practice and insights bring a new depth of understanding to the Jewish traditions of prayer and text study—and that the mystics of our own tradition open new gates of understanding that move me. The Buddhist meditative practice gives me the cloth to clean the lens of perception—the lens I look through is a Jewish lens. The Jewish philosopher Philo gives me permission to use what the Buddhists know in order to further explore and refine our Jewish spiritual lives. In his essay "Every Good Man Is Free," Philo explains that the Essenes, the Zoroastrians, and the sages of India are all really good at sitting in silence in order to "sanctify their minds."[4] Jonathan Omer-Man showed me how to read Jewish texts in a contemplative way, and for many years, I have been doing this work with my congregation in Pittsburgh. I believe that each one of us is responsible for one letter of all the Oral and Written Torah. Each of us is called to hold up our letter. These teachings may be my one letter. I have no way of knowing. But I do want to make this one contribution to understanding.

Let's see if it is helpful to anyone.

Buddhists have refined how to sit in silence. They know how to deliberately work with attention, to continuously clean the windows of our perception, to stay earthbound while we ground ourselves in faith. My small piece of our collective soul can hold up what I know about the Jewish perspective to the continuous light of Divine Mystery. That is the only thing I know how to do. I am that simpleton at the back of the synagogue, sounding out the letters and raising them to God.

Deep humility is foundational to any spiritual practice. We need to continually work to let go of our attachment to ideas about ourselves, about the meaning and purpose of our lives. We need to open ourselves to the continuum of possibilities and keep working to make choices that are wholesome on the levels of action, thought, and emotion. Philo speaks of the need to toil, to continue to work on the refinement of our perception and passions. Humility is necessary to not fall into the grave error of divorcing the sense of the immanent presence from the transcendent.[6] To help us from committing this error, we begin each blessing by acknowledging both the immanent, the indwelling, and the infinite unknowable when we say:

בָּרוּךְ אַתָּה, יי אֱלֹהֵינוּ, מֶלֶךְ הָעוֹלָם . . .

Baruch atah, Adonai Eloheinu, Melech haolam . . .
Blessed are You, Eternal our God [the Immanent],
Sovereign of this world [the Transcendent] . . .

We are continually reminded that both are essential: experiences of transcendence and a deep connection to the earthy conditions of human existence. Without humility, this is quite impossible. Without access to awe, we are bound to a very limited view.

At this point, I would like to introduce the Buddhist list of the five faculties of mind: mindfulness, concentration, absorption, wisdom, and faith. The Buddhists work with attention in order to refine their perception and concept of self and then, in a second step, learn to tame and harness their passions. I will lay out how we can integrate these practices into our Jewish spiritual lives.

Mindfulness

The first faculty is mindfulness. You can never have too much mindfulness. Mindfulness is a cultivated skill of being awake to whatever my heart, body, and mind are busy doing in the moment. I am just sitting here, being here, as I am wakeful to the ongoing sense of being alive, here, now.

Mindfulness, awakened attention, can be cultivated by sitting still. We learn not to scratch the itch as we are just sitting here breathing. We are trying to observe the relationship of cause and effect and create the possibility of something new happening. The intention not to move is a good place to start. By deciding not to scratch the itch, we are learning to make the habitual reflex optional. This is a process of leaving the familiar and moving into the unknown. What happens when I don't have to scratch the itch? With the decision not to move, we learn that sensations arise and then disappear. As I just sit here, feeling what I feel as I feel it, it turns out okay. This is the beginning of cultivating faith in the process. The itchy feeling is temporary; I don't need to do anything about it.

Concentration and Absorption

Supporting mindfulness are two linked pairs. The first of the two linked pairs is concentration in relationship to absorption. You can think of this pair as a directional arrow with a certain amount of energy, aiming in a prescribed direction. When everything else falls away except the prescribed object, this is absorption.

The other pair of linked qualities is wisdom and faith. They grow together. Wisdom knows that everything—every thought, every feeling, and all mortal life—is temporary. As we integrate this understanding on deeper and deeper levels, our capacity for faith grows, independent of any fixed thing or idea.

We can tie all these qualities to the Jewish path. We can bring the process of the investigation of the mind and the teachings of the five faculties to our own wisdom tradition. We do this in order to make these techniques useful to us.

Concentration and absorption seems to be the favorite pair of those interested in the cultivation of states. With concentration, I intend to pay attention to just one thing (the breath at the nostrils can be a useful starting point), letting all other matters and thoughts fade into the background, until there is absorption into the one thing. This practice can become really interesting. If there is too much energy, I will get agitated and restless; if there is too little, I will nod off and fall asleep. We can learn to regulate the amount of energy to prevent either extreme, unless we are too tired, in which case we just fall asleep.

Absorption without awareness is trancelike. We may easily end up focusing on only one thing or aspect of our existence, unable to hold onto a sense of the whole. This is the state in which most of us unintentionally live our lives. Sometimes, when used deliberately, absorption is a useful tool when we try to fall asleep or cultivate relaxed states. Knowing how to relax is necessary. Comfort and ease and the capacity for contentment should be valued. The capacity to patiently wait is extraordinarily useful. These can all be cultivated as possibilities for immanent indwelling, creating a home base within ourselves. Pragmatically, being able to stay awake during those states sure beats falling into mindless rumination about things that make us miserable.

In our Jewish vocabulary, this practice might be a Shabbat practice. I can practice ceasing to work; I learn to value comfort and ease, to let go, and to be receptive. Let the eyes receive light. Let the ears receive sound. Let the heart be open and receptive. We are taught in our tradition that if we are incapable of keeping Shabbat, this inability will kill us (Exodus 31:14). The practice of Shabbat becomes an obligation. We keep the Sabbath religiously. And we are taught that the Sabbath will keep us.

Some Jews and some Buddhists love cultivating states of absorption. Sometimes we can identify, catalogue, and rank the steps of our "progress" through them. The Chasidim practice holding God in their hearts and minds at all times. The Yitzhak Buxbaum book *Jewish Spiritual Practices* has 679 pages of suggestions of how to train the mind and heart this way—to focus solely on God at all times.[7] Those folks with a bent toward Abulafia's meditation methods focus on letters and sounds.[8]

However, I want to add a word of warning. At the time I was reading Aryeh Kaplan's seminal book *Jewish Meditation*,[9] I met a fellow named Paul Bindler. I met him at a professional conference, and we did some committee work together on insurance reimbursement for biofeedback. I asked him if he was the Paul Bindler who was part of Kaplan's inner circle, as mentioned in the acknowledgments. Paul was one of those guys in constant movement, even when he was standing still.

Sparks circled around him like dust around the *Peanuts* character Pig Pen. When I asked him, he paused and then said with a chuckle, "We were into some really crazy [stuff]," using a more colorful term. They had been doing intensive concentration and absorption meditations. He then became pensive, and the sparks all sank around his feet. He paused again, looked up thoughtfully, and then said, "I am the only one left alive." He looked a bit lost. I was sad with him. Paul died in 2002.[10] His story underscores my own experience with the cultivation of states. It reinforces my attachment to an embodied practice. When I was with a group of chanting Jews, doing the permutations of the *Yod-Hei-Vav-Hei*, I found myself floating above Encino in a nanosecond. The same thing happened at Elat Chayyim. I lost sight of the room, and a vortex opened up. I did not like it. There is danger in finding the light and forgetting about gravity.

In 1973 I went on my first meditation retreat, thirty days with S. N. Goenka in Madras.[11] He implored us all to "stay in our bodies." I like staying in my body. It is my home, for now. Being alive is important to me. However, the directional arrow (the mental faculties pair of concentration and absorption) is essential to a meditative practice, also beyond the cultivation of ecstatic states. States arise naturally. For me, that is good enough and makes the meditative practice much more applicable to daily life, as well as for my ongoing, day-to-day relationship with the Divine Mystery. When I speak to Buddhist groups, I talk about "de-stupidment," rather than "enlightenment." I am much more interested in the ways habitual reactivity causes the painful separation between immanence and transcendence and in learning ways to cultivate and refine skills of connection. It turns out that careful and kind attention can untangle the knots of perceptual habits. With deliberate use of attention, we can begin to pull apart the factors of habitual reactivity and create a possibility for change. Interested and kind awareness facilitates the alchemy.

There is so much more present than the few things we are aware of as we just sit here. We have moods, thoughts, and hormones affecting our reactivity, habits, problems, pains, and unsolvable conundrums making up this rich soup of experience. Among them, there is the possibility of awareness itself. Our consciousness can expand to hold all, or at least more, content without any prejudice or judgment. We can awaken to this. The content is not the point. The light of consciousness simply shines. Consciousness, supported by equanimity, becomes our resting point.

Wisdom and Faith

With that said, we can now consider the other pair of mental factors that supports awareness—wisdom and faith. These are terms with which Jews are much more familiar. This pair is extremely useful for what the more mystically inclined Jews call the "nullification of the self" (a loose translation of *bitul hayeish*, ביטול היש, the "erasure of what exists"). Our selves are fabrications. Consequently, we get to make adjustments when our habits of perception and identification are no longer working for us. We get to observe our habits of understanding and learn that there is no absolute truth. As one of my daughters once said as I was tucking her in bed, "You know, these lives of ours, I think we make them up as we go along."

We can cultivate the willingness to hold perceptions lightly and let something new arise in the often repeated habitual chain of perception. This is part of not scratching the itch. Letting go of the familiar way of perceiving the world opens us up to not knowing, to silence, to simply being. This can scare us. This is where faith gets cultivated. I can rest on the ground of nothingness, no-thing-ness, for a moment, as I continue to just sit here. I learn to have faith in the process of letting go. Faith is a cultivated and direct experience. It becomes the anchor in the endless sea of unknowing. Wisdom knows awe. It knows that all is temporary, all is mere breath (Ecclesiastes 1). Faith helps us to just sit here and know what we now know. And then perception re-forms around a new temporary truth. With a honed intention, we move closer to living well, living with the knowledge of our relationship with eternity and our responsibility to make what the Buddhists call wholesome choices.

We need to take a look at our behavior and our intentions before we can even begin this process of deconstructing the unconsciously (or consciously) crafted defense systems that we utilize for self-protection.

Many times, these defenses do not serve us well. We need to take on the obligation to cultivate patterns of thought, speech, and action, which lead us closer to loving ourselves and others.

As Jews, we add yet another kind of love to this list that the Buddhists do not overtly have: we have a personal relationship with the Divine we can draw upon. We can use the responsibility to that relationship to discover where we fall short. We are told to love God with all our heart, all our might, and all our soul. Being open to a relationship with the Divine Mystery calls upon us to work on our fear of the infinite and our fear of mortality and to cultivate our willingness to rest on what the Buddhist call the "firm ground of no-thing-ness." Our personal relationship with the Divine also creates an immediate obligation: How do we begin to make space for God in every aspect of our lives? In this moment, in this setting, with these people, how can I contain all this as an active element of my awareness? How do I shift from "God, help me" to "God is helping me"?[12]

We practice both as we sit silently and as we interact. Judaism is not a monastic practice. We are asked to learn to love within the context of the people who are closest to us, those whom we can call our "familiars," and even beyond that context: Love God, love your familiars, and love the strangers, as you love yourself (Leviticus 19:34).

Learning with Love and Humility

How do we learn to do this while we cannot even be kind to ourselves? My teacher Jonathan Omer-Man taught that our relationship with God, ourselves, and others is exactly the same. I found wisdom in this. This teaching frames my work and describes my experience.

What is our capacity to love and receive love? Fear certainly seems to come to me more easily than love. The path of the contemplative, the path of all the resilient Isaacs, unfolds like this: First, I know awe. I have seen the glint of the knife in the sunlight and know how the ground beneath me gives way. All that is left is the unarticulated. Only after I figure out how to live after experiencing true awe, only then can I begin to re-dig my father Abraham's wells[13] and find the source of love. Only then I can dig my own wells, as did Isaac.

Jonathan Omer-Man has another teaching that is really helpful to me. I am paraphrasing it and giving it to you in the way that I have integrated it. I don't know where he got it from, but I want to thank whoever taught it to him, for pulling this idea down from the heavens. New ideas can change us.

We have four kinds of relationships with God. One is no greater than the other, and we move through them throughout the day or month or year, depending on what is the most helpful or necessary at the moment. The first is the relationship of lower-level awe—*I better do the right thing or I will get smote*. This relationship has us working to determine what is the next right thing to do. It can move us toward acts of *t'shuvah*.

The second relationship is lower-level love—*I am loved*. This is the love that fills us completely. It is the love we frequently yearn for. This relationship is especially sweet on Shabbat. If we make even the smallest opening, we are filled.

The next kind of relationship is higher-level love—the kind of love that is simply available in the universe. This kind of love is not personal. It is sublime.

And then there is the relationship of higher-level awe—the Hubble telescope perspective—*I am a wee, small part of the universe*. This relationship leads us to humility. It is the largest container, which puts all my petty concerns in perspective. It eliminates everything but faith and awe.

A Story from Our Tradition

At this point, as we begin to remember the obstacles that naturally lie on our path, I would like to remember Cain. One of my favorite moments of the Torah narrative is when God says to Cain, who is suffering from jealousy, "Why are you incensed, and why is your face fallen? For whether you offer well, or whether you do not, at the tent flap sin crouches and for you it's longing but you will rule over it" (Genesis 4:6–7, translation by Robert Alter). Paraphrasing God: "Cain, all you have to do is do the right thing." Of course, he then killed his brother. Why is doing the right thing so difficult? This difficulty is constantly reminding us that sin is always crouching at our tent flap.

In our Jewish vocabulary, we often speak about the *yetzer hara*, the so-called "evil inclination," as opposed to *yetzer hatov*, the "good inclination." Those two include what the Buddhists call our "passions." They cannot be eliminated, but they can be harnessed for the good. We need to be trained to regulate our passions. Buddhists instruct us neither to repress nor to act out. We do not repress because we need to know what those destructive inclinations are up to in order not to act them out. Both Jews and Buddhists agree that this practice of increasing awareness and the harnessing of our passions leads to spiritual transformation.[14]

The *Zohar* has a loving and compassionate view of Cain, which is essential. We will mess up and we will learn something new, over and over again. We consistently need to keep relearning and refining what we keep forgetting. We continually need to practice *t'shuvah*. We are taught that *t'shuvah* was put into place even before Creation. The cure for the inevitable wounding was put in place before the beginning.[15]

> Rabbi Yitzchak said, "Come and see: As Cain was killing Abel, he did not know how his soul would expire, as the Companions have established. At that moment the Blessed Holy One cursed him, and he wandered the world, everywhere rejected, till finally he slapped himself on the head and returned to the presence of his God."[16]

Cain moved from ignorance to understanding. Every good insight comes with a "duh" moment, because it was there all along. Cain slapped himself on the head and returned to God. And as Philo described, we continuously refine our tendencies, our passions, our knee-jerk reactions. Philo called this our "toil."[17]

Meditation is but one possible way to do the work. It supports us in cleaning the lens of perception; it unhooks our habits; it provides us with access to our soul; it brings new life to Jewish wisdom practices. Perhaps through cultivating Buddhist meditation tools, we become ready to sit in silence for an hour before we pray, read Torah, or go on the journey of ascent and descent and ascent and descent within the magnificent poetry of the *Zohar*.[18] And then, when we pray and study, we will find that we are assisted. It turns out that I am not the center of the universe. You are not the center of the universe. We live in relationship to all that is. It is a dynamic, living relationship. The Divine Mystery connects the immanent presence to the transcendent, without a single moment of separation.[19]

I have a metaphor I find useful to describe this unfolding process: The meditator learns to sit on the side of the stream of consciousness and watch whatever flows by. We call this mindfulness. Eventually, there is a natural deepening. There is the discovery that she who is aware is standing awake in the middle of the stream, with all the stuff of personality, mood, disposition, habit of perception, and intentionality, all in constant flux. Consciousness holds the stream, with equanimity and interest. From that vantage point, the more mystically inclined can look upstream toward the source of the flow.

We, as Jews, we might find ourselves shouting, "Who??" The *Zohar* suggests that the answer is "This."

בָּרוּךְ אַתָּה, יי אֱלֹהֵינוּ, מֶלֶךְ הָעוֹלָם, הַיֵּשׁ וְהָאַיִן.

Baruch atah, Adonai Eloheinu, Melech haolam, hayeish v'ha-ayin.

Blessed are You, Adonai our God, Sovereign of the universe, what-is and no-thing-ness.

Notes

1. Adin Even-Israel Steinsaltz, *The Soul* (Jerusalem: Steinsaltz Center/Maggid Books, 2018).
2. In *Mishnah B'rachot* 5:1, we read, "The ancient Chasidim used to meditate for an hour and then pray, so that they could direct their hearts to the Omnipresent."
3. Kalonymus Kalman Shapira, *Conscious Community: A Guide to Inner Work*, trans. Andrea Cohen-Kiener (Lanham, MD: Jason Aronson, 1996).
4. *Philo*, trans. F. H. Colson and G. H. Whitaker, vol. 9 (Cambridge, MA: Harvard University Press, 1991), 53–54.
5. *Philo*, vol. 7, 121–25.
6. Daniel Matt, trans., *The Zohar: Pritzker Edition*, vol. 7 (Stanford, CA: Stanford University Press, 2012), 304–5.
7. Yitzhak Buxbaum, *Jewish Spiritual Practices* (Lanham, MD: Jason Aronson, 1990).
8. See, for example, Abraham Abulafia, *Meditations on the Divine Name*, trans.

Avi Salomon (self-pub., 2012).

9. Aryeh Kaplan, *Jewish Meditation: A Practical Guide* (New York: Schocken Books, 1985).

10. P. Bindler, "Meditative Prayer and Rabbinic Perspectives on the Psychology of Consciousness: Environmental, Physiological, and Attentional Variables," *Journal of Psychology and Judaism* 4, no. 4 (1980): 228–48.

11. S. N. Goenka, *The Discourse Summaries of S. N. Goenka* (Onalaska, WA: Vipassana Research Publications, 1987).

12. To deepen that question, see Daniel Matt, *The Essential Kabbalah: The Heart of Jewish Mysticism* (San Francisco: HarperSanFrancisco, 1994).

13. See Genesis 26:15–33; and Matt, *The Zohar: Pritzker Edition*, vol. 2, 257–319.

14. There is an image (Aizen-my-oo, thirteenth century) in the National Museum in Tokyo I fell in love with. The meditator is sitting peacefully on the ever-present lotus flower. And as your eyes rise to see his face, it is beet red and in obvious, extreme distress. On top of his head is the head of a roaring lion. Yes, sometimes raising up the energy of the passions feels just like that.

15. Babylonian Talmud, *N'darim* 39b.

16. Matt, *The Zohar: Pritzker Edition*, vol. 7, 306.

17. *Philo*, vol. 2, 121–25.

18. Melila Hellner-Eshed, *A River Flows from Eden: The Language of Mystical Experience in the Zohar* (Stanford, CA: Stanford University Press, 2009), 309–39.

19. Matt, *The Zohar: Pritzker Edition*, vol. 7, 304–6.

CONCLUSION

Putting It All Together

Rabbi Edwin C. Goldberg and Rabbi Elaine S. Zecher

Tell me: What is it you plan to do with your one wild
and precious life?
—Mary Oliver, "The Summer Day"

When Eddie was a child, growing up in a large mainstream Reform temple in Kansas City, he thought he had God figured out. God lived behind the *Guinness Book*–recorded gigantically long curtains of the architecturally awesome sanctuary. At *Kol Nidrei*, he half expected God to be revealed between the curtains.

Eddie came to see that God is not to be conveniently placed into a certain sacred spot. God is everywhere. God is in El Capitan at Yosemite, in the cancer ward at Children's Hospital, in the bloodied streets of yesterday, today, and tomorrow, in the fight for justice, and in the delicious *Shabbes* meal enjoyed with beloved family. God is in a little two-year-old asleep in his bed and in the eyes of the psychologist explaining to his worried parents about his lifelong limitations. God was with Eddie's mother when her six-year-old son died of cancer and also back when she slipped out of the murderous clutches of National Socialism.

The purpose of the essays in this book has been to present various ways to experience God in our daily lives. Far from being a linear exercise, however, the authors featured found God in the unexpected places, in the questions, the struggles, the boredom, the challenges, and the simple joys. The authors showcase how they experience God in their lives . . . and how they slowly, over time, found the theological language to integrate these experiences into their day-to-day parlance—at times combining different views of God into their possible personal theologies. Those integrated theologies are integrated into lives of deep spiritual meaning. The experience of God is embodied and celebrated in the constant and sometimes random stream of life. As is pointed out in the introduction, this is a book about depth theology, about the experience of God, not the concept of God. We are not explaining God any more than we would explain a meal to someone who wasn't there to enjoy it. We are expressing what it feels like to enjoy the food—to enjoy a life lived with the experience of God.

Some common themes appear in the essays in this book. First, there is the wisdom of John Lennon, who said that life is what happens when you are making other plans. Experiences of God don't happen when scheduled in prayer services or even life-cycle events. They happen most often in the midst of ordinary life. It's been said that genuine spiritual experiences cannot be planned at all. They can only happen by accident. Nevertheless, cultivation of certain practices can make us more spiritually accident prone. These practices include being in nature, listening to music, sitting in silence, focusing on our body, enjoying time with others, studying Torah, engaging in social justice work, and preparing sustenance for ourselves and our loved ones. By definition, the list is not close ended. We can always find a new way to experience the Divine if we are open to it.

Second, there is a general understanding that spirituality is dedicated to what is real, be it our feelings, our passions, the fact that we have a body, or the premise that we all are seeking a connection to something greater than ourselves. For too long many religious leaders have argued that spirituality and materiality are separate. Even in Judaism this artificial barrier has been erected. The essays in this book dispute that idea, showing that God is embodied in our entire experience.

Finally, from this book we see that the onus is on us. If we want a deeper theology, we will have to work for it. The work is not about enrolling in a theology class, any more than reading a book about tennis will by itself do much for our tennis game. It couldn't hurt, of course, but it will not make us adept either. Especially in a time with so much uncertainty, the notion that we can discover enlightenment in the things we are already doing is seductive and comforting.

After experiencing this book, please take some time to reflect on these questions: Where are you in the journey of inviting holiness into your life? Where might you consider going? What else is out there to read, to live, to try? Forest bathing in the great and salubrious wilderness? Do you endow your regular prayer practice with new Chasidic insights? Is your Shabbat table transformed through culinary creativity? Do you appreciate anew the power of group song in a time when singing itself is not easy? Do you find God in the suffering, in your personal darkness? In your conflict with God, with others, and with yourself? Can you feel God's presence in your breath? In your dancing? In your silence?

We Reform Jews always secretly knew that God is more than a Pittsburgh Platform God-idea. As if we could disembody God! This volume celebrates our coming-out party. We are no longer ashamed to admit that God is everywhere! To the well-meaning rabbi who taught us in rabbinical school that God has no place being spoken of in a sermon, we say, "Thank you for teaching me about God despite your greatest efforts to avoid it."

In the end, Mary Oliver said it best:

> I do know how to pay attention, how to fall down
> into the grass, how to kneel in the grass,
> how to be idle and blessed, how to stroll through the fields
> which is what I have been doing all day.
> Tell me, what else should I have done? [1]

Thank you for reading this book! God bless you on your journey.

NOTE

1. Mary Oliver, *New and Selected Poems* (Boston: Beacon Press, 1992), 94.

Glossary

aggadah: A Rabbinic narrative or category of classic Jewish text that does not relate to law.

alef: The first letter of the Hebrew alphabet: א.

Aleinu: Lit. "it is upon us"; a prayer that comes toward the end of a Jewish service accepting the responsibility to do our share to build God's kingdom in our world.

Amidah: The "standing" or "silent prayer," traditionally recited at least three times per day.

aron kodesh: Lit. "holy ark"; the ark where the Torah scroll is kept in a synagogue.

ashrei yoshvei veitecha: Lit. "Happy are those who dwell in Your house"; Psalm 84:5, liturgically prefacing Psalm 145, recited traditionally three times a day, in prasie of God for life's blessings.

autoethnographies: Studies that utilize personal stories and reflections within their wider cultural and sociopolitical context.

Avinu Malkeinu: Lit. "Our Father, our King"; a liturgical text, recited predominately on the High Holy Days, on the themes of repentance and forgiveness.

baruch atah: Lit. "Blessed are You"; the beginning of the Hebrew blessing formula.

bat kol: Lit. "daughter of a voice"; a heavenly voice in the Hebrew Bible, or a type of low-level prophecy. For example, in Babylonian Talmud, *Eiruvin* 13b, God's voice is described as a *bat kol*, proclaiming *Eilu v'eilu divrei Elohim chayim!* "These words [of Hillel] and these words [of Shammai] are *both* the words of a living God!"

bimah: Platform in the synagogue from where services are led and sacred text is chanted.

bitul hayeish: Lit. "the erasure of existence"; also known as the concept of "the negation of the self" found throughout mystical literature.

b'nei mitzvah: Lit. "children of the commandment"; in colloquial American English, a coming-of-age ceremony celebrated by reading from and reciting the blessings over the Torah for the first time, traditionally at age twelve for girls and age thirteen for boys.

B'rachot: Lit. "blessings"; the first tractate of the Talmud, which focuses on laws regarding prayers and blessings.

b'tzelem Elohim: Lit. "in the image of God"; a quote from Genesis 1:27. The idea that all humanity was created equally and deserves equal respect and dignity.

chameitz: Translated as "leavened bread," but refers to any leavened food made with the five grains prohibited on Passover: wheat, barley, oats, spelt, and rye.

charoset: A traditional Passover dish made out of fruits, nuts, and spices, symbolizing the mortar that the Hebrew slaves used in ancient Egypt.

Chasidism: Mystical Jewish movement founded by the Baal Shem Tov, with roots in eighteenth-century Poland.

chasidut: Lit. "piety"; the philosophy of Chasidism, which draws on ancient kabbalistic mystical traditions to emphasize the embodied human experience as a way of connecting to God.

chavruta: Study system with pairings of study partners, derived from the Hebrew word *chaver*, "friend."

chol: Ordinary or non-holiday times, often juxtaposed with *kodesh*, "holy."

dunam: Unit of land measurement used by the Ottoman Empire, approximately equivalent to an acre.

Echad: Lit. "one"; the last word in the *Sh'ma* text, indicating God's Oneness.

Elohai N'shamah: Lit. "my God, my soul"; a blessing in the morning service for the gift of the pure soul returned to us each morning.

El Shaddai: A biblical name for God often translated as "God Almighty" (Genesis 17:1).

eilu v'eilu: Lit. "these and these"; a Rabbinic phrase indicating that there are different perspectives in any argument. For example, in *Babylonian Talmud, Eiruvin* 13b, God's voice proclaims, *Eilu v'eilu divrei Elohim chayim!* "These words [of Hillel] and these words [of Shammai] are *both* the words of a living God!"

Erev Rosh HaShanah: Lit. "the eve of the head of the year," or "the eve of Rosh HaShanah"; the beginning of Rosh HaShanah, the Jewish new year.

gelfilte fish: A traditional Ashkenazi dish made from ground fish.

golem: Lit. "incomplete" or "unfinished"; a creature of Jewish folklore usually made out of mud or clay and animated through magic.

hachnasat orchim: Lit. "bringing in strangers"; the Jewish value of welcoming guests, exemplified by Abraham in Genesis 18.

halachah: Jewish law, as opposed to aggadah (see above). Halachah and aggadah make up the corpus of classic Rabbinic literature.

hamantaschen: Triangle-shaped cookies filled with fruit jam or chocolate, traditionally eaten on the holiday of Purim.

hechsher: A kosher certification; a symbol appearing on a package or premises that indicates that a regulatory body has determined that the product or business is in compliance with the laws of kashrut. The Orthodox Union is the largest kosher-certification agency in the country; however, there are now many organizations that have developed their own supervisors and symbols.

hineini: Lit. "here I am," "I am present"; Abraham's response when God calls out to him at the site of the *Akeidah*, the sacrifice of his son Isaac (Genesis 22:1).

Kaddish: A prayer said at multiple times during any given religious service, praising God's name and power. Often "the *Kaddish*," when used colloquially, refers to the *Kaddish Yatom*, the Mourner's *Kaddish*, said at the end of prayer services by people in the period of mourning after an immediate family member has died or on the Hebrew calendar date of their death in subsequent years.

kashrut: Jewish laws concerning food and eating, ranging from which kinds of animals can be eaten to which kinds of dishes may be used for different kinds of food.

kavanah: Lit. "intention" or "direction"; colloquially, a Jewish value often meaning to set one's intention in the right spiritual and emotional place to be present for the sanctity of prayer.

K'dushah: Lit. "holiness" or "sanctity"; the name of a blessing delineating God's sanctity that is part of the *Amidah*.

kosher: When something fits into the laws of kashrut (see above).

kuchen: Lit. "cake" (in German and Yiddish); may refer to a specific kind of cake, often eaten with coffee.

kugel: A traditional Ashkenazi baked dish usually made with noodles or potatoes.

L'chah Dodi: Lit. "To you, my love"; a poetic song sung on Friday nights to welcome in Shabbat, described as a beautiful bride.

machloket: Lit. "an argument"; a Rabbinic term indicating a disagreement about a biblical interpretation.

matzah: Unleavened bread traditionally eaten on Passover.

m'chitzah: The dividing barrier between the men and women's sections in Orthodox synagogues.

midrash: Rabbinic exegesis on or expansion of Torah. Midrashim are documented in Talmud as well as other rabbinic books of Jewish teachings and interpretations.

Minchah: The afternoon prayer service.

minyan: The quorum of ten Jews that make up the minimum required for a full prayer service.

Mishkan: The Tabernacle that the Israelites built in order to worship God in the wilderness.

mishlo-ach manot: Lit. "sending of meals"; the Jewish mitzvah of giving gifts of food and sustenance to friends and family during the holiday of Purim.

mitzvah, mitzvot: Lit. "commandment, commandments"; refers to the prescriptions and prohibitions in the Torah, Mishnah, and later Jewish legal works.

Modeh Ani: Lit. "I am grateful"; prayer of gratitude traditionally recited in the morning service.

N'ilah: Lit. "to lock" or "to seal"; the final prayer service of Yom Kippur.

n'shamah: Lit. "spirit, soul."

Oseh Shalom: Lit. "creator of peace," referring to God; also the name of a prayer for peace at the end of the *Amidah* and several forms of the *Kaddish*, including the Mourner's *Kaddish*.

parashat hashavua: The weekly Torah portion.

parve: Within the laws of kashrut, the category of food that is neither meat nor dairy, including fish, eggs, and produce.

pushke: Yiddish for *tzedakah* box, a container in which one puts money to be donated to charity

Sephardic: Jews who originate in Sefarad (Spain and Portugal). Starting during the time of the Roman Empire and stretching until the fifteenth century, there was a large Jewish population in this region, which was exiled during the Spanish Inquisition and has since spread all over the world.

Shechalak Meichochmato: Lit. "who imparted of his wisdom"; blessing traditionally recited when we encounter a great scholar and usually spoken when we are standing in their presence. See Babylonian Talmud, *B'rachot* 58a for an example.

Shechinah: Lit. "dwelling"; the female name and aspect of God. *Shechinah* is associated with exile, as this is the aspect of God that dwells with the Israelite people also outside the Land of Israel. Also the lowest of the ten *s'firot*, the mystical layers of God's emanation, also called *Malchut* ("kingdom").

Shehecheyanu: Lit. "that gave us life"; the name of a blessing recited upon doing something for the first time or when marking a special occasion.

shivah: Lit. "seven"; the traditional seven-day mourning period after a loved one has passed away, commemorated by daily gatherings at the mourner's home for the first week after the funeral.

Sh'ma: The central creed of Judaism, said as a prayer three times daily. The full text means "Hear, O Israel, *Adonai* is our God, *Adonai* is One."

shomeret: Lit. "one who keeps"; refers to a woman who keeps the mitzvot or, more specifically, the laws of Shabbat.

shukkel: Lit. "to shake" in Yiddish; the swaying back and forth that Jews traditionally do while praying.

shul: The Yiddish word for "synagogue."

siddur: Lit. "order"; the Jewish prayer book.

simchah: Lit. "joy" or "happiness"; a celebration or joyful moment.

s'michah: Lit. "rely on" or "trust"; ordination, the act of making someone into a clergyperson (traditionally a rabbi, more recently expanded to include cantors).

sukkah: A temporary hut built outdoors with three sides and a partial-
ly open roof used on the holiday of Sukkot to symbolize the tem-
porality of life, the Israelite Exodus from Egypt, and the autumnal
harvest.

Talmud: A work of Jewish law from late antiquity based on Rabbinic
discussions of the behaviors prescribed and prohibited in the Mishnah, a compendium of Jewish law compiled in the second century.
The Babylonian Talmud has been for centuries the core legal source
of Rabbinic Judaism.

t'fillin: Phylacteries traditionally worn during weekday morning
prayer. They consist of two black leather boxes with parchment
scrolls containing text from the Torah inside them, which are
mounted on the arm and head with leather straps.

t'hilah: Psalm or praise.

tikkun olam: Lit. "repairing the world"; often refers to the Jewish call
to social justice. In traditionally Orthodox spaces, *tikkun olam* refers
to Jews doing mitzvot to bring about the Messiah and the messianic
redemption. In liberal Jewish spaces, *tikkun olam* can mean anything
from social action to the performance of mitzvot.

tohu vavohu: Lit. "chaos," referring to Genesis 1:2, in which God
forms the world out of the empty, amorphous chaos that existed.

t'shuvah: "Repentance" or "return"; one of the guiding themes of the
High Holy Days.

Contributors

Rabbi Nicole Auerbach is the director of congregational engagement at Central Synagogue in New York City. She is the author, with Dr. Ron Wolfson and Rabbi Lydia Medwin, of *The Relational Judaism Handbook: How to Create a Relational Engagement Campaign to Build and Deepen Relationships in Your Community* (2018). She was ordained by Hebrew Union College–Jewish Institute of Religion in 2016.

Rabbi Anne Brener, LCSW, professor of ritual and spiritual development at the Academy for Jewish Religion, California, is the author of *Mourning and Mitzvah: Walking the Mourners' Path*, now in its third edition. She is a psychotherapist, spiritual director, and meditation teacher, whose writing appears in many anthologies and periodicals. Ordained by the Reform Movement, she is a board member of Aleph: Alliance for Jewish Renewal, a trans-denominational organization that seeds the Jewish world with a creative integration of socially progressive values and traditional practices.

Rabbi Ken Chasen is the senior rabbi of Leo Baeck Temple in Los Angeles, California. He is a leading activist and prolific author on a wide variety of social justice matters in the United States and Israel, with writings appearing in numerous books and print and digital media publications. In addition, he is a nationally recognized composer whose original liturgical and educational works are regularly heard in synagogues, religious schools, Jewish camps, and sanctuaries across North America, Israel, and Europe.

Cantor Jonathan Comisar is a pianist and eclectic composer of vocal, chamber, choral, and orchestral music. His musical training includes the Eastman School of Music, Oberlin, and Manhattan School of Music. Cantor Comisar received his cantorial ordination from the Hebrew Union College–Jewish Institute of Religion School of Sacred

Music, where he now serves on the adjunct faculty. He is an award-winning musical theater composer and a sought-after composer of Jewish music throughout North America.

Rabbi Rebecca L. Dubowe was ordained by the Hebrew Union College–Jewish Institute of Religion as the world's first female Deaf rabbi in 1993. Rabbi Dubowe is the full-time rabbi for Moses Montefiore Congregation in Bloomington, Illinois, having previously served two congregations, Temple Adat Elohim in Thousand Oaks, California, and Anshe Emeth Memorial Temple in New Brunswick, New Jersey. Besides leading her congregation, Rabbi Dubowe serves as a spiritual mentor to the Jewish Deaf community across the nation, helping to inspire and educate Deaf individuals on connecting with their Jewish identities. A Los Angeles native, Rabbi Dubowe spends her free time exploring the prairies of the Midwest with her husband, Michael Dubowe. They have two adult daughters, Rachel and Arielle.

Rabbi Susan Freeman is a rabbi and ACPE certified educator, teaching clinical pastoral education (CPE) in San Diego. Her most recent book is *To Dwell in Your House: Vignettes and Spiritual Reflections on Caregiving at Home*. She is a certified yoga therapist (IAYT).

Rabbi Edwin C. Goldberg serves Congregation Beth Shalom of The Woodlands, outside of Houston, Texas. He is the author of several books and was coeditor of *Mishkan HaNefesh*, the Reform Movement's prayer book for the High Holy Days. He earned a doctorate in Hebrew Letters from Hebrew Union College–Jewish Institute of Religion.

Melanie Cole Goldberg, RJE, is a Jewish nonprofit management professional and Jewish educator who graduated from the joint master's program for Jewish education and Jewish communal service at Hebrew Union College–Jewish Institute of Religion. She currently serves as the volunteer coordinator for Jewish Family Service Houston. Her beloved sons and husband love to eat the food she makes, especially challah.

Rabbi Suzie Jacobson (she/they) serves as associate rabbi and education director at Temple Israel of Boston, a community that has long been her home. Suzie was ordained as rabbi by Hebrew College in

Newton, Massachusetts, where she also received a master's in Jewish education. Prior to her rabbinical studies, she received an AM in Jewish philosophy from the University of Chicago Divinity School, a BA in Jewish thought from the Jewish Theological Seminary, and a BA in history from Columbia University. Rabbi Jacobson is passionate about ensuring that Jewish communities are inclusive and just, that educational programs allow students to bring their whole selves, and that prayer is meaningful, authentic, and full of immense joy.

Rabbi Marc Katz is the rabbi at Temple Ner Tamid in Bloomfield, New Jersey. He is author of the book *The Heart of Loneliness: How Jewish Wisdom Can Help You Cope and Find Comfort*, which was chosen as a finalist for the National Jewish Book Award.

Cantor Evan Kent currently lives in Jerusalem, Israel, and is currently on the faculty of Hebrew Union College–Jewish Institute of Religion in Israel. He was the cantor at Temple Isaiah in Los Angeles for twenty-five years before making *aliyah* in 2013.

Rabbi Myriam Klotz (she/they) is senior program director at the Institute for Jewish Spirituality, where they have taught yoga and embodied practice since 2003, and a spiritual director. They were the founding director of the Spirituality Initiative and the Bekhol Levavkha Jewish spiritual director training program at Hebrew Union College–Jewish Institute of Religion, New York.

Ilana Kurshan is the author of *If All the Seas Were Ink* (St. Martin's Press, 2017), winner of the Sami Rohr Prize for Jewish Literature. She has translated books of Jewish interest by Ruth Calderon, Benjamin Lau, Yemima Mizrahi, and Micah Goodman, and she is a regular contributor to *Lilith Magazine*, where she is the book reviews editor. Kurshan is a graduate of Harvard University (BA, summa cum laude, history of science) and Cambridge University (MPhil, English literature), and she teaches at the Conservative Yeshiva in Jerusalem, where she lives with her family.

Rabbi Hara E. Person is the chief executive of the Central Conference of American Rabbis. She was previously the publisher of CCAR Press and the editor-in-chief of URJ Books and Music. She is the coeditor of *Mishkan HaSeder: A Passover Haggadah* and managing editor of *The Torah: A Women's Commentary*, among many other books.

Rabbi Sonja K. Pilz, PhD, earned her doctorate from the Department of Rabbinic Literature at Potsdam University in Germany and holds rabbinic ordination from Abraham Geiger College in Germany. Prior to becoming the spiritual leader of Congregation Beth Shalom in Bozeman, Montana, she worked for the Central Conference of American Rabbis as the editor at CCAR Press. She also taught worship, liturgy, and ritual at Hebrew Union College–Jewish Institute of Religion in New York and the School of Jewish Theology at Potsdam University, and she served as a rabbinic intern, adjunct rabbi, and cantorial soloist for congregations in Germany, Switzerland, Israel, and the United States. Not surprisingly, she loves to write poetry, midrashim, and prayers. Her work has been published in *Ergon*, *Liturgy*, *Worship*, *CCAR Journal*, Ritualwell, and a number of anthologies. She lives with her husband and son in Bozeman, Montana.

Rabbi Gayle Pomerantz is the senior rabbi of Temple Beth Sholom in Miami Beach, Florida. Since her ordination by Hebrew Union College–Jewish Institute of Religion in 1989, she has been serving the Jewish people and organizing for a more just world.

Rhonda Karlton Rosen became a dedicated student of Buddhist forms of meditation almost fifty years ago and became a student of Jewish contemplative practice and text study with Jonathan Omer-Man twenty-five years ago. These interests blossomed within her work as a social worker in private practice and as a clinical supervisor of graduate students in the clinical training program at the University of Pittsburgh Department of Psychology. She is a leader of meditation and Jewish contemplative practices at Temple Sinai in Pittsburgh and of Jewish contemplative practices for Beit T'Shuvah in Los Angeles.

Rabbi John L. Rosove is senior rabbi emeritus of Temple Israel of Hollywood in Los Angeles, a national co-chair of the Rabbinic and Cantorial Cabinet of J Street, the immediate past national chairman of the Association of Reform Zionists of America (ARZA), and the author of two books: *Why Judaism Matters: Letters of a Liberal Rabbi to His Children and the Millennial Generation* and *Why Israel [and Its Future] Matters: Letters of a Liberal Rabbi to His Children and the Millennial Generation*. He is the coeditor of *Deepening the Dialogue: Jewish-Americans and Israelis Envisioning the Jewish-Democratic State*, published by CCAR Press.

Rabbi Efrat Rotem was ordained by Hebrew Union College–Jewish Institute of Religion in Jerusalem in 2015. She served as the rabbi of Kehilat HaLev in central Tel Aviv and now serves as an independent rabbi in Israel. She is a queer environmental activist who integrates pluralist Judaism, critical feminism, and queer identity and worldview into her work as a rabbi. In addition, she holds an MA in literature from Tel Aviv University and is a translator and editor.

Rabbi Joseph A. Skloot, PhD, is the Rabbi Aaron D. Panken Assistant Professor of Modern Jewish Intellectual History at Hebrew Union College–Jewish Institute of Religion, New York. He is a historian of Jewish culture and religious thought.

Miriam Heller Stern, PhD, is the national director of the School of Education and associate professor at Hebrew Union College–Jewish Institute of Religion, based on the Skirball Campus in Los Angeles. A frequent presenter at professional and academic conferences, Dr. Stern serves as a consultant, mentor, and advisor to Jewish educational leaders, institutions, and initiatives across North America and Israel. She is the editor of *Revelation Is Just the Beginning* and numerous articles for academic journals and popular media.

Rabbi Elaine S. Zecher found her experience of working on *Mishkan T'filah* and *Mishkan HaNefesh* a profound and nourishing pathway toward the Divine. She currently serves as the senior rabbi of Temple Israel of Boston and is grateful for her community›s passionate exploration of that which is sacred. She has served in many leadership roles for the Central Conference of American Rabbis and is grateful for its mission to support colleagues and to ensure that liturgy and the written word foster spiritual encounters with that which is sacred and holy.